NATIONAL GEOGRAPHIC

TRAVELER

San Francisco

Jerry Camarillo Dunn, Jr.

CITY LIGHTS B

National Geographic
Washington, D.C.

Contents

Page 1: Cable car
Pages 2–3: Vesuvio and
City Lights Bookstore
by night
Left: Traffic negotiates
California Street's
steep slope.

How to use this guide

See back flap for keys to text and map symbols

The *National Geographic Traveler* brings you the best of San Francisco in text, pictures, and maps. Divided into three sections, the guide begins with an overview of history and culture. Following are 10 area chapters with featured sites selected by the author for their particular interest. Each chapter opens with its own contents list for easy reference. A final chapter suggests possible excursions from San Francisco.

A pictorial map introduces each area of the city, highlighting the featured sites and locating other places of interest. Walks, plotted on their own maps, suggest routes

for discovering the most about an area. Features and boxes offer intriguing detail on history, culture, or contemporary life.

The final section, Travelwise, lists essential information for the traveler—pre-trip planning, getting around, communications, money matters, and emergencies—plus a selection of hotels and restaurants arranged by area, shops, and entertainment possibilities.

To the best of our knowledge, site information is accurate as of the press date. However, it is always advisable to call ahead whenever possible.

Color coding

126

Each region is color coded for easy reference. Find the area you want on the map on the front flap, and look for the color bar at the top of the pages of the relevant chapter. Information in **Travelwise** is also color coded to each region.

Exploratorium
www.exploratorium.edu
- ✉ Behind the Palace of Fine Arts
- ☎ 415/561-0360 or 415/561-0362 (Tactile Dome reservations)
- 🕐 Closed Mon. except some holidays
- 💲 $$. Free 1st Wed.
- 🚌 Bus: 22, 28, 30, 41, 43, 45

Visitor information

Practical information for most sites is given in the side column (see key to symbols on back flap). The map reference gives the page number where the site is shown on a map. Further details include address, telephone number, website, days closed, entrance charge in a range from $ (under $4) to $$$$$ (over $25), and nearest bus, cable car, streetcar, or BART stop. Other sites have information in italics and parentheses in the text.

TRAVELWISE

- Color-coded area name
- Category name
- Hotel name & price range
- Address, telephone & fax numbers, website
- Brief description of hotel
- Hotel facilities & credit card details
- Category name
- Restaurant name & price range
- Address & telephone number
- Brief description of restaurant
- Restaurant closures & credit card details

Hotel & restaurant prices

An explanation of the price ranges used in entries is given in the Hotels & restaurants section (see p. 246).

AREA MAPS

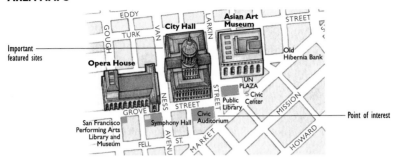

Important featured sites

Point of interest

- A locator map accompanies each area map and shows the location of that area in the city.

WALKING TOURS

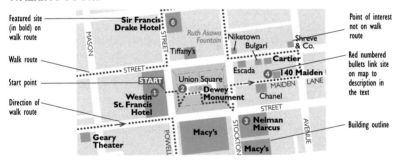

Featured site (in bold) on walk route

Walk route

Start point

Direction of walk route

Point of interest not on walk route

Red numbered bullets link site on map to description in the text

Building outline

- An information box gives the starting and ending points, time and length of the walk, and places not to be missed along the route.

EXCURSION MAPS

Point of interest

Important featured town

Road number

Grid number

- Towns and cities described in the Excursions chapter (pp. 207–40) are highlighted in yellow on the map. Other suggested places to visit are also highlighted and are shown with a diamond symbol.

NATIONAL GEOGRAPHIC

TRAVELER

San Francisco

About the author

A third generation Californian, Jerry Camarillo Dunn, Jr., was born and raised in
Los Angeles—a fact that elicits pity (at best) in San Francisco, but for which he makes
no apology. San Francisco became a second home during college at nearby Stanford
University. In later years, Jerry lived in the city and also in Marin County across the
Golden Gate Bridge. He is the author of numerous books, including *National Geographic's
Driving Guides to America: California, Nevada, and Hawaii;* the *Smithsonian Guide to
Historic America: The Rocky Mountain States;* and *Idiom Savant: Slang As It Is Slung.*
A former staff editor and writer for National Geographic *Traveler* magazine, he has
won three Lowell Thomas Awards from the Society of American Travel Writers for his
feature stories. Jerry lives with his wife, Merry, and two sons, Graham and Lachie,
in southern California. Their tucked-away valley is still filled with orange blossoms
and not with smog.

History & culture

Panning for gold at Sutter's Mill

San Francisco today

IT'S NO WONDER THAT SO MANY PEOPLE DO WHAT THE FAMOUS SONG SAYS: They leave their hearts in San Francisco. The love affair may be purely physical, of course: No American city offers such gorgeous sights, from the painted gingerbread trim on a Victorian house to a sparkling panorama of the bay with Alcatraz in the middle.

But San Francisco's appeal is far more than skin-deep. The constantly changing views, the interplay of water, hills, and sky, lend the city a rhythm, an effervescent beat, like jazz. You get the feeling that the city is improvising out of some deep well of experience and expressing a singular personality. It always plays inspired new riffs on an old refrain.

Some San Francisco scenes are urban classics: When the fog rolls in, for instance, a cloak of mystery and romance drapes the city's shoulders, like local detective Sam Spade's overcoat thrown around a blonde on a darkened street. Shadows fall, music rises, ice cubes clink in cocktail glasses, and anything goes. The city has a definite mystique. Of course, this mood is only one of many that make up San Francisco's personality. Other experiences that a visitor can take home to remember might include:

- gasping at the unexpected view of the bay as your cable car crests a hill;
- buying crab cocktails at Fisherman's Wharf from an Italian vendor who sports a big waxed moustache;
- walking across the Golden Gate Bridge as a cargo ship traces a white streak on the blue bay below;
- inhaling the steamy aroma of cappuccino in a North Beach café where the Beat Generation once hung its beret;
- gazing at the ruined Sutro Baths and picturing the era when 20,000 swimmers at once frolicked beneath its glass dome;

Below: A modern view of a historic city
Right: The farmer's market behind the Ferry Building

- musing on what Rodin's "The Thinker" is thinking about, at the California Palace of the Legion of Honor;
- sipping California wine at the Cliff House with a sunset view of sea lions on the rocks;
- giving your change to a street magician at the Cannery;
- watching radio-controlled boats scoot across a lake at Golden Gate Park;
- Christmas shopping at Union Square, the epicenter of high style and glittering, conspicuous consumption in San Francisco;
- eating dim sum in Chinatown restaurants where the only language heard is Chinese;
- dancing till you drop at a hip club in SoMa;
- touching thick adobe walls made by long-vanished hands at Mission Dolores, the oldest building in the city;

- braking your automobile downhill on Lombard, the "crookedest street in the world."

Such experiences make many visitors feel that San Francisco is their favorite American city. In fact, it has been repeatedly chosen in surveys as travelers' favorite city in the world. Europeans often compare it to Europe, meaning they find it picturesque and charming. New Yorkers feel at home with the world-class hotels, restaurants, museums, and opera. Folks from small towns discover a city built on a remarkably human scale.

And no one loves San Francisco more than San Franciscans themselves. Sometimes the city grows dewy-eyed with self-appreciation. It could give itself a big hug. But you can't blame it, really. Part of the city's appeal lies in the way it manages to balance the old or traditional

Trading at the Pacific Exchange

with the new and offbeat. The city is, paradoxically, both provincial and worldly.

THE PROVINCIAL

In many ways, San Francisco maintains itself in an insular world, guarded by its 43 hills and locked behind the Golden Gate. For more than half a century the city's symbols, now visual clichés, have remained the same: cable cars, the Golden Gate Bridge, Chinatown.

Provincial San Francisco carefully preserves its past. Lovingly restored Victorian houses and Edwardian buildings lend the city an old-fashioned look. In fact, a street of Victorians seems like something out of a child's pop-up storybook.

San Francisco is also a city of provincial manners. Like the residents of a small town, people are hospitable, cordial, and even mercifully slow to honk their car horns.

Older citizens remember a time when ladies never ventured downtown without their hats and gloves. Even today San Francisco is always called the City, and never "Frisco"—just one more gesture of civility.

To the knowing eye, San Francisco is a collection of provincial neighborhoods, districts that bind residents to the corner grocery stores and familiar faces they see every day. Home is home. It may be Pacific Heights, where the elite can walk their pedigree pups in a hilltop park. Or Chinatown, where old women in bulky sweaters practice the slow meditative dance of Tai Chi Chuan. Or North Beach, where aspiring poets who hope to emulate the 1950s Beats sit at café tables, scribbling in notebooks and sipping coffee for inspiration.

San Francisco icons: Golden Gate Bridge (1937) and the Transamerica Pyramid (1972)

THE WORLDLY

Among the many features that make San Francisco a beloved city, one of them can't be depicted in a color postcard. But it's there in the eyes of residents who return your friendly gaze. This quality is open-mindedness, a receptiveness to new and different ideas, and a willingness to let you do your own thing.

For a century and a half, the provincial city has been opened up to the outside world through waves of immigrants. (Just think of Italian fishermen and Chinese herbalists.) They have come from all directions: Europe, Asia, Latin America, Russia, the Philippines, and more. Their languages, religions, and cultures have created a uniquely diverse and tolerant place to live.

San Francisco's broad-mindedness first took root during the California gold rush. Everyday life was a wild pageant, and San Franciscans embraced all sorts of characters in the passing parade. Ravishing entertainer Lola

Montez (famous for her Spider Dance) strolled the streets with a riding whip to discourage male admirers who became too enthusiastic. Silk-cuffed gamblers and grizzled miners mixed with writers and millionaires. Around the infamous Barbary Coast a character named Oofty Goofty wore fur and feathers left over from his days as a sideshow "wild man." He launched a new career by permitting anyone to kick him for a dime (whacking him with a baseball bat cost a quarter).

At the Golden Gate, ships—and ideas— come and go from around the world.

But San Francisco's most enduring character was its favorite (and only) monarch, Joshua Abraham Norton. After arriving in San Francisco in 1849 and losing his fortune, he took to wearing an old blue army uniform and a dusty plumed hat. He proclaimed that he would be known as "Norton I, Emperor of the United States and Protector of Mexico."

San Franciscans played along happily with this bearded eccentric. When Emperor Norton entered a theater, the audiences would rise to their feet. Newspapers published his letters, whose "crazy" suggestions included building the Bay Bridge, as well as decorating a colossal Christmas tree in Union Square for the children of San Francisco—a tradition that is still followed to this day. The emperor frequently asked city financiers for loans of millions of dollars, but happily settled for 50 cents.

Everyone was a soft touch for Emperor Norton, and he touched them in turn. In 1880 he died while waving to tourists on a passing cable car. More than 30,000 people attended his funeral. Although Emperor Norton died nearly penniless, he was the undisputed monarch of San Francisco's heart.

Like Emperor Norton, over the decades countless other characters have proved one truth about this city: San Francisco will let you do pretty much what you feel like doing.

This liberating philosophy makes room for people of all social and political persuasions. Consider, for example, the Sisters of Perpetual Indulgence, motorbiking and in-line skating "nuns" who are actually amusing guys in drag. The city has always fostered outrageous characters, individualists, and bohemians—from turn-of-the-century painters and poets to the Beat Generation of the fifties and the 1960s flower children who "did their own thing" during the Summer of Love. But even

One province in a provincial city, Chinatown never seems to change.

if you're a buttoned-down type, a solid family man, a wife and mother, you'll find that San Francisco takes hold of you with all the giddy joy of riding a cable car down a dizzying hill, with the sunshine on your face and the bay breeze in your hair. Suddenly you come alive. What a rush! What freedom! What a beautiful city! ∎

Physical setting

SAN FRANCISCO OCCUPIES THE TIP OF A PENINSULA BETWEEN THE PACIFIC Ocean and the San Francisco Bay. The bay is both an inlet that stretches for 50 miles and an estuary fed by 16 rivers that drain the Sierra Nevada and Central Valley.

GEOGRAPHY

About 500,000 years ago, the ocean level offshore began to fall about 300 feet as ice built up at the Poles during the ice ages. The San Francisco coastline was near the Farallon Islands, 27 miles west. What is now the bay was a dry, grassy valley in the Coast Range where mammoths grazed. A river flowed from the Sierra Nevada and through the valley into the Pacific, passing through the Golden Gate. Then about 12,000 years ago, the glacial ice melted and the ocean level rose. Water flooded inland to fill the ancient valley, which became San Francisco Bay.

The peninsula was left high and dry, with water on three sides, a setting that lends San Francisco an exhilarating beauty, especially when viewed from one of its 43 hills.

San Francisco's climate is maritime and Mediterranean, with both summer and winter temperatures moderated by ocean air. But in a city famous for nonconformity, even the weather is eccentric. The warmest season is early autumn, rather than summer. At any time of year, fog and chill may envelop the Sunset District, while "banana belt" neighborhoods such as North Beach and Potrero Hill bask in sunshine. These weather pockets, or microclimates, are created as the result of cooled sea air entering the Golden Gate and being deflected off the city's irregular hills in divergent patterns.

EARTHQUAKE TERRITORY

San Francisco has a neighbor with a bad reputation: the San Andreas Fault. Constantly threatening an earthquake, the fault runs from the northwest part of the state more than 700 miles to the Gulf of California. It doesn't actually pass beneath San Francisco, but veers offshore between Daly City and Point Reyes. The fault is the unstable boundary between two tectonic plates—the Pacific and North American—which move in opposite directions against each other about two inches each year. Occasionally, the plates lock along the fault. Pressure builds, only to be released in sudden cataclysmic fury.

In 1906 the earth shifted more than 15 feet along the fault line, and the force shook buildings for 200 miles. The great earthquake was estimated at 8.3 (out of 10) on the Richter scale. Nowadays earthquakes occur every week, most of them less than magnitude 3.0 and therefore unnoticed (see the box below for the main exception). Seismologists predict that a "Big One" is coming. They just don't know when or where.

Loma Prieta earthquake

On October 17, 1989, fans at Candlestick Park were waiting for the third game of the World Series when a tremor of magnitude 7.1 rocked the stadium—and the entire Bay Area. The force of the earthquake, the most powerful since 1906, jerked the Bay Bridge five inches north, shearing bolts and causing a 50-foot upper section of the span to fall onto the lower section. On the Nimitz Freeway, a collapsing upper lane smashed automobiles and killed 43 people. In the Marina District, a number of houses and apartment buildings sagged, shifted off their foundations, or collapsed. They stood on unstable landfill (ironically, made of rubble from the 1906 earthquake) that liquefied during the tremor. Fire spread, and as in 1906 residents formed bucket brigades to help firefighters.

In all, 68 people died and damages exceeded six billion dollars. The quake had one positive effect, however. The Embarcadero Freeway that blighted the eastern waterfront was so damaged that it was torn down, opening up a panoramic view of the bay. ■

Foggy vanishing act by the Golden Gate, viewed from the Marin Headlands

Fog

San Francisco's fog is a shape-shifting shaman that casts a spell of white magic over the city. At the headlands of the Golden Gate, moisture-carrying Pacific winds meet the upwelling chilly waters of the bay, causing the moisture to condense like droplets on an iced-tea glass. The result: fog. Common in summer, it pours through the Golden Gate at between 10 and 20 miles an hour, sucked inland because high temperatures in the Central Valley cause air to rise there and pull the fog toward it. Conversely, on winter mornings, a dense, low-lying tule fog forms inland and drifts toward the ocean, often blanketing the entire bay. ■

VIEWPOINTS

Nearly everywhere you go in San Francisco, you encounter a view that is affecting or downright jaw-dropping: the Golden Gate Bridge seemingly suspended in midair as its towers vanish into the fog; cherry trees in bloom at the Japanese Tea Garden; rows of pastel-hued houses against the backdrop of the blue bay. For great views of the city, take to the water, the hills, or a tall building.

Water level

A bay cruise (see p. 105) gives a fresh vantage point on both the city and Fisherman's Wharf, plus a look *under* the Golden Gate Bridge. **Alcatraz Island** (see pp. 106–111) has an achingly lovely views of San Francisco (which must have driven the prisoners nuts). At **Fort Point** (see p. 131) you see the Golden Gate Bridge from beneath, all metal and bolts, and the Golden Gate itself, with powerful currents surging through it. (Watch for windsurfers here.) From **Baker Beach** (see p. 131) you'll see the distant Marin Headlands, the Golden Gate Bridge, the Pacific waves—and probably some nude sunbathers on the sand.

Hills & high buildings

Coit Tower (see pp. 94–96) has a 360-degree view of the Financial District and Chinatown (south); the Bay Bridge and East Bay (east); Fisherman's Wharf and Alcatraz (north); and Russian Hill and the Golden Gate Bridge (west). **Twin Peaks** (east of the Castro) gives you a clear shot of the city's northern and eastern sections. For a multimillion-dollar view with interest, try the **Bank of America** building (see p. 51), whose Carnelian Room restaurant on the 52nd floor overlooks everything, from the Transamerica Pyramid to the bay. For cocktails-with-a-view, sample the sky-high lounges atop **Nob Hill hotels** (see p. 63) such as the Mark Hopkins. At the Fairmont, you can ride the outside glass elevator for added thrills. ■

Food & drink

SAN FRANCISCO HAS SOME 3,300 RESTAURANTS—MORE PER CAPITA THAN any other American city—which makes eating out a major recreation. In fact, it often seems more like a religion. Devoted foodies worship at such shrines as Gary Danko, Slanted Door, Fleur de Lys, and Jardinière. But the humblest Mexican taco stand or Italian trattoria may also turn out great meals, and at low cost. The city has enjoyed good food since the gold rush. If you were a Forty-Niner with a pocketful of nuggets, you came to San Francisco and splurged on oysters and imported French champagne.

Today's San Francisco cuisine has three distinctive elements that make it world-class: (1) fresh vegetables, fruit, meats, cheeses, nuts, herbs, and wines, all locally produced; (2) a melting pot of cooking styles that immigrants have brought to this port city from all over the world—particularly Italy, China/Asia, and Mexico/Latin America (although you'll also find Moroccan, Swiss, and even Istrian restaurants); and (3) groundbreaking new approaches to cooking, notably the "California cuisine" created in the early 1970s at Berkeley's Chez Panisse by Alice Waters, whose menus offered the freshest seasonal ingredients, cooked and presented with imagination and art. As this style became popular and widely interpreted, consumers eventually reacted against sometimes small portions and overly precious presentations. The result: a late 1980s upsurge in country-style or "new American" restaurants, which serve up hearty portions of homey American dishes such as roasted chicken and Maryland crab cakes.

In San Francisco, culinary cross-fertilization produces some wonderful hybrid dishes. You'll find pumpkin ravioli with ginger, Caesar salad with Caribbean jerk chicken, and roasted salmon with red curry sauce. Also popular is "Pacific Rim fusion" cuisine, whose menus blend dishes from across Asia.

The Napa and Sonoma Valleys, north of San Francisco, produce some of the world's great wines, along with very drinkable table varieties. Especially successful are Cabernet Sauvignon and Pinot Noir among the reds, Chardonnay and Sauvignon Blanc among the whites. Other drinks include beer (local Anchor Steam, various microbreweries), coffees (espresso, cappuccino, latte), and mineral water (Calistoga, from the Napa Valley).

During your visit, try some of these San Francisco specialties:

Cioppino Italian fish-and-shellfish stew in a tomato stock.

Dim Sum Bite-size Chinese food that includes dumplings stuffed with seafood, meat, or vegetables. Served from carts. (There's no menu, so ask questions to avoid taking an unexpected bite of pig stomach or duck foot.) The bill is tallied by counting the plates on your table. A Chinatown bargain.

Dungeness crab Light and delicate; goes perfectly with sourdough bread and white wine; in season mid-November through June.

Fortune cookies Folded cookies with printed fortunes or proverbs inside (see p. 78).

Ghirardelli chocolate Made in San Francisco since 1852 and available at the company's historic factory, now a shopping-dining complex called Ghirardelli Square at Fisherman's Wharf.

Hangtown Fry Oyster-and-bacon omelette that dates back to gold rush days. You can try it for lunch at the downtown eatery once favored by mystery writer Dashiell Hammett, John's Grill (63 Ellis St., tel 415/986-0069).

Irish coffee A soul-warming blend of Irish whiskey, coffee, and whipped cream, introduced to the U.S. in 1952 at the Buena Vista Café (see p. 120).

Sourdough bread Crusty French bread with a sour tang (see p. 113). A large roll may be hollowed out as a "bread bowl" and filled with steaming clam chowder.

Walkaway crab cocktail Dungeness crabs cracked and sold by Fisherman's Wharf vendors since 1916 (see p. 112); served with a sharp cocktail sauce. ∎

At the Stinking Rose garlic restaurant

History

ONLY 230 YEARS AGO, THE SAN FRANCISCO BAY AREA WAS A WORLD unknown—at least, unknown to Europeans. It was the domain of Indians: Coast Miwok, Wintun, Yokut, and, most numerous, the 10,000 Ohlone who dwelled on the San Francisco peninsula, the East Bay, and south to Big Sur.

INDIANS & EARLY EXPLORERS

The Native Americans enjoyed a bountiful diet of shellfish, deer, and acorn mush. They used tule, a marsh bulrush, to weave masterful watertight baskets. Ideas such as the wheel and agriculture never dawned, but neither did warfare. In this land of plenty, each tribe had

Padre Francisco Palóu planned an adobe mission church to convert Indians.

its respective territory, with peace safeguarded by trade and marriage between groups.

Their splendid isolation couldn't last. Spain controlled an empire that included Mexico, and in 1542 it sent Portuguese navigator Juan Rodríguez Cabrillo north to explore "Alta California." (He was also to seek the Northwest Passage, a hoped-for link between the Pacific and Atlantic Oceans that would offer a shortcut to Asia. It was eventually

navigated far to the north between 1903 and 1906 by Roald Amundsen.) Cabrillo sailed past the entrance to San Francisco Bay, later named the Golden Gate, but didn't notice it.

Next came English freebooter Francis Drake, who in 1579 at the helm of the *Golden Hind* also missed the bay's entrance. Drake refitted his ship 25 miles north in what was likely Drakes Bay, below Point Reyes. With grand words he claimed the area for Queen Elizabeth I, calling it "Nova Albion" (New Britain in poetical Latin). But the claim languished through English inactivity.

Two centuries passed before Spain realized that to keep dominion over Alta California, it must establish colonies. In 1769 an expedition under Capt. Gaspar de Portolá left Baja California bound for Monterey Bay. At length,

suspecting that he had overshot his goal, Portolá sent Sgt. José Ortega with a party to scout the terrain. Ortega crested a ridge and saw a great body of water stretching north and south. Thus the first outsiders spied San Francisco Bay. (It's odd that the discovery was made by a land expedition, after centuries of exploration by sea.) Remarkably enough, Portolá didn't recognize what this sighting meant, and doubled back toward Monterey.

1775–1834: SPANISH SETTLEMENT

Only in 1775 did the first European sail through the Golden Gate—Juan Manuel de Ayala in the supply ship *San Carlos*. He charted the bay and named features such as Angel Island.

Meanwhile, an expedition under Capt. Juan Bautista de Anza was traveling overland to the bay. In 1776 he dedicated the site of the future Spanish *presidio*, or military post, at the tip of the peninsula near the entrance to the bay. Three miles southeast, he situated the mission. And so the sword and the cross arrived together—emblems of Spanish power and aspiration.

Colonists celebrated Mass at the mission site on Laguna de los Dolores, or Lake of Sorrows, on June 29, 1776. (San Francisco was therefore established before the Declaration of Independence was signed.) In 1791 the mission that stands today was built of adobe bricks and redwood timbers. Formally named San Francisco de Asís, to honor the padres' patron St. Francis of Assisi, it is usually called Mission Dolores. Here Indians were yoked to Christianity and to field labor. In 1816 a French traveler noted that after a few months the Indian converts "usually begin to grow fretful and thin, and they constantly gaze with sadness at the mountains...." Some slipped away to their old life.

After Mexico's independence from Spain in 1821, the Mexican government secularized the missions and gave Indians much of the mission land—which was quickly absorbed by Mexican property holders. Rootless, racked by European-imported smallpox and measles, stripped of their culture, the Indians were doomed. They drifted or worked on *ranchos*— cattle spreads on vast land grants that the government gave to settlers and retired soldiers.

33   34

VIEW OF SAN FRANCISCO, FORMERLY YERBA BUENA,
BEFORE THE DISCOVERY OF GOLD

WE THE UNDERSIGNED HEREBY CERTIFY THAT THIS PICTURE IS A FAITHFUL AND ACCURATE REPRESENTATION OF SAN FRANCISCO AS IT REAL

J. D. Stevenson
COMMANDING OFFICER OF N.Y. VOLS. IN THE WAR WITH MEXICO.

Gen'l M. G. Vallejo   *George*

The favored families, known as *Californios*, dominated Alta California, holding fiestas while the Indians labored as virtual serfs.

Neglected by Mexico, San Francisco's presidio fell into disrepair, although a few soldiers stayed on. Mission Dolores closed in 1834, and was later used as a tavern where outdoor bull-and-bear fights attracted frenzied crowds. Meanwhile, a settlement on a nearby cove was growing into a trading port that would soon bring the world to San Francisco.

1835–1848: YANKEE TOWN

California cattle ranches produced hides and tallow, which Yankee ships carried from San Francisco to New England's leather tanners. The trade would soon end the settlement's isolation.

Commerce centered on a sheltered cove at the northeastern edge of the peninsula with deep water for anchoring ships. The major businessman was English sailor William Richardson, who married the daughter of the

13—John Sullivan's Residence.
14—Peter T. Sherback's do.
15—Juan C. Davis' do.
16—G. Reynolds do.
17—A. J. Ellis Boarding House.
18—Fitch & McKurley's building.
19—Capt. Vioget's Residence.
20—John Fuller's Residence.
21—Jesus Noe's do.
22—Juan N. Padilla's do.
23—A. A. Andrew's do.
24—Capt. Antonio Ortega's Residence.
25—Francisco Caceres's Residence.
26—Capt. Wm. Hinckley's do.
27—Gen. M. G. Vallejo's building
29—C. L. Ross' building
29—Mill.
30—Capt. John Paty's Adobe building.
31—Doctor E. P. Jones' Residence.
32—Robert Ridley's Residence.
33—Los Pechos de la Choca.
34—Lone Mountain.
35—Sill's Blacksmith Shop.
←→ Trail to Presidio.
←→ Trail to Mission Dolores.

San Francisco as a small frontier town

presidio's commander and started the first commercial boat service on the bay. In 1835 he put up the cove's first "house"—a tent made from a sail—and a trading post.

Whaling ships and other vessels called. More buildings rose along a dirt track grandly called Calle de la Fundación (Foundation Street, roughly equivalent to today's Grant Avenue). Richardson named the settlement

Yerba Buena ("good herb"), after an aromatic, mintlike shrub that locals brewed to make a kind of tea. The Mexican authorities commissioned a Swiss grocer, Jean Jacques Vioget, to lay out streets for the expanding community. On the central plaza an adobe customhouse served the growing port.

U.S. officials in Washington were starting to eye the fertile valleys and lucrative trade in California, taking note of the weak grip that Mexico had on its remote possession. Americans felt they had a "Manifest Destiny" to expand the nation from sea to sea. In 1846 war broke out with Mexico over Texas and California. On July 9 Capt. John B. Montgomery of the warship U.S.S. *Portsmouth* came ashore with 70 sailors and marines. Without meeting resistance, he raised the Stars and Stripes above Yerba Buena's plaza (which was later named after his ship).

The Americans renamed the town San Francisco in 1847. Irish surveyor Jasper O'Farrell extended the street grid and added 120-foot-wide Market Street, which sliced diagonally across the city blocks—creating difficulties in getting across town that plague residents to this day.

In 1847 John Augustus Sutter, who ran a trading post and fort in the area that became Sacramento, saw that the growing community of San Francisco would be needing lumber. So he hired carpenter James W. Marshall to build a sawmill on the American River at Coloma, in the foothills of the Sierra Nevada. When the Mexican War ended in 1848, the U.S. took possession of California. But a few days before the treaty signing, something happened that would transform sleepy California. On January 24, 1848, Marshall was inspecting the tailrace of the mill when he saw a gleam in the water. "I reached my hand down and picked it up," he said. "It made my heart thump, for I was certain it was gold."

1848–1859: GOLD RUSH BOOMTOWN

Although San Francisco in 1847 was growing steadily, it was still a tiny settlement thousands of miles from civilization. Who could foretell that in two years it would explode from 500 people to 20,000, a boomtown whose name stoked gold fever in hearts around the globe?

Soon after his discovery, Marshall's workers were spending most of their time washing gravel for more nuggets. As word spread, San Francisco newspapers reported the find, but residents were at first skeptical. It took Sam Brannan to fan the flames of gold fever. The colorful Brannan had come to San Francisco heading a group of 200 Mormons but quickly

The lure of gold tempted many to make the long sea journey from the East Coast.

became an entrepreneur. He founded the city's first newspaper, the *California Star*, and owned hardware stores in San Francisco and Sacramento. In May, Brannan strode through Portsmouth Square holding a small bottle filled with nuggets and hollering: "Gold! Gold! Gold from the American River!" San Francisco emptied like a theater on fire. Every able-bodied man lit out for the diggings.

The California gold rush had begun. Hopeful miners snatched up every pick and shovel in town and headed for the Sierra. Sam Brannan became California's first millionaire. Before trumpeting the news of gold, he had stocked his stores with all the equipment the miners would need, priced at a premium.

After President James Polk confirmed the rumors of an "abundance of gold" in California, the news electrified the East Coast and the world beyond. In 1849 an incredible 100,000 fortune seekers headed for California as if it were a golden magnet. In legend they will live forever as the Forty-Niners.

Some trekked overland across mountains and deserts. One emigrant tallied 469 wagons on a single 9-mile stretch. At night so many campfires flickered that they looked like the lights of a great city. Other argonauts came by sea, crammed onto ships around Cape Horn or crossing Panama at the risk of yellow fever.

As fortune seekers arrived in San Francisco by ship, crews promptly deserted for the gold-fields, leaving Yerba Buena Cove a forest of masts. Some abandoned vessels were hauled ashore to be warehouses.

San Francisco provided food, mining equipment, and services, but not cheaply. Ham, eggs, and coffee cost $6, or a shovel $50. Land prices soared; one man sold a lot for $18,000 two years after trading a barrel of whiskey for it. Men walked the streets toting bags of gold dust.

In 1848, when a day's wages east of the Mississippi averaged $1, a typical California miner made $10 to $15 a day. Crime flourished. Australian hooligans, called the Sydney Ducks, robbed people and set fires to distract attention so they could loot. Finally entrepreneur Sam Brannan galvanized civic leaders to form a Committee of Vigilance to drive out the criminals. The "vigilantes" hanged several lawbreakers and murderers in 1851 and 1856, effectively cowing the undesirables.

About half the goldseekers were Americans, but the balance made San Francisco a cosmopolitan place, bursting with the languages and cultures of Mexico and Chile, Germany and France, Hawaii and Ireland, China and Italy. This diversity still marks San Francisco—a fine legacy from the days of '49.

At first nuggets were easy to pluck from the rivers, and some claims produced five pounds of gold a day. Men swirled dirt and gravel in frying pans, washing away the lighter material to leave the heavier gold. The "flash in the pan" of surface gold soon gave out, though, and more equipment was needed to extract the deeper-lying gold. Using cradles and wooden filter boxes, miners worked the deeper placers, which were pretty much exhausted by 1852. At this point corporate financing was required. (Many Forty-Niners with dreams of riches ended up as laborers in hard-rock mines.) Hydraulic nozzles called monitors blasted away hillsides to get at the gold—with disastrous environmental consequences.

1859–1905: FROM COMSTOCK BONANZA TO HARD TIMES

In the waning days of California gold, a bonanza of a different color was discovered in 1859, northeast of Carson City, Nevada. History's richest silver find, the Comstock Lode produced more than 300 million dollars from a stretch of ground just a few hundred

Between 1848 and 1851 San Francisco was swept by six severe fires. The early city was a recipe for conflagration: wood and cloth houses, ocean winds, and whale-oil lamps and wood stoves used for light and heat. After the 1851 blaze—which burned a quarter-mile swath and destroyed more than 1,500 houses—citizens rebuilt in more substantial brick and stone. Yerba Buena Cove was landfilled for a new financial district. Banks, churches, schools, theaters, and a horse-drawn streetcar line reflected a prosperous city grown up almost overnight from a frontier hamlet.

As gold production declined by the mid-1850s, San Francisco's economy turned to banking and manufacturing. But the city would never forget the California gold rush, which turned San Francisco into an instant city, rich beyond its wildest dreams.

Chinese, Mexicans, and Europeans soon joined the American gold seekers.

feet wide and two miles long. It brought fabulous wealth to San Francisco, whose citizens financed and controlled the mines, made or imported 90 percent of the miners' supplies, and reaped the profits.

The four "Bonanza Kings" who controlled the big Consolidated Virginia mine raked in up to $500,000 per month: John W. Mackay, James C. Fair, James L. Flood, and William S. O'Brien. William C. Ralston of the Bank of California provided financing that kept the mines going despite flooding and debt, in return taking shares that made him rich. He and his partners stripped Lake Tahoe of trees for mine timbers and held a railroad monopoly to Virginia City, the main mining town.

A large proportion of San Francisco's growing population arrived by sea.

The Comstock deluged San Francisco with capital. New banks, brokerage houses, and office buildings went up in the district around Montgomery and California Streets, which became the West Coast's financial center. (More than a thousand new buildings were erected in 1864 alone.) When Andrew Hallidie introduced the cable car in 1873, it stimulated development on Russian Hill and in Pacific Heights. Two years later the 800-room Palace Hotel opened on Market Street.

Meanwhile, San Francisco was instrumental in building the 1869 transcontinental railroad. California business interests expected to benefit by this link to East Coast markets. The Union Pacific built westward to meet the Central Pacific heading east. Engineer Theodore Judah laid out the Central Pacific route from Sacramento across the Sierra

Nevada to the meeting place at Promontory Point, Utah. Financing for the Central Pacific came from four canny Sacramento merchants: Leland Stanford, Mark Hopkins, Collis P. Huntington, and Charles T. Crocker. The "Big Four" earned huge profits and gathered vast amounts of real estate through government land grants along the railroad right-of-way. They built a transportation monopoly (known after 1884 as the Southern Pacific) that charged inflated rates and ran California politics, bribing politicians freely. Much hated, the Southern Pacific was known as the "Octopus" for its stranglehold on the West.

Although Californians expected the transcontinental railroad to bring trading advantages, instead it brought cheaper East Coast goods to San Francisco that undercut local high prices. Factories closed, unemployment rose, and the mid-1870s brought a depression. Chinese immigrants, whose labor was vital in building the Central Pacific, found themselves out of work when the project was finished. Thousands came to San Francisco and took jobs at low wages, angering unemployed white workers and provoking abuse, violence, and unfair laws such as the Chinese Exclusion Act of 1882, which blocked most Chinese immigration.

Despite turbulence, the 1880s blossomed into a so-called Gilded Age that turned the city into the "Paris of the West." The economy grew on fishing, whaling, and the shipping of wheat from California's Central Valley to Europe. Restaurants proliferated. (San Francisco remains a capital of great dining.) Golden Gate Park played host to the 1894 California Midwinter Exposition.

On the flip side, the Barbary Coast district on the southern margin of Telegraph Hill peddled the seedier pleasures of the Victorian era—gambling and prostitution. The sordid could watch a woman have sex with a boar, or see a man called "Dirty Tom" who ate any disgusting substance offered. The area was rife with crime, and unwary men were "shanghaied," or kidnapped as seamen on departing ships. Under Mayor Eugene Schmitz and powerful boss Abe Ruef, political corruption rotted the fabric of civic life.

In 1898 a small industrial and shipping boom occurred when San Francisco became a base for military operations during the Spanish-American War. The new Ferry Building opened as an embarkation point to Marin and Oakland, while early skyscrapers rose in the business district. The arts also flourished. Bohemian poets lived on Russian Hill, Ambrose Bierce wrote his acerbic newspaper columns, and Mark Twain penned amused descriptions of the city.

1906–1915: EARTHQUAKE, FIRE, & RECOVERY

Residents said it sounded like a cattle stampede, or a locomotive thundering at full speed. It was the sound of the worst natural disaster ever to hit a U.S. city. At 5:12 a.m. on April 18, 1906, citizens were jolted from sleep by tremors that lasted a total of 65 seconds and unleashed the energy of 15 million tons of dynamite. The earthquake (later estimated at 8.3 on the Richter scale) took place along the notorious San Andreas Fault (see p. 18), a

fracture in the Earth's crust that runs along the California coastline. It veers offshore around San Francisco, but if the fault had run beneath the city, the catastrophe would have been much worse. People from Los Angeles to Coos Bay, Oregon, felt the earth move.

The temblor warped sidewalks, twisted streetcar rails out of alignment, and sent brick chimneys toppling through roofs, killing several people in their beds. Terrible damage occurred in reclaimed areas such as the former Yerba Buena Cove, where building foundations rested on unstable landfill. Downtown, whole fronts of buildings crashed to the streets. A woman's house was bumped four feet down the street, making her feel like "corn in a popper."

Accustomed to occasional quakes, San Franciscans weren't panicked. Then they saw smoke rising across the city. Leaking gas pipes, broken electrical connections, and overturned wood stoves had started fires. Aid was hampered because the earthquake had not only knocked out the city's fire alarm system and killed the fire chief, but ruptured water mains so that the ample supply in reservoirs couldn't be delivered to fires. Telephone and telegraph lines went down, hindering emergency operations.

By noon 52 fires raged in the city. Embers showered onto rooftops, spreading the blaze. That evening a witness reported "the whole front of San Francisco was ablaze, the flames shooting upward…with the glowing discharge of a blast furnace." The inferno reached 2,700°F, so hot that marble melted in buildings and silverware fused in kitchens. Smoke reached a height of 5 miles, and people 50 miles away could see the fire's light and "desolating splendor."

Brig. Gen. Frederick Funston dynamited buildings to clear a firebreak along the east side of Van Ness Avenue, but cinders blew across the street. Only a lucky shift in the wind turned the fire from continuing westward. Meanwhile, the mayor issued a proclamation that looters would be killed on sight.

After three days and two nights, the fire burned out. Four square miles of the city were consumed, including the waterfront, business district, and industrial section—a total of 514 blocks and 28,000 buildings. The dead and

Ansel Adams captured the dramatic character of the Golden Gate.

missing numbered 674. Property damage was estimated at up to 500 million dollars.

Now the city had to house and feed 250,000 residents left homeless. They camped in tents in Golden Gate Park and the Presidio, and later occupied thousands of "refugee shacks" lined up in rows in the parks. Relief donations came in from around the country.

Through it all, San Franciscans managed to keep their sense of humor. A sign on a ruined building read: "The cow is in the hammock/ The cat is in the lake/The baby in the garbage can/What difference does it make?/There is no water and still less soap/We have no city, but lots of hope."

Optimistic San Franciscans rebuilt at an energetic pace. The first job was clearing streets of tons of debris, which legions of horse-drawn wagons hauled to the bay for dumping. The work was so arduous that 15,000 horses died. Three-quarters of the lost buildings were replaced within three years, usually using better materials and workmanship. Although civic leaders hoped to rebuild San Francisco in a more gracious

layout planned by beaux arts architect Daniel Burnham, local businessmen quickly re-occupied their old locations, and little changed. At Civic Center Plaza, though, impressive new government buildings included the 1915 City Hall, with a dome taller than the Capitol's in Washington.

1915–1941: AN ERA OF GROWTH

Having resurrected San Francisco, residents were ready to show off their phoenix of a city to the world. Popular mayor "Sunny Jim" Rolph boosted the Panama-Pacific International Exposition of 1915, which celebrated the newly completed Panama Canal—and San Francisco's recovery from the earthquake. Held in today's Marina district, this world's fair was a misty vision of gently lighted beaux arts buildings, with exhibits from many states and nations.

During this era electric streetcars served the city. Housing was developed in the Richmond and Sunset Districts. (To free up more real estate, the city ordered cemeteries vacated and the coffins relocated to Colma.)

San Francisco became a major financial center, providing capital for California's booming agriculture. To bring water from the high Sierra, the city built dams and reservoirs in the Tuolumne River watershed at Hetch Hetchy Canyon in Yosemite National Park. In 1934 a 156-mile aqueduct began carrying water for San Francisco.

unionists opposed the buildup as an unfair load on the working class, and a court convicted militant labor activists Tom Mooney and Warren Billings for the bombing deaths. They became martyrs to the labor cause. Later photographs contradicted witnesses who placed Mooney at the crime scene, and his death sentence was commuted; both men were eventu-

Survivors of the 1906 earthquake and fire among the rubble that it left behind

Despite the Great Depression, the city managed to complete some spectacular building projects—the Golden Gate Bridge, and the San Francisco-Oakland Bay Bridge, which was anchored to the world's largest man-made island. Here on Treasure Island in 1939 the city staged its third world's fair, the Golden Gate International Exposition, which focused on the cultures of the Pacific Rim and trade relations in Asia and the Pacific.

San Francisco became a union stronghold. Labor strife dated back to the Gilded Age (see p. 32), when sandlot orator Dennis Kearney criticized the rapacious railroad barons. In 1916 a bomb killed nine people during a parade that supported a military buildup before the U.S. entry into World War I. Many

ally released. In 1930 longshoremen held the biggest walkout in U.S. labor annals. The union gained better conditions, but only after strikebreakers had sparked off rioting that killed two people.

WORLD WAR II & AFTER

During World War II San Francisco thrived. About 1.6 million soldiers, sailors, and marines shipped out through the Golden Gate for action in the Pacific. The Bay Area became a complex of military installations. The Navy took over Treasure Island, constructing an airfield. Yards in Richmond (East Bay) and Sausalito (Marin County) built more than a thousand ships. About half were 7,000-ton supply vessels called Liberty ships, constructed in just 45 to 60 days. At the Opera House in the Civic Center, international diplomats wrote the United Nations charter in spring 1945. That summer the cruiser *Indianapolis* sailed from the bay, carrying the atomic bombs that were later dropped on Japan. (Early in the war, 5,000 Japanese Americans had been removed to internment camps.)

California at Berkeley, just across the bay, erupted with student activism and the Free Speech Movement, which among other things attacked racism and precipitated anti-war protests around the world.

By 1967, however, the flower children's ideals of sharing and "good vibes" had given way to media exploitation, destructive hard

The remains of Oakland's Cypress Freeway after the 1989 Loma Prieta earthquake

Many wartime workers were women and members of minorities, including Hispanics and blacks. The city's diverse population took shape as these workers and returning military personnel settled after the war. During the prosperous 1950s, bohemians disenchanted with conformity and mainstream society moved into North Beach, where the Beat Generation was led by writers such as Ferlinghetti, Ginsberg, and Kerouac.

In 1965 another offbeat movement emerged with the hippies of Haight-Ashbury. Through them, San Francisco generated seismic shifts in American life (recreational drugs, "free love"), along with its own music (psychedelic or acid rock) and clothing style (thrift-store Victorian). The University of

drugs, and crime in Haight-Ashbury. A positive legacy for America was greater social tolerance as society opened more to women, gays, and minorities. San Francisco became a capital of gay liberation during the 1970s, and for the first time, a U.S. city elected out-of-the-closet politicians.

In October 1989 the Loma Prieta earthquake killed 68 people and caused extensive damage, much of which was quickly repaired—the Golden Gate Bridge reopened after only a month. In 1991, fires raged across the Oakland Hills to the east of San Francisco Bay, killing 25 people and destroying 3,000 homes. Today San Francisco is a vibrant place where business, the arts, tourism, and an unconventional spirit happily coexist. ■

The arts

IT'S NO ACCIDENT THAT THE CITY WHERE JACK LONDON WAS BORN ALSO inspired Jack Kerouac and the Grateful Dead. San Francisco seems to draw out the artistic adventurers, the questioners, the seekers of an alternative view. The best of the city's creative output turns things on their heads, makes you see the world afresh—either openly, as in Allen Ginsberg's poem "Howl," or a lot more subtly, as in the photographs of Ansel Adams.

LITERARY SAN FRANCISCO

San Franciscans have always liked to read. The city had a newspaper by January 1847, when colorful Mormon-leader-turned-entrepreneur Sam Brannan launched the weekly *California Star*. The paper later merged with the rival *Californian* as the *Alta California*, the West's first daily. Pioneer newspapers were produced on hand presses, often with battered old type. When newsprint was scarce occasionally, they were printed on any handy substitute, from Chinese tea paper to brown manila.

Writers developed their craft in the city's literary journals. The first was the *Golden Era* (1852), which ran early poems and sketches by its typesetter, Bret Harte. Harte's short

story, "The Luck of Roaring Camp," made him famous. He romanticized the life of the mining towns, portraying the gambler and the "prostitute with a heart of gold"— before they were stock characters. Harte's romanticism was counterbalanced by the amused satire of Mark Twain, who moved to San Francisco in 1864, stayed more than two years, and made his early reputation with a tall tale ("The Celebrated Jumping Frog of Calaveras County") and an account of his travels in the West called *Roughing It*.

San Francisco's literary and Bohemian circles included the future poet laureate of California, Ina Coolbrith (see p. 100); she

San Francisco co-stars with James Stewart and Kim Novak in Hitchcock's *Vertigo*.

nurtured many writers, including the young Jack London (1876–1916). The unlikely son of an astrologer and a spiritualist medium, London worked in a cannery, became an "oyster pirate," and sought adventure on a schooner in the South Pacific. He wrote more than 50 books (including *The Sea-Wolf, The Call of the Wild,* and *Martin Eden)* and more than 100 short stories, in which he tackled stark action and themes of social philosophy.

Poet Cincinnatus Heine Miller changed his name to Joaquin (inspired by bandit Joaquin Murrieta) and wrote about larger-than-life Western characters: frontiersmen, Indians, outlaws. He strode around in tall boots, a red flannel shirt, and a sombrero. Known as the Poet of the Sierra, he was more famous for his eccentricity than for his poetry.

By the 1880s the city's dominant literary voice was that of Ambrose Bierce, whose "Prattle" column attacked people and issues with a bludgeon of black wit. He also produced the acerbic *The Devil's Dictionary*. During this period, Robert Louis Stevenson and Rudyard Kipling passed through and wrote about San Francisco. On the light side, in the mid-1890s Gelett Burgess edited the gleefully anarchic *The Lark,* which published stories and poems with a silly streak. His "Purple Cow" became a classic of nonsense verse, and he wrote a response to the unsought fame it brought: "Ah yes, I Wrote the 'Purple Cow'/I'm sorry, now, I Wrote it!/But I can Tell you Anyhow/I'll Kill you if you Quote it."

At the turn of the century, Frank Norris set his realist novel *McTeague* in San Francisco, while *The Octopus* showed the Southern Pacific railroad's stranglehold on California. During the 1920s Dashiell Hammett lived in San Francisco, the shadowy setting for *The Maltese Falcon*. He finished this hard-boiled detective classic in an apartment on Leavenworth Street. After 1929, novelist Gertrude Atherton held literary gatherings at her Pacific Heights apartment.

The Beats

The best known literary movement to come out of San Francisco spun out of North Beach and the 1950s Beat Generation, exemplified by Jack Kerouac. He wrote *On The Road* (1957) in the spontaneous style of jazz in a

three-week burst of almost continuous typing on a long roll of teletype paper. Kerouac's success spread Beat ideas of wandering the open road, partying, and yearning for freedom to the larger American culture, previously dominated by conformity and complacency.

A poetry renaissance began in 1955 when Allen Ginsberg erupted with "Howl" at the Six Gallery on Fillmore Street. (An obscenity trial followed its subsequent publication by Lawrence Ferlinghetti.) Among other local poets were Kenneth Rexroth, the Zen-influenced Gary Snyder, and Ferlinghetti, whose City Lights Bookstore in North Beach was, and still is, a hub of literary life.

During the mid-1970s Armistead Maupin wrote in the *San Francisco Chronicle* a serialized story of life and love among young San Franciscans, both straight and gay, which was collected in the book *Tales of the City.* Other San Francisco writers include Herbert Gold *(Fathers),* Alice Walker *(The Color*

Purple), and Amy Tan, whose *The Joy Luck Club* unfolds partly in Chinatown.

IN THE MOVIES

As photogenic as a movie star, San Francisco has been the setting or subject of more than 500 films. Among early ones are *Frisco Kid* (1935, James Cagney), *San Francisco* (1936, Clark Gable), *After the Thin Man* (1936, William Powell), and *The Maltese Falcon* (1941, Humphrey Bogart).

The Grateful Dead, once known as the Warlocks, were for a time financed by LSD chemist Owsley Stanley.

Later films include *It Came From Beneath the Sea* (1955), *Vertigo* (1958), *The Birdman of Alcatraz* (1962), *Bullitt* (1968), *Gimme Shelter* (1970), *Dirty Harry* (1971), *What's Up Doc* (1972), *The Conversation* (1974), *Towering Inferno* (1974), *Escape from Alcatraz* (1979), *The Presidio* (1988), *Pacific Heights* (1990),

Visitors cross the catwalk in the skylit tower at the San Francisco Museum of Modern Art.

Sister Act (1992), *The Joy Luck Club* (1993), *Mrs. Doubtfire* (1993), *Golden Gate* (1993), *The Rock* (1996), and *Bedazzled* (2000).

THEATER & BALLET

San Francisco's love for the performing arts dates back to the gold rush. In June 1849, the city's first theatrical event featured a New York actor singing and doing impressions in the Portsmouth Square schoolhouse. By 1850 Shakespeare productions competed with less elevated saloon shows and circuses. Illiterate cab driver Tom Maguire opened the first of several Jenny Lind Theaters and then Maguire's Opera House. Spanish dancer Lola Montez came to town with her Spider Dance, which involved shaking whalebone "spiders" from her skimpy costume and stomping on them. The city was also a stop for touring East Coast performers such as actor Edwin Booth.

Shows in today's theater district, west of Union Square, range from avant-garde to mainstream musical. Broadway hits run at the Curran Theatre, while the Geary Theater has repertory works by ACT/American Conservatory Theater (see p. 62). Other venues include Golden Gate Theater (major shows),

the 70-seat Cable Car Theater, and the off-Broadway Theater On The Square. Campy *Beach Blanket Babylon* plays perennially at Club Fugazi in North Beach. The San Francisco Mime Troupe has presented smart, satirical pieces for 40 years, while the San Francisco Shakespeare Festival and experimental San Francisco Fringe Festival are annual events.

Founded in 1933, the San Francisco Ballet ranks among the nation's top companies. It was the first company to stage *The Nutcracker* in the U.S., and at Christmas it regularly mounts a spectacular production of this ballet.

MUSIC

The sound track for the 1960s was partly played by San Francisco bands, which blossomed with the flower children and marijuana-LSD culture of Haight-Ashbury. The San Francisco Sound (a.k.a. psychedelic rock) was created by major groups (the Jefferson Airplane, the Grateful Dead, Big Brother and the Holding Company with Janis Joplin) as well as minor and forgotten ones.

A common thread was experimentation with LSD and other psychedelics. As a result, the bands' songs became longer and more

The audience awaits the overture at the magnificent War Memorial Opera House.

improvised, with extended jams. New electronics altered rock music with echo, fuzztone, and wah-wah effects. Concerts were often accompanied by hallucinatory light shows.

In the late sixties, the hippie scene was exploited in songs such as Scott McKenzie's "San Francisco (Be Sure to Wear Some Flowers in Your Hair)" and Eric Burdon and the Animals' "San Franciscan Nights." The seminal Grateful Dead, though, stayed active for decades, keeping the spirit of the sixties alive.

In serious music, the dazzling San Francisco Opera at the War Memorial Opera House features top performers and imaginative sets. (English translations are projected above the stage.) The San Francisco Symphony Orchestra performs at the Louise M. Davies Symphony Hall. (Violinists Yehudi Menuhin and Isaac Stern debuted with the orchestra.) The Herbst Theater presents baroque and chamber music. The annual San Francisco Jazz Festival is intelligently programmed, with top stars in intriguing venues.

PAINTING, PHOTOGRAPHY, & SCULPTURE

The visual arts in San Francisco form a composite image of the city's life and times. The oldest "work of art" is Mission Dolores (1791), whose Mexican altars and bronze bells reflect the era of the mission-founding padres, while its painted ceiling decorations evoke the basketry patterns of the Ohlone people.

The California gold rush brought an influx of influences and cultural styles from the world outside, notably from Europe. Painter Charles Christian Nahl used classical technique to depict life in the mining camps. His canvases, such as "Sunday Morning in the Mine" (1872), show telling details and wry humor, and, like the stories of Bret Harte, offer a living picture of early California.

At mid-century a school of landscape took root, its best known painter being Albert Bierstadt (1830-1902), who first traveled west with a surveying expedition. His monumental canvases depict the vast gorges and towering mountains of the West. Thomas Hill painted Yosemite and other outdoor subjects, while William Keith produced tranquil, dappled landscapes of oak groves, hills, and brooks.

San Francisco's newly rich art patrons were a rather conservative, stiff-collared lot who preferred works that would decorate their mansions and lend prestige. (California's railroad and mining millionaires, such as Mark Hopkins and James Flood, scoured Europe for works of art, furniture, and tapestries.)

A group of painters helped form the Bohemian Club in 1872, about the same time that the San Francisco Art Association opened a gallery and school. Later the association occupied the Mark Hopkins mansion on Nob Hill, then moved to Russian Hill. Its members included painters Bierstadt and Keith, and pioneering photographer Eadweard Muybridge, whose motion studies of a galloping horse (1872), taken by a series of still cameras, made photographic history.

Around the turn of the 20th century, Douglas Tilden created heroic sculptures, including the "Mechanics' Monument" on Market Street, depicting muscled men wrestling with a lever and wheel. His pupil Robert Aitken created the figure of "Victory" that graces the Dewey Monument in Union Square. Meanwhile, Arthur Putnam produced snarling bronze jaguars and mountain lions, and various other creatures, all carefully observed. (His previous experience with animals included driving cattle and working in a forest.)

New artistic styles and influences flowed into San Francisco after the Panama-Pacific International Exposition of 1915, where works by Monet and Degas were shown. When passing through San Francisco, Henri Matisse made colorful pictures of tropical fish at the Steinhart Aquarium. Mexican muralist Diego Rivera came to paint frescoes, including one at the San Francisco Art Institute. His style and technique influenced the government-subsidized artists who decorated the interior of Coit Tower during the 1930s Depression.

Watercolorist Dong Kingman used a bright palette to depict San Francisco scenes. In 1932 Ansel Adams, Edward Weston, and other photographers founded the influential Group f.64, whose ultrasharp images were a reaction against the romantic soft focus then in fashion. Sculptor Beniamino Bufano dotted the city's parks and playgrounds with huge stylized figures, including one of Sun Yat-sen (1938) in St. Mary's Square. But San Franciscans rejected his proposal to erect a 156-foot-tall statue of St. Francis atop Twin Peaks. (The stainless-steel saint would have

had his arms upraised, prompting a critic to quip: "It looks like a holdup.")

After World War II abstract art came to the city under the tutelage of Mark Rothko and Clyfford Still at the San Francisco Art Institute, where they influenced students Sam Francis and Robert Motherwell. In reaction, Bay Area figurative painters such as Richard Diebenkorn produced representational work. (Diebenkorn's "Seated Woman" is part of the M.H. de Young collection.)

The sixties were reflected in work by artists such as Wayne Thiebaud, who portrayed features of popular culture. Psychedelic posters, created to promote San Francisco rock concerts, were raised to the level of art. They influenced advertising, graphic art, and fashion in the larger American culture with intense colors and typography that seemed to warp and flow together as if the viewer were on LSD. Today, these posters are valuable collectibles.

Today's San Francisco art scene focuses around private galleries and the SoMa axis: the San Francisco Museum of Modern Art, specialized museums, and the more experimental Center for the Arts at Yerba Buena Gardens.

ARCHITECTURE

The earliest structures around San Francisco Bay have long vanished—the huts of the Ohlone and Coast Miwok people, which were fashioned of a marsh bulrush called *tule*. European architecture was introduced after 1776 by Franciscan padres of the mission period. For their California missions they employed 17th- and 18th-century Spanish designs and construction methods, adapting them to a remote frontier with limited building materials: mud and wood. The resulting Mission style was distinguished by thick walls of adobe (mud stabilized with straw), massive timbers, tile floors, and red-tile roofs. The only original example in San Francisco is Mission Dolores, the city's oldest building (1791). Three-foot-thick walls have kept it standing despite earthquakes. Of the original Spanish *presidio*, or military post, nothing remains but an adobe wall fragment that is now part of the Officers' Club.

The Bank of America building looms 779 feet above the Financial District.

With the California gold rush of 1848, wooden buildings predominated. After a series of fires raged through the canvas and wooden structures downtown, solid brick buildings were erected, often with iron shutters. Some commercial buildings survive in Jackson Square, next to the Financial District. Notable are the Golden Era Building (1852) and the Hotaling Warehouse (1866).

For the rest of the 19th century Victorian architecture (see pp. 44–45) dominated.

Architects of the ensuing Arts and Crafts style emphasized a natural appearance by using redwood, stone, and dark-stained shingles, often adapting decorative devices from Japan.

After the turn of the 20th century, San Francisco was caught up in the City Beautiful movement to redesign America's urban environments more aesthetically. The dominant style was beaux arts, derived from principles taught at the École des Beaux-Arts in Paris. A revival of classical and Renaissance design, the

style was used chiefly for public buildings.
Highlights include the Bank of California and
the Fairmont Hotel, whose resurrection after
the 1906 earthquake was overseen by Julia
Morgan. The 1915 City Hall has a classical
dome, Doric pillars, and Greek temple motifs.
The pinnacle of beaux arts achievement in the
city is the Palace of Fine Arts, sole survivor of
the 1915 Panama-Pacific International
Exposition. The California Palace of the Legion
of Honor (1924) was designed by George

**Study in contrast: Victorian houses at
Alamo Square against the modern skyline**

Applegarth, who studied at the École des
Beaux-Arts in Paris.

Modern architectural innovations appeared
as early as the 1890s, when steel frames helped
San Francisco buildings rise high. In 1917
Willis Polk produced a design four decades
ahead of its time for the eight-story Hallidie
Building, the grandfather of modern steel-and-

San Francisco's painted ladies

San Francisco's exuberance during the second half of the 19th century found perfect expression in Victorian architecture, with its nothing-exceeds-like-excess ornamentation. Its Victorian houses ran riot with fanciful towers, bay windows, gingerbread decoration, art glass, turned posts and spindles, shingles, and gables. Oddly, most houses were mass-produced with similar floor plans on narrow plots of land. Their individuality came from the choice of embellishments and mixture of colors with which they were dressed up.

About 15,000 Victorian houses still stand in San Francisco, many of them in Pacific Heights, the Western Addition, Haight-Ashbury, the Mission District, and the Castro District. These areas, situated west and south of downtown, escaped both the 1906 fire and subsequent re-development. In recent years numerous Victorians have been lovingly restored, in many cases after various ill-conceived "modernizations" have first been corrected. Homeowners often paint the facades and trim with a vibrant palette of colors, quite unlike the pale hues typically

Gothic Revival

Italianate

Ornamentation and structural framing were of wood—redwood, pine, fir—which was in plentiful supply in nearby coastal forests and therefore inexpensive. Houses were designed to fit San Francisco's narrow lots, generally 25 feet wide by 100 feet deep, a size that allowed developers to squeeze more houses onto a parcel of land ... and more profits out. Bay windows eased the sense of narrowness by affording more sunlight, fresh air, and floor space.

used in the Victorian era itself. (The period takes its name from the virtuous and duty-bound Queen Victoria, who ruled Great Britain between 1837 and 1901.)

Four major styles of architecture appeared successively in San Francisco during the Victorian period.

Gothic revival: Popular in the 1850s and 1860s, this style (also known as Carpenter Gothic) draws on features of Medieval

Gothic architecture, and is distinguished by its use of spacious porches and balconies, pointed arches, and especially by carved or pierced bargeboards (trim attached to the projecting edges of gable roofs). Many dwellings of this style were modest cottages, usually painted white. (1978 Filbert Street is a good example.)

Italianate: A feature of the 1870s, the Italianate style evoked the villas and palazzos of Italy. Straight roof lines were topped with high cornices (horizontal molded projections). Neoclassic decorations framed the doors and windows, and porches often had pediments (triangular elements of classical Greek style).

Stick

The facade was flat and formal, with symmetrically placed windows. The overall effect was a palatial look, even for a small house. As the style developed, later designs also incorporated bay windows. (The Pacific Union Club at 1000 California Street, originally a private mansion, is built in an Italianate style; see p. 68.)

Stick: In vogue in the 1880s, this style is also called Stick Eastlake (in honor of Charles Locke Eastlake, a British writer and

designer who influenced both furniture and architectural tastes of the late Victorian era). It can be identified by its strong vertical lines, which are created by long "sticks" of ornamental wood trim. Other characteristic features include square bay windows, square corners, false gables, and ornately decorative brackets. Embellishments were created by skilled woodcarvers, as well as being machine-produced by newly developed steam-powered saws and lathes. (111–115 Liberty Street is an example of Stick architecture.)

Queen Anne: Widely favored during the 1890s, this inventive, exuberant style showed off contrasts in texture (decorative shingles,

Queen Anne

stone, clapboard, brick, sunburst patterns, and other ornamentations) and form (turrets, pointed roofs, corner towers with witch's cap roofs, pediments, Venetian windows, high chimneys). Designs were asymmetrical, with stronger horizontal lines than in earlier styles. (Good examples of Queen Anne architecture include the Haas-Lilienthal house, 2007 Franklin Street, featured on p. 147; and the much photographed strip of houses on Alamo Square, 710–720 Steiner St. , on pp. 42–43). ■

"Eclipse" by Charles Perry, in the 17-story atrium lobby of the Hyatt Regency Hotel

glass skyscrapers; its glass curtain wall was a radical innovation. Among early skyscrapers, the 30-story Pacific Telephone and Telegraph Company headquarters (1925) appeared to soar heavenward, an effect achieved with stepped-back levels. Other notable buildings included 450 Sutter Street, an art deco building in Mayan style, and the neo-Gothic Russ Building (1927), whose E-shaped footprint allowed light and air to penetrate to the offices.

Major construction in San Francisco then took a 30-year hiatus, mostly caused by the Great Depression and World War II. In the 1960s, urban renewal in the Western Addition saw thousands of pre-1906 houses, flats, and shops razed to make way for multiple-family units. (The realization of the loss of so many early buildings helped give rise to the city's his-

toric preservation movement.) The downtown skyline began to bristle with office towers, notably the Crown Zellerbach building (1959), which rests upon piers, and the cross-braced Alcoa building (1964). Later came the Bank of America headquarters (1971) on California Street, with 52 floors and almost two million square feet of offices, and the Hyatt Regency Hotel (1973), with a tiered design and the world's largest atrium lobby. The Transamerica Pyramid (1972) rises 853 feet, the city's tallest building and a most recognizable emblem.

Notable contemporary architecture includes the Museum of Modern Art (1995) in SoMa, with brick blocks and a slant-topped glass cylinder. The Main Public Library (also 1995) is a postmodern take on beaux arts design, with deconstructionist elements. ■

The Financial District—a wedge roughly bounded by Market Street, Kearny Street, Pacific Avenue, and the Embarcadero—gives the city its distinctive skyline.

Financial District

Skyscrapers tower over the Financial District.

Financial District

YOU CAN ALMOST HEAR THE MONEY PILING UP…RUSTLE, RUSTLE, CLATTER, clink…in this powerhouse center of San Francisco's financial life. Steel-and-glass skyscrapers of modern mega-corporations tower above turn-of-the-20th-century banking halls that resemble Roman temples of commerce. Pioneer skyscrapers from the 1920s still soar gracefully. Both old and new buildings represent imposing feats of engineering and, in some cases, high points of American architecture. The white Transamerica Pyramid cleaves the drifting fog. The red granite Bank of America building, when the sunset light is right, glows like a tower of gold (which, in a sense, it is).

The district's roots go back to the 1830s, when it was the site of Yerba Buena Cove, a small trading settlement. American forces under Capt. John Montgomery took it over from Mexico in 1846. The next year Jasper O'Farrell extended the street layout of the fledgling city. He laid out Market Street, a wide boulevard that slices across the downtown grid at a 36-degree angle, essentially making hash of the traffic pattern for years to come. Market Street later became a line of social demarcation, with financial institutions and the upper classes to the north, and industry and the working class to the south.

During the gold rush, the arrival of droves of Forty-Niners (see pp. 25–27) transformed what was then a backwater settlement of 500 people into a teeming throng of 20,000. The city had no option but to expand. Its eastern shoreline lay at Montgomery Street, from which wharves were built into the bay to serve the merchants' warehouses. Soon the mudflats between the wharves were filled in with sand, trash, and even abandoned ships whose crews had lit out for the goldfields. Over a hundred such ships were buried beneath the city as the shoreline pushed steadily eastward to today's Embarcadero.

As San Francisco got rich on gold and silver in the 1850s and 1860s, new banks and financial institutions arose on the old waterfront, earning the area based around Montgomery Street the title of the "Wall Street of the West." When the Bank of California opened in 1866 on California Street, this became the area's most prestigious commercial address.

Around 1890 the downtown area began to grow up—literally. The first steel-frame skyscrapers began to rise, among them the Mills Building, a Romanesque revival design by Daniel Burnham that still stands on Montgomery Street. Most of the Financial District was reduced to rubble and ashes in the 1906 earthquake and fire, but it was quickly rebuilt. Today, apart from the area around Jackson Square, little remains of the city created by the gold rush. By the 1920s innovative taller buildings were scraping the sky. Like other tall art deco buildings, the Shell Building incorporated stepped-back towers and vertical design elements that made it appear to rocket upward. But the advent of the 1930s Great Depression put a lid on this new thrust.

Not until the end of the 1950s did construction start again, big time. It began with the Crown Zellerbach Building in 1959, and culminated in the 1970s with the Bank of America headquarters and Transamerica Pyramid that dominated the city's skyline. Still more towers joined the high-flying parade in the 1980s. There are approximately 38 million square feet of office space contained within these few blocks, so it is no surprise that new development has lately shifted south of Market Street (where new laws restrict the height and bulk of developments). Despite this, the Financial District remains the heart of the city's business life, and Montgomery Street is still the main artery of this area.

Wander around the Financial District at lunchtime with office workers enjoying the fresh air. Step aside as power brokers in power suits stride past. Peek into the often exceptional lobbies of the buildings. Stroll the streets—the Financial District is compact and easy to walk—and gaze upward to see the art of building at its loftiest. But watch out for speeding bicycle messengers! ∎

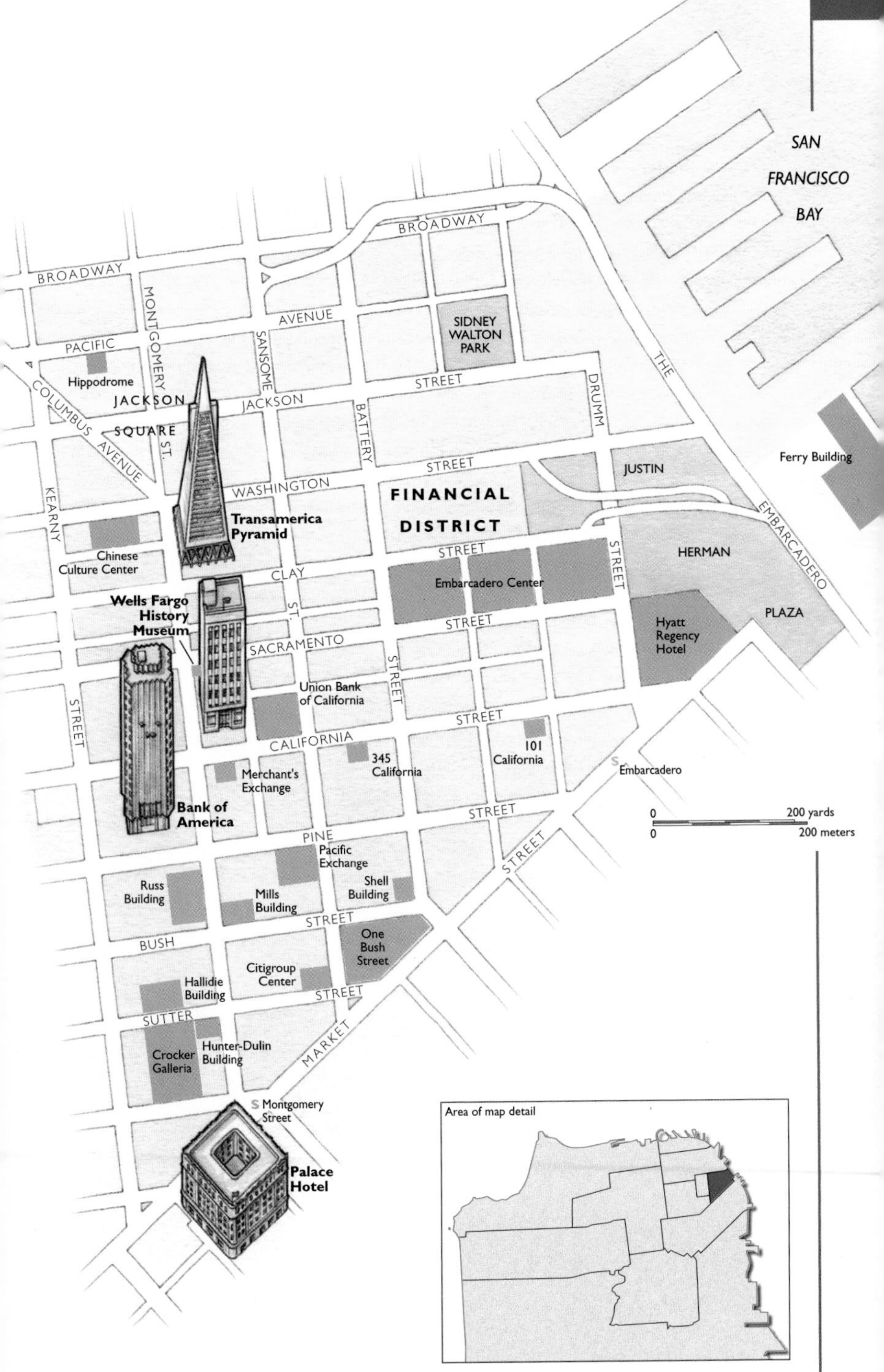

SAN

FRANCISCO

BAY

BROADWAY

BROADWAY

SIDNEY
WALTON
PARK

STREET

THE

PACIFIC

Hippodrome

MONTGOMERY ST.

SANSOME

JACKSON

JACKSON

STREET

BATTERY

DRUMM

Ferry Building

SQUARE

COLUMBUS AVENUE

STREET

JUSTIN

WASHINGTON

FINANCIAL

Transamerica
Pyramid

DISTRICT

KEARNY

EMBARCADERO

STREET

HERMAN

Chinese
Culture Center

CLAY

Embarcadero Center

ST.

PLAZA

Wells Fargo
History
Museum

STREET

Hyatt
Regency
Hotel

SACRAMENTO

STREET

Union Bank
of California

S

Embarcadero

CALIFORNIA

STREET

Bank of
America

Merchant's
Exchange

345
California

101
California

STREET

STREET

PINE

Pacific
Exchange

Russ
Building

Mills
Building

Shell
Building

STREET

BUSH

One
Bush
Street

Hallidie
Building

Citigroup
Center

STREET

SUTTER

Crocker
Galleria

Hunter-Dulin
Building

MARKET

S Montgomery
Street

Palace
Hotel

0   200 yards
0   200 meters

Area of map detail

Around the Financial District

Transamerica Pyramid
 600 Montgomery St.
CC: California St.;
Bus: 1, 15, 42;
BART: Montgomery

THE FINANCIAL DISTRICT IS AN OPEN-AIR TEXTBOOK OF architectural periods, with stunning new skyscrapers and resplendent old banking halls that draw on classical styles. These are working buildings, so they may not provide access for tourists.

TRANSAMERICA PYRAMID

As San Franciscan as a cable car, this is the most easily recognized building in the city. Built in 1972 with 48 stories and a spire, it pokes 853 feet into the sky—taller than any other building in the city. Why a pyramid? Architect William Pereira realized that its slender shape would allow more light to reach the street than a standard box design. Transamerica, an insurance and financial company, realized that as a corporate logo, the pyramid would put them on the map.

Here are Amazing Pyramid Facts, from the ground up: The base is a 30,000-ton concrete slab laced

with more than 300 miles of steel reinforcing rods. The walls slope at five degrees; their 3,000 quartz aggregate panels weigh 3.5 tons each and are spaced to allow movement in an earthquake. Exactly 3,678 windows pierce the building. (They pivot for washing from inside, a one-month job.) Two windowless wings begin at the 29th floor, the east holding elevators, the west a stairwell and smoke tower. The largest floor is the fifth at 145 feet per side; the smallest is the 48th, only 45 feet per side. The 212-foot spire is hollow and illuminated from inside. On the east side, this mountainous skyscraper has a California redwood grove (a good picnic spot).

The pyramid occupies the site of the 1853 Montgomery Block, once the biggest building west of the Mississippi. With prestigious offices for lawyers, businessmen, and newspapers, it was visited by everyone from Mark Twain (who met the original Tom Sawyer, a fireman, here) to Sun Yat-sen (who wrote the proclamation of the Republic of China in a lawyer's office).

CALIFORNIA STREET

The **Bank of America building** soars 779 feet (52 stories) and contains almost two million square feet of office space, where 5,000 people work. The facades zigzag to make bay windows and are clad in polished carnelian granite, creating a looming, deep red presence in the cityscape. On the top floor is the Carnelian Room, where cocktails or dinner come with a stupendous view. In the California Street plaza, a massive granite lump of a sculpture, "Transcendence" (1969) by Masayuki Nagare, is nicknamed "The Banker's Heart."

Bank of America founder Amadeo P. Giannini started his bank in 1904 for Italian immigrants whom other banks wouldn't serve. His Bank of Italy (as it was first called) accepted deposits as small as a dollar. During the 1906 fire, Giannini himself hauled deposits to safety, hidden in fruit crates. Giannini created the branch banking system, and by 1945 the Bank of America was the nation's largest (it no longer holds this position).

In 1864 William Ralston and Darius Mills founded the **Bank of California** (now the Union Bank of California, at 400 California St.). Ralston had made a fortune investing in Nevada's Comstock mines,

Bank of America building

- ✉ 555 California St.
- ☎ 415/433-7500 (Carnelian Room)
- 🕐 Carnelian Room open from 3 p.m.
- 🚇 CC: California St.; Bus: 1, 15; BART: Montgomery

Market Street seen from a dizzying height in the city's business center

Museum of Money of the American West
- ✉ 400 California St.
- 🕐 Closed Sat.–Sun.
- 🚇 CC: California St.; Bus: 1, 42

Wells Fargo History Museum
- ✉ 420 Montgomery St.
- ☎ 415/396-2619
- 🕐 Closed Sat.–Sun.
- 🚇 CC: California St.; Bus: 1, 12, 15, 42

and used it to finance projects such as the city's first iron mill. This banking temple (1907, Bliss and Faville) has Corinthian columns, a marble interior, and windows soaring toward a 60-foot-high coffered ceiling. The basement **Museum of Money of the American West** displays gold rush and Comstock artifacts: nuggets, banknotes, and privately minted coins. (One is inscribed "In Gold We Trust.")

The entrance of **345 California** (1987, Skidmore, Owings & Merrill) retains the fronts of two historic buildings (1919, 1920) that housed the Dollar Lines steamship company. The top 11 floors make up the elegant Mandarin Oriental Hotel, with twin towers linked by dizzying glass "sky bridges." **101 California** (1982, Johnson & Burgee) is a round glass silo. A slanted glass gallery cutting across the lower floors gives the tower above a weightless appearance.

MONTGOMERY STREET

The 31-story **Russ Building** (235 Montgomery St., private) was designed in 1927 in Gothic Revival style by George Kelham, whose E-shaped plan allows light and ventilation to penetrate to the offices. The lobby has inlaid floors, stone vaults, and ornate bronze elevator doors. The city's first all-steel-frame structure, the 1891 **Mills Building** (220 Montgomery St., private) was designed by Daniel Burnham in the Chicago school style, with an exterior of marble, buff brick, and terra-cotta, and a Romanesque entry arch. A 21-story tower by Lewis Hobart was added in 1931.

Also in this area, the **Wells Fargo History Museum** tells of the company that Henry Wells and William Fargo established in 1852

to provide banking, express, and mail services to the West. You'll see a century-old Concord stagecoach (and upstairs, a reproduction to sit in), a re-created Wells Fargo office, a telegraph key to try, raw gold and coins, and Wells Fargo strongboxes.

OTHER BUILDINGS

Designed by George Kelham in 1929, the soaring art deco **Shell Building** (100 Bush St.) is clad in terra-cotta. Its entrance is topped with a scallop shell, one of many such motifs honoring the builder, Shell Oil. The design was influenced by Eliel Saarinen's second-place entry in the Chicago Tribune Tower competition, a design never executed but of great impact.

The International Style shows its best face at **One Bush Street**, whose two components are a tower of green glass set atop stilts, and a low round pavilion. Designed in 1959 (Hertzka & Knowles/ Skidmore, Owings & Merrill), it also features a sunken plaza and an elevator tower of uniform mosaic.

Citigroup Center (1 Sansome St.), a 1984 design by William Pereira, preserves part of a 1910 beaux arts bank. Its forecourt displays a 1983 copy of the 1870 A. Stirling Calder statue from the 1915 Panama-Pacific International Exposition, "Star Girl," a woman in diaphanous gown and radiant star headdress. A block west, the 1926 **Hunter-Dulin Building** (111 Sutter St.) is where Sam Spade has his office in Dashiell Hammett's mystery stories.

Next door is the glass-roofed **Crocker Galleria** (1982, Skidmore, Owings & Merrill), an arcade of boutiques and cafés. The third level connects to the rooftop garden of the 1908 bank at **One Montgomery** (Willis Polk). ∎

Jackson Square

IN JACKSON SQUARE YOU CAN IMAGINE YOU'RE IN THE commercial zone of gold rush San Francisco. Miners once weighed glittering nuggets on Gold and Balance Streets. Wells Fargo stage-coaches rattled into livery stables on Hotaling Place. The district—four blocks bounded by Washington Street, Columbus Avenue, Pacific Avenue, and Sansome Street—preserves masonry buildings and cast-iron facades that date back as far as the 1850s. The streets are narrow and most buildings are under 40 feet high.

Jackson Square
🔼 See map p. 49
🚌 Bus: 12, 15, 42, 83

In the 19th century this part of town, particularly Pacific Avenue, was infamous as the **Barbary Coast** (named after pirate waters off North Africa). In this rough-and-tumble tenderloin, men were men and women were prosti-tutes—hundreds of them working in tiny "cribs." The most depraved acts became entertainment: On stage women had sex with horses. For a few pennies a man named Oofty Goofty let people beat him with a baseball bat; another man ate any disgusting glop presented to him. The streets jumped with saloons called the Morgue, Devil's Kitchen, and the like. "Give it a wide berth as you value your life," said an 1878 tourist guide, describ-ing "the precise locality, so that our readers may *keep away*." Dance hall entertainers included the Little Lost Chicken, who cried at the end of her songs and later picked the pockets of the crowd. A sister act called the Dancing Heifer and the Galloping Cow made the audience—and the boards of the stage—groan. Of all the dance halls, the old **Hippodrome** *(555 Pacific Ave., private)* still shows off its bas-relief facade of busty girls.

Buildings here largely survived the 1906 earthquake and fire. In 1908 San Francisco's first gay bar, The Dash, opened at Pacific Avenue and Kearny Street. But after 1913 the government slowly

expunged sin from the Barbary Coast. When the 1930s Depression lowered rents, artists moved in. Twenty years later, the district was taken over by interior decorators, then by today's antique dealers, architects, ad agencies, and design studios. Restored and glittering, this quarter makes a pleasant place to stroll along tree-shaded streets.

One axis is Montgomery Street.

Grand old buildings in the Jackson Square historic district

The Financial District rises in the heart of the City.

Among past tenants of the 1851 building at **722 Montgomery** were an auctioneer, a Turkish bathhouse, and a theater where frontier chanteuse Lotta Crabtree performed. In the late 1950s a flamboyant lawyer, the late Melvin Belli, moved in. Whenever he won a big tort case, the building flew a Jolly Roger flag. The three-story brick building at **728 Montgomery** (1854) occupies the site where California's first Masonic Lodge meeting took place in 1849. Reputedly, Bret Harte wrote his short story "The Luck of Roaring Camp" here in the 1850s. Artists later occupied the top floors, where they entertained Oscar Wilde in 1882. More literary history was made at **730–32 Montgomery,** the 1852 Golden Era Building, home to the literary weekly that published early work by Harte and Twain.

The **400 block** of **Jackson Street** is lined with historic buildings, many adapted as high-end antiques shops. The former French consulate at **472 Jackson** (1852) has simple brick walls and its original iron shutters upstairs for fire protection. The 1860s masonry buildings on each side of Hotaling Place—**445, 455,** and **463 Jackson**—were the domain of liquor distiller Anson Hotaling, purveyor of booze to the Barbary Coast. When his Italianate warehouse survived the 1906 fire, a local wit wrote the famous jingle: "If, as they say, God spanked the town/For being over-frisky/Why did He burn all the churches down/And spare Hotaling's whiskey?" Possible answer: Firemen worked *really* hard to save this particular building. In 1893, Domingo Ghirardelli opened his pioneering chocolate factory (see pp. 118–19) in an 1853 building at **415 Jackson.**

Off Jackson, **Balance Street** was reputedly named for a ship buried here as landfill, a common practice during gold rush fever. ■

Palace Hotel

IT WOULD BE ACCURATE TO DESCRIBE THE PALACE HOTEL as a phoenix, because the building you see today rose out of the ashes of an earlier one and carries on some of its extraordinary style.

Occupying a whole block, the city's grande dame original Palace Hotel was financed by William Ralston of the Bank of California in 1875. Guests entered a central courtyard edged with tiers of balconies and capped by a vast skylight. With seven stories and ample white paint, the hotel was compared to a combination of riverboat and wedding cake. There were newfangled elevators (or "rising rooms" in the parlance of the day). Each guest room boasted a fireplace and discreet water closet, from which the "water is carried off without producing the horrid noise one usually hears." Guests ranged from President Ulysses S. Grant to actress Sarah Bernhardt, who arrived in 1887 with her pet baby tiger.

In 1906 tenor Enrico Caruso checked in with 40 pairs of boots and an equal number of portraits of himself, but fled in a bath towel when the great earthquake struck. The Palace withstood the temblor, but burned in the ensuing fire. Overextended, banker Ralston apparently drowned himself.

The hotel rose again in 1909, with a new design by New York's Trowbridge and Livingston (famous for the St. Regis Hotel). The former carriage entrance was transformed into the beaux arts style **Garden Court restaurant,** crowned by a spectacular dome of 70,000 pieces of leaded art glass. Austrian crystal chandeliers twinkle above the potted palms and Ionic columns of Italian marble.

Like the Garden Court restaurant, **Maxfield's cocktail lounge** is in itself worth a visit to the hotel. Above the bar stretches a glowing Maxfield Parrish mural of the Pied Piper of Hamelin, like a page from the illustrated fairy tales of an earlier day.

The hotel underwent complete restoration between 1989 and 1991, and once again ranks as one of the city's top hotels. The traditional mahogany furnishings have been combined with modern fixtures, and original fireplaces can be found in the Palace, Bridal, Governor's, and Presidential Suites. ■

Palace Hotel

✉ 2 New Montgomery St. (at Market St.)

☎ 415/512-1111

🚌 Bus: 7, 9, 21, 31, 66, 71; Streetcar: J, K, L, M, N

Note: See p. 245 for further information.

Social San Francisco takes tea in the Palace's opulent Garden Court.

The entrance to the Embarcadero Center

More places to visit

EMBARCADERO CENTER

A cluster of four 35- and 40-story office towers linked by pedestrian bridges, and bounded by the Justin Herman Plaza, Clay Street, Sacramento Street, and Battery Street, was designed by John Portman and Associates from 1967 to 1982 and partly financed by David Rockefeller. This is San Francisco's largest redevelopment project, so extensive that it includes more than 150 shops and restaurants.

Don't miss the magnificent 17-story atrium of the **Hyatt Regency Hotel** (*California St. at Drumm St., see p. 245*), the world's largest hotel lobby. The vast irregular space incorporates a "creek" and trees, an immense spherical sculpture by Charles Perry ("Eclipse," 1973), cafés, and twinkling glass elevators rising to a revolving cocktail bar. On the bay side, **Justin Herman Plaza** is popular with skaters and features the Vaillancourt Fountain of monumental tubes with flowing water.

🅰 Map p. 49 🚋 CC: California; Bus: 1, 32, 42

HALLIDIE BUILDING

With the design of this 1917 building, architect Willis Polk made history. This was the world's first example of the glass curtain wall, an amazing innovation at a time when walls were supposed to be solid and substantial. The facade is a grid of panes suspended in front of the seven-story concrete structure, so it bears no weight. Decades ahead of its time, the design later found wide use in commercial architecture. Decorative iron fire escapes frame the expanse of glass. The building is named for Andrew Hallidie, developer of the cable car.

✉ 130–150 Sutter St. 🚋 Bus: 4 🕐 Not open to the public

MERCHANT'S EXCHANGE BUILDING

Designed by Willis Polk, this 1903 building was once the hub of San Francisco commerce. In the Grain Exchange Hall, traders, investors, and shipowners made deals for merchandise arriving on ships—which were spotted by lookouts on the roof of the 14-story building. Visitors are allowed access to the present-day bank, where fine paintings by William Coulter trace the maritime history of San Francisco.

✉ 465 California St. ☎ 415/421-7710
🚋 Bus: 3, 4, 15

PACIFIC EXCHANGE

Formerly occupied by the largest stock exchange in the U.S. outside New York (and now a gymnasium), this is the 1915 U.S. Subtreasury building, a columned granite hall remodeled and expanded in 1930 by Miller & Pfleuger. At the entrance to the building are Ralph Stackpole's monumental sculptures in 1930s social-realist style: "Man and His Inventions" and "Mother Earth."

✉ 301 Pine St. 🚋 CC: California St.; Bus: 3, 4, 15, 42 ■

Union Square is to serious shoppers what Christmas is to children. Nearby Nob Hill rises a mere 376 feet above sea level, but has a high-flown air and stunning views of the bay, the Financial District, and Russian and Telegraph Hills.

Union Square & Nob Hill

Sensible sign at the Cable Car Museum

Union Square & Nob Hill

IF SAN FRANCISCO WERE A THEATER, ITS MAIN STAGE WOULD BE UNION Square. Nob Hill would be a box seat for viewing the urban drama from lofty heights, both geographically and socially. The two districts are linked by the Powell and California cable car lines.

UNION SQUARE

Union Square is the heart of traditional San Francisco. It is a lively hub of elegant stores, bell-clanging cable cars, and flower stalls.

Union Square Park in 2002 got a $25 million makeover—a granite plaza with a terraced stage big enough to hold a symphony orchestra, a café, grassy terraces for relaxing, and somewhat underwhelming "light sculptures." It's a rest spot for office workers, homeless people, and exhausted shoppers. Stores range from vast Macy's and Neiman Marcus to Tiffany and Chanel. East of the park are boutiques; to the west, hotels and theaters.

The neighborhood wasn't always commercial. When Union Square Park was given to the city in 1850 by Mayor John Geary, churches, Victorian houses, and private men's clubs clustered round it. When residents moved away from fashionable Sutter Street in the late 19th century, their houses were converted to stores. The City of Paris department store appeared in 1896, and the St. Francis Hotel opened in 1904. Now Union Square was a destination in itself.

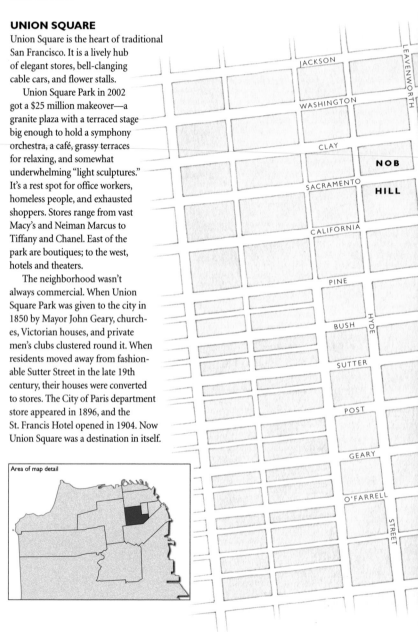

Area of map detail

NOB HILL

After the cable car conquered San Francisco's hills in 1873 Nob Hill began to look like prime real estate to wealthy men. In 1876 Leland Stanford of the "Big Four" (see p. 63)

erected an Italianate mansion, soon overshadowed by an edifice of Gothic towers, gables, and gingerbread that Stanford's partner, Mark Hopkins, built next door at his wife's urging.

Collis P. Huntington and Charles Crocker of the Big Four also had Nob Hill mansions that trumpeted their owners' conspicuous consumption. The mansions of James Fair and James Flood, two of the "Bonanza Kings"(see p. 27), were filled with European antiques. Most mansions on so-called Snob Hill were built of wood and destroyed in the 1906 fire. Only the brownstone Flood Mansion (now the Pacific Union Club on California St.) survived. Over time, rebuilding brought Edwardian houses, apartments, luxury hotels, and the vast Grace Cathedral. ∎

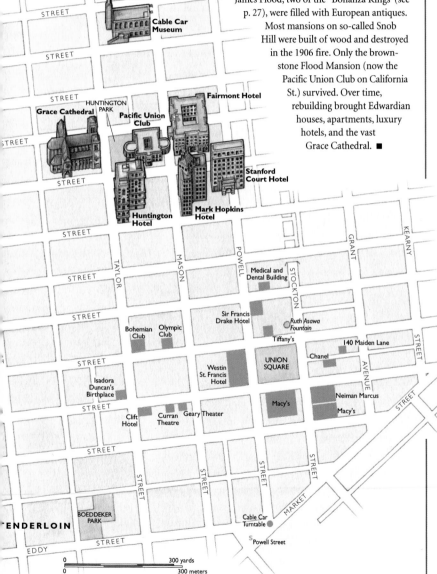

UNION SQUARE WALK

Union Square walk

Stroll among grand hotels, theaters, and throngs of shoppers in San Francisco's most famous retail district. Credit card ready? Cha-a-a-arge!

Begin in the lobby of the **Westin St. Francis Hotel ❶** (*335 Powell St., tel 415/397-7000*). Its marble and gilt reflect the opulent vision of railroad millionaire Charles T. Crocker, who promoted the idea of a world-class hotel for the city. Opened in 1904, the St. Francis has welcomed monarchs and U.S. Presidents (including Richard Nixon, whose midnight craving for Oreo cookies was duly fulfilled). The lobby's 1856 Viennese Magneta clock, with its carved rosewood cabinet, is a meeting spot for social San Franciscans. For a dizzying thrill, go to the rear lobby and ride a glass elevator up the outside of the tower.

Newly revamped Union Square

Across Powell Street is **Union Square Park ❷**, a central place to rendezvous with friends or just to rest your weary feet and do some people watching. Once a sand bank, the 2.6-acre park was set aside as open space in Jasper O'Farrell's 1847 plan of the city. Named when pro-Union rallies were held here just before the Civil War, the park has provided a soapbox for public expression since 1930s labor demonstrations. In 1958 beatniks in sandals and beards paraded here to a bongo-drum beat on the "Squaresville Tour," designed to express wry annoyance at having become tourist attractions in North Beach. In 1987 a group of gay activists called the Sisters of Perpetual Indulgence protested Pope John Paul II's visit.

The park's Dewey Monument honors Adm. George Dewey for his 1898 victory in Manila Bay during the Spanish-American War. Atop its 97-foot Corinthian column stands Robert Aitken's 1903 bronze figure of "Victory." (His lithe model was San Francisco grande dame Alma de Bretteville Spreckels in her youth.) Beneath the park is a pioneer underground parking garage built in 1942.

Along Geary Street sprawls an immense **Macy's** department store. At Stockton stands the postmodern **Neiman Marcus** ❸ (1982, Johnson and Burgee), clad in multicolored Italian granite. Step into the rotunda to see a 2,600-piece stained-glass dome of pale gold and white, preserved from the 1909 City of Paris store, on whose site it stands. The ship it depicts is the emblem of Paris, France, whose Latin municipal motto (*Fluctuat nec Mergitur*) translates, "It floats but does not sink." In 1982 the fine beaux arts City of Paris did sink, however, to the sorrow of San Franciscans.

As you walk up Stockton Street, here's a typical scene: A homeless man seated by an open suitcase full of black kittens. Behind him in a store window, a mannequin slouches in a chic black dress. Enter **Maiden Lane,** an ironic name, considering that at the turn of the 20th century harlots lined the narrow street. Beckoning from windows and naked from the waist up, they charged passing men a dime to fondle one breast, or two for fifteen

---

🗺 See area map page 58
▶ St. Francis Hotel
🔄 less than 1 mile
🕐 2 hours
▶ Powell at Market Street

NOT TO BE MISSED
- St. Francis Hotel
- 140 Maiden Lane

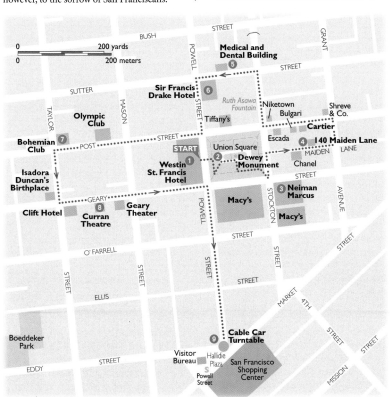

The Tenderloin

An unsavory district with sex for sale and a high crime rate, the Tenderloin lies near Union Square and is bounded roughly by Larkin, Mason, O'Farrell, and Market. This is not a good place to venture at night. ∎

cents; further intimacies cost a quarter. With sex came violence; the street averaged one murder a week. All this sin was reformed by the 1906 earthquake and fire. Today the lane is lined with upscale shops and café tables.

The highlight is **140 Maiden Lane** ④ *(now Folk Art International gallery, tel 415/392-9999)*. The city's only building designed by Frank Lloyd Wright (1949), it has been called one of the gems of 20th-century American architecture. The facade of honey-hued brick has a splayed entry arch of glass and brick that funnels passing shoppers inside. The sweeping circular ramp to the mezzanine prefigures Wright's design for the New York Guggenheim Museum. Circular wall cut-outs and other round motifs echo the building's original use—as a china shop. The architect signed his creation on a red tile at the left of the entrance.

At Grant Avenue, turn left to Post Street. Turn left here and explore a block of stores both traditional and chic that include Shreve & Co., Cartier, Bulgari, Escada, Yves Saint Laurent, and Niketown.

Near Post and Stockton you'll find the **Ruth Asawa Fountain,** set into stairs outside the Grand Hyatt Union Square. The 1972 fountain is faced in whimsical San Francisco scenes including Cliff House, the Transamerica Pyramid, and Victorian houses.

Continue up Stockton to Sutter and turn left to the **450 Sutter Medical and Dental Building** ⑤ (1928, Pflueger & Miller), an art deco skyscraper whose facade and gilded entrance canopy are rampant with Mayan designs. The elevator lobby is a fantasy temple with a stepped roof and hanging lamps adorned with Mayan faces.

At Powell Street, turn left downhill past the 1928 **Sir Francis Drake** ⑥ hotel *(450 Powell St.),* whose doorman famously wears a red Beefeater uniform.

At Post Street, turn right and walk two blocks to see two of San Francisco's elite private clubs. Housed in a Renaissance-style palazzo, the **Olympic Club** *(524 Post St.)* is the nation's oldest amateur athletic organization (1860). World heavyweight champion "Gentleman Jim" Corbett was once the boxing instructor; the Australian crawl was first demonstrated to Americans in the glass-roofed swimming pool. Next door, at the corner of Taylor Street and Post Street, stands the vine-covered premises of the **Bohemian Club** ⑦. Although it was founded in 1872 by artists, writers, and journalists, and the group's early members included luminaries such as Jack London and Ambrose Bierce, business leaders now fill the ranks. On the Post Street side, a 1919 bronze bas-relief by J. J. Mora depicts characters from Bret Harte tales.

Turn left down Taylor to see the **birthplace of Isadora Duncan** *(601 Taylor St.);* the free-spirited dancer of the early 20th century was the first to perform barefoot and to interpret music through improvised movement.

At the corner of Geary Street, the Clift Hotel *(tel 415/775-4700)* is a San Francisco classic redone by tragically hip hotelier Ian Schrager. The 1933 **Redwood Room,** paneled entirely from one 2,000-year-old redwood tree, now has television screens glowing with digital art.

You are now in the theater district. Walk along Geary Street toward Union Square to reach the **Curran Theatre** ⑧ *(445 Geary St., tel 415/551-2000),* with its mansard roof and Romanesque arches (1922, Alfred Henry Jacobs). Next door is the ornate facade of the **Geary Theater** *(415 Geary St., tel 415/749-2228),* where colorful terra-cotta fruit entwines the columns, and masks of comedy and tragedy mark the entrance doors. Designed by Bliss & Faville in 1909, it has showcased stars from Fanny Brice to Helen Hayes (who debuted here); it now presents the celebrated productions of ACT/American Conservatory Theater.

Continue to Powell Street at Union Square. If you turn right to Market Street you will see the **Powell Street cable car turntable** ⑨, a device with which a single-ended cable car can be rotated by hand. ∎

Hotels of Nob Hill

THE GRANDEUR OF NOB HILL'S MANSIONS TURNED TO smoke in the 1906 fire, but in their place rose great hotels.

The **Stanford Court Hotel** occupies the mansion site of Leland Stanford, who financed the steep California cable car line largely to make it easier to come home. Lobby murals show Nob Hill's mansions.

Of Mark Hopkins' three-million-dollar Victorian mansion, with its rampant excesses, only granite retaining walls survive. These edge the 1926 **Mark Hopkins** hotel, designed by Weeks & Day. High above the city in the Top of the Mark bar, World War II servicemen bound for the Pacific whispered goodbyes to their sweethearts.

The **Fairmont Hotel** occupies land once owned by Comstock silver king "Bonanza Jim" Fair. The Renaissance Revival building was gutted by the 1906 fire before opening day. Architect Julia Morgan oversaw its resurrection. Don't miss the Tonga Room, a wonderfully over-the-top bamboo cocktail lounge with a lagoon and regular tropical "thunderstorm."

The brick-and-ivy **Huntington Hotel** occupies a 1924 apartment house designed by Weeks & Day. Known for discretion and impec-

Mark Hopkins hotel entrance

cable service, it attracts celebrities who shun publicity. The lobby has the feel of an English country house, with 19th-century paintings. Decorated in green leather and wood, the Big Four Restaurant is hung with railroad memorabilia. ∎

Note: see p. 246 for further information on all four hotels.

The Big Four

Four Sacramento merchants—Leland Stanford, Mark Hopkins, Charles Crocker, and Collis P. Huntington—made one of the shrewdest business deals in U.S. history, financing the Central Pacific Railroad (later the Southern Pacific) to build the 1869 transcontinental rail line. The "Big Four," called "robber barons" for their unscrupulous tactics, soon - controlled California transportation and politics. All owned Nob Hill mansions. ∎

Nob Hill

⊠ See map pp. 58–59

🚌 CC: All lines; Bus: 1

Renaissance Stanford Court Hotel

✉ 905 California St.

☎ 415/989-3500

InterContinental Mark Hopkins

✉ 1 Nob Hill

☎ 415/392-3434

Fairmont

✉ 950 Mason St.

☎ 415/772-5000

Huntington Hotel

✉ 1075 California St.

☎ 415/474-5400

Grace Cathedral

Grace Cathedral
- See map p. 59
- 1100 California St. at Taylor St.
- 415/749-6300
- CC: All lines; Bus: 1

THE NATION'S THIRD LARGEST EPISCOPAL CATHEDRAL measures 329 feet long, with a spire rising 247 feet. It is modeled on Paris's Notre Dame, and, like a European cathedral, took many years to complete (1928–1964). Unlike a European cathedral, it was built not of stone but of reinforced concrete—a material perhaps incongruous for a sacred space. (It was used for earthquake safety.)

Heaven and earth: Sunbathing in Huntington Park near Grace Cathedral

The French Gothic architecture by Lewis Hobart sets off some fine features. In the **east portal** are copies of Lorenzo Ghiberti's bronze "Doors of Paradise" created for the Baptistry in Florence in 1445, with panels of Old Testament scenes. Above the 2.75-ton doors glows a rose window made in Chartres. In the **Singing Tower,** a carillon has 44 bronze bells from England that weigh 12 pounds to 6 tons. A joyful noise rises in the cathedral when the bells ring, or when the baroque organ (1930, Aeolian Skinner Co.) thunders through its 1,422 pipes.

To the left of the main altar, the **Chapel of Grace** has a limestone French altar of 1430. The fine Gospel windows in the nave are by Charles Connick (1930) and contain 20,000 pieces of richly colored glass. Other windows depict Jesus Christ and a somewhat baffling range of other figures, including Henry Ford and Albert Einstein.

A **tapestry labyrinth** on the floor duplicates the stone original at Chartres Cathedral. The single looping path symbolizes a religious pilgrimage. To tread it is a walking meditation, while reaching the center may bring a sense of illumination, guidance, or union. An identical labyrinth of terrazzo is in the Interfaith Meditation Garden in the Cathedral grounds (open to the public 24 hours a day).

Between the Diocesan House and the Chapter House once stood the cottage of undertaker Nicholas Yung, who refused to sell his lot to railroad baron Charles Crocker. Thwarted in owning the entire block, Crocker erected a 30-foot-high "spite fence" around three sides of Yung's property. Crocker's heirs obtained the parcel on Yung's death. After the 1906 fire, the family donated the block for Grace Cathedral. ∎

Cable Car Museum

IT SEEMS IMPOSSIBLE: THE STEEL ROPES THAT WHIZ IN AND out of this building power every cable car in San Francisco. The 1909 brick structure contains the system's powerhouse, repair shop, car barn, and a museum about the world's first (and now last) working cable cars.

Cable Car Museum
www.cablecarmuseum.com
- See map p. 59
- 1201 Mason St. at Washington St.
- 415/474-1887
- CC: Powell-Hyde, Powell-Mason

A cable car has no power of its own, but is towed by an endless loop of cable moving beneath the street. Downstairs in the Sheave Room, you'll see the cables come in underground and thread around large grooved wheels called sheaves. The cables figure-eight their way upstairs, then around other huge sheaves whose electric motors drive the system. Plaques and a video explain how everything works.

On display is **Cable Car #8,** sole survivor of the city's first cable car line, the 1873 Clay Street Hill Railroad. It looks like a comic-strip Toonerville Trolley, with simple wooden benches and a grip that's nothing more than a screw and nut attached to a hand-wheel. Other museum attractions include a couple of early cars, historical photos, transit apparatus (ticket

punches, coin changers), and model cable cars. At night, the city's cable cars are garaged in the barn on the building's upper level. ■

Huge wheels power the cable car system.

Mr. Hallidie aboard the very first version of his cable car

Hallidie's Folly

In 1869, London-born Andrew Smith Hallidie watched in horror as an overloaded streetcar slipped backwards down a San Francisco hill, cruelly dragging the horses trying to pull it.

Hallidie was a maker of wire rope, with a factory near today's Fisherman's Wharf, and he had designed cable systems for the gold country—including an overhead loop with a system for attaching ore buckets by gripping and ungripping. He imagined that a loop of wire rope could be made to move under the street, and that a rolling car could be attached or released at will.

People laughed at "Hallidie's Folly." But on August 1, 1873, the world's first cable car made its maiden run. The conductor chickened out when he saw the steep grade down five blocks of Clay Street, so Hallidie himself took the controls. ■

Powell-Hyde line outside the Cable Car Museum

Cable cars

A San Francisco trademark, the cable car is an endearing marvel of 19th-century mechanical ingenuity. Climb aboard a colorful Victorian car with its Bombay roof and clanging bells, and you slow down to the pace of an earlier day, taking time to enjoy the trip, and views of city and bay. Cable cars have appeared in movies, television commercials, and even wedding pictures.

Introduced by Andrew Hallidie in 1873 (see p. 65), the cable car replaced the horsedrawn streetcar. Horses couldn't struggle up a number of the city's hills and left tons of manure in the streets. Cable cars solved these problems. In the system's heyday, eight cable car lines crisscrossed the city with 112 miles of track.

By the early 1890s, more efficient electric streetcars made cable cars seem past their prime. But they remained in the hearts of San Franciscans. When officials decided to replace cable cars with buses, citizens launched a successful protest in 1947. ("San Francisco without its cable cars would be like a kid without his yo-yo!" said a radio comedian.)

Three lines survived along 10.5 miles of Hyde, California, Mason, and Powell Streets. In 1964, the system became the nation's only moving landmark on the National Register of Historic Places. In 1982 the system shut down for rehabilitation, reopening in 1984 with a gala celebration.

Among the system's 40 cars (of which 26 operate at one time), there are two types. Single-ended cars run on the two Powell lines, and must be manually reversed on a turntable at the end. Double-ended cars operate on the California line and don't require turning around, since they can be driven in either direction.

WHAT MAKES CABLE CARS GO?

A cable car has no motor—it is towed by a cable moving beneath the pavement. A complex network of pulleys supports and guides the cable around sharp turns and through crossings.

To make a cable car move, the gripman pulls a lever ("grip") that passes down through a slot in the pavement and clamps jaws onto the whizzing cable, something like a pair of pliers. The car's speed depends on how loosely or tightly the grip is closed. (The cable moves at a steady 9.55 miles an hour.) To stop, the gripman lets the cable drop, and the brakeman applies the brakes. The two coordinate through bell signals.

Cable car operators are chosen for their strength and outgoing personalities. The job must be a thrill, especially when a cable car rolls down the seemingly vertical stretch of Hyde Street between Bay and Francisco Streets, the system's steepest grade at 21.3 percent. (Relax: Each car has three sets of brakes.)

CABLES & GRIPS

Each 1.5-inch-diameter steel cable is made up of six strands of nineteen wires, which are woven around a core of sisal manila rope for more flexibility. Worn-out cables are replaced at night when the system is shut down. The old cable is cut and attached at one end to the new cable, then pulled through the entire channel and back to the powerhouse. The California line's cable is 21,500 feet long. Skilled splicers fasten the ends of the new cable into a loop, interweaving strands for 90 feet—a job that takes five hours.

Under constant stress and friction, a cable lasts 100 to 300 days. The grip's soft metal dies, which clamp the cable, must be replaced every four days. ■

Where they go

Three cable car lines serve the city:
California line Market Street to Van Ness Avenue. Sights include the Financial District, Chinatown, and Nob Hill.
Powell-Hyde line Market Street to Victorian Park near Fisherman's Wharf. Sights include Union Square, Nob Hill, Cable Car Barn Museum, Russian Hill, and stunning city and bay views.
Powell-Mason line Market Street to Bay Street near Fisherman's Wharf. Sights include Nob Hill, Cable Car Museum, North Beach, and city and bay views. See "Getting Around" on p. 243 for information on how to use the cable car system. ■

More places to visit

HUNTINGTON PARK

Opposite the Pacific Union Club, this slightly elevated 1.75-acre park was designed by John McLaren (superintendent of Golden Gate Park, see p. 156) on the site of the 1872 mansion of David Colton, attorney for the Big Four railway millionaires. The neoclassic

mansion later belonged to Big Four member Collis P. Huntington, whose widow gave the land (bereft of the house, which was destroyed in the 1906 fire) to the city. The central **Fountain of the Tortoises,** copied from a fountain in Rome, has bronze figures atop dolphins, shells, and tortoises. Mornings in the park bring practitioners of Tai Chi Chuan, a system of rhythmic Chinese exercise with a meditative quality. In the evening, look across at Grace Cathedral's rose window, illuminated from within in rich emerald and cobalt blue. ⊠ Bounded by California St., Taylor St., Sacramento St., and Cushman St. 🚇 CC: All lines; Bus: 1

PACIFIC UNION CLUB/FLOOD MANSION

In 1886 silver king James Flood (see p. 27) built a 42-room mansion for 1.5 million dollars. Around it he erected a lacy-patterned bronze fence that cost $30,000 and required a full-time employee just to keep it polished. A contemporary noted that the fence "flashed for the entire length of two blocks." The mansion's walls of Connecticut brownstone managed to survive the 1906 fire, while other Nob Hill palaces, being built of wood, went up like kindling. After the exclusive Pacific Union Club bought the landmark building in 1907, architect member Willis Polk added two wings in 1908. In the basement he installed a pool with Minoan columns and an illuminated ceiling of stained glass, which historian Randolph Delehanty ranks "among the most astounding private rooms in the city."

The club is a merger of two earlier groups: the Pacific Club (founded in a saloon in 1852 as the city's first gentlemen's club) and the 1854 Union Club. The best time to view the exterior is in early evening, when the windows of the shaded, hulking mansion shine warmly, as if turn-of-the-20th-century gas lamps were aglow in the richly appointed rooms. ⊠ 1000 California St. 🕐 Not open to the public 🚇 CC: All lines; Bus: 1 ■

Nob Hill's sole survivor of the 1906 fire, the stone Flood Mansion now houses an exclusive men's club.

C hinatown has often been called a "city within a city." By far the most densely populated area of San Francisco, it is best explored on foot.

Chinatown

Traditional Chinatown against the backdrop of the Financial District

Chinatown

STEP THROUGH THE JADE GREEN CHINATOWN GATE ON GRANT AVENUE AND you enter another world, a place at once exotic and ambiguous. Ahead stretches what appears to be a Cantonese marketplace, all pagoda roofs with upturned eaves (to ward off evil spirits), colorfully painted balconies, and signs in Chinese calligraphy.

There is an underlying layer of turn-of-the-20th-century America in the Edwardian buildings, not to mention a spot of carnival midway, with popping firecrackers, and shops selling all kinds of gimcracks from plastic kung-fu weapons to wicker "finger traps." Pot-bellied Ho Tai, the god of happiness, smiles in ivory and porcelain from a hundred store windows.

More than one cultural Chinatown exists within the traditional borders of Bush, Broadway, Powell, and Kearny Streets. The first is the colorful tourist attraction that stretches along Grant Avenue. Visitors from around the world come to sample exotic foods such as fishball soup (and never dream that "chop suey" is nothing more exotic than the Chinese name for "hash"). Tourists also shop for trinkets, as well as jade carvings, gold jewelry, and silk gowns.

This is also a true neighborhood, rather than a kind of improvised theme park. More than 30,000 people live in just 24 blocks, making this second Chinatown not only the

A close game in Portsmouth Square

most densely populated section of San Francisco, but also one of the most congested neighborhoods in the nation. Because of housing conditions—too many people per room, too little plumbing—this Chinatown has been characterized as a ghetto. The average income here is low, the number of people who don't speak English is high. The majority of residents were born outside the U.S. Women in small garment factories work long hours at whirring sewing machines for low wages. Residents must make use of whatever space they can find. Elderly men gather in Portsmouth Square, which functions as their community living room for chatting and playing Chinese chess. Children scamper in narrow alleys. On Stockton Street, locals shop for groceries, eat dim sum, and attend high school.

The third Chinatown forms a heartland for Chinese Americans who live elsewhere in the city. (Some have escaped the crowded conditions of Chinatown. Many younger, better educated, and more affluent Chinese never lived here but settled in the Richmond and Sunset Districts.) They come to buy snow peas, bamboo shoots, roast duck, oyster sauce, and other ingredients for holiday feasts. They read Chinese newspapers or see a Chinese movie. They enjoy big family dinners in upstairs banquet halls. In Waverly Place, they climb stairs to temples where incense rises above altars and oranges are left as offerings.

All three Chinatowns join together in joyful celebration of festivals such as Chinese New Year. Drums beat a cadence, dancing dragons weave along the street, and costumes of embroidered silk come out of closets to lend an air of the Far East to San Francisco.

You won't want to squeeze your car through the crowded streets, or search for a parking space. Walk around, so you can explore the neighborhood's maze of streets and alleys. Slowly, all three aspects of Chinatown will reveal themselves to you. ■

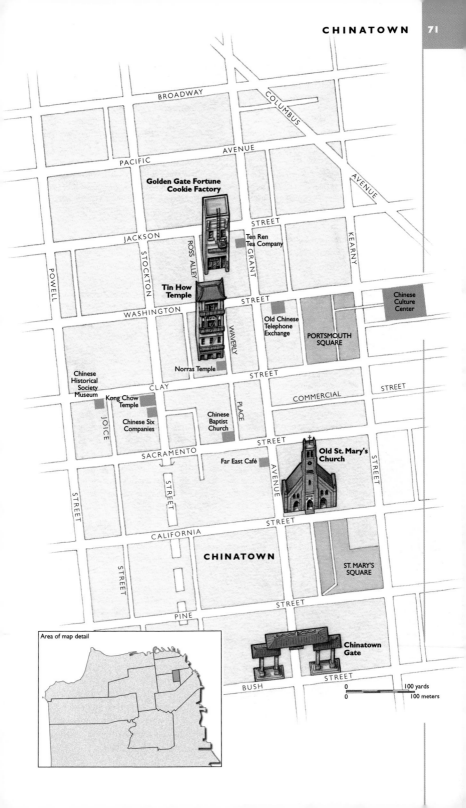

BROADWAY

COLUMBUS

PACIFIC AVENUE

AVENUE

Golden Gate Fortune Cookie Factory

JACKSON STREET

POWELL

STOCKTON

ROSS ALLEY

GRANT

KEARNY

Ten Ren Tea Company

Tin How Temple

WASHINGTON STREET

WAVERLY

Old Chinese Telephone Exchange

PORTSMOUTH SQUARE

Chinese Culture Center

Norras Temple

Chinese Historical Society Museum

CLAY STREET

COMMERCIAL STREET

JOICE

Kong Chow Temple

Chinese Six Companies

PLACE

Chinese Baptist Church

STREET

SACRAMENTO STREET

Far East Café

STREET

AVENUE

Old St. Mary's Church

STREET

CALIFORNIA STREET

STREET

CHINATOWN

ST. MARY'S SQUARE

PINE STREET

STREET

Area of map detail

Chinatown Gate

BUSH STREET

| 0 | 100 yards |
| 0 | 100 meters |

Chinese San Francisco

Chinese treasure seekers arrived in California in the late 1840s and headed for the gold diggings. (California was known as Gum San, or "golden mountain.") Most passed through San Francisco, and by 1849 the city's first Chinese restaurant opened, followed by laundries. Within 35 years San Francisco had 7,500 Chinese laundries.

By the late 1850s, the Chinese had gathered around Portsmouth Square, which American merchants had abandoned for new commercial districts. Most Chinese were unmarried male laborers, fleeing floods and famine in southern China's Guangdong Province, whose capital was Canton (now called Guangzhou). The Cantonese newcomers wore knee-length trousers and quilted jackets, with wide hats of split bamboo. As sojourners, most planned to save money and return home with improved chances for business and marriage.

Most men were indentured servants, having borrowed their ship passage from brokers in Asia, and were now compelled to work off their obligation. They joined associations that secured jobs, repaid their passage, provided a social life, and, if the men died, even organized the shipping of their bodies back to China for interment. In return, members paid dues. District associations recruited arrivals from various geographical regions of Guangdong, while family associations assembled men with the same family names (Lee, Eng, Wong, and so on). The immigration process was soon dominated by powerful merchants who established the Canton Company, or Sam Yup Association. They delivered peasant laborers to mines, railroads, and factories. In 1869 about 12,000 Chinese worked on the transcontinental railroad. Laborers formed an alliance of their own called the Sze Yup Association.

A third type of association was the Tong, or secret society. Some were organized for legitimate purposes, others for criminal. Tongs ran Chinatown's gambling, opium dens, and prostitution—understandable vices in a society of lonely single men, who in early days outnumbered women by two thousand to one.

Tongs also protected and avenged wrongs for members. Turf wars flared up, and Tong "hatchet men" (the source of this term) hacked and killed their rivals in illicit enterprises. Chinatown became a place of dark alleys and shadowy violence. To arbitrate disputes and promote civic activities, several district associations in the late 1850s united as the Chinese Six Companies, whose power dominated the community.

Chinese workers flooded the job market after the completion of the transcontinental railroad. American industrialists hired them at cheap wages, so white workers blamed the Chinese for taking away jobs. Resentment and xenophobia raged. Newspapers built hysteria over the "Yellow Peril." As it was, the Chinese were already isolated from American society. They kept to their own language, customs, and dress (including the long braided queues that China's Manchu emperors required as a sign of loyalty). Increasing white hostility led to beatings and murders, and in 1877 a mob attempted to burn down Chinatown. In 1882 racism reached a peak in the Chinese Exclusion Act, which prevented Chinese laborers from immigrating to the U.S. Another law barred Chinese women, thus condemning the working men of Chinatown to lifelong bachelorhood. No wives meant no families. Chinatown's population dwindled.

The 1906 earthquake and fire virtually erased Chinatown. But it also destroyed the citizenship records of the western U.S., which meant the government couldn't dispute Chinese claims of citizenship. "Paper sons" from China, asserting dubious kinship with U.S. residents, began to immigrate.

After 1906, city officials talked about relocating Chinatown, but local merchants argued that it would be better to create a district that appealed to tourists. In the 1920s an architectural style unique to San Francisco appeared, as American designers embellished plain Edwardian buildings with stylized pagoda roofs, painted balconies, and other bits of chinoiserie. Shops and restaurants proliferated, luring both tourists and Chinese, as they do to this day. ■

Chinatown life includes the Chinese New Year Parade and (below) traditional medicine.

Chinese medicine

Wooden drawers filled with leaves, barks, seeds, nuts, flowers, and roots—this is a Chinatown version of a pharmacy. The pharmacist is skilled in a 5,000-year-old art, using 600 different substances. You'll see chrysanthemum leaves (vision), dried sea slugs (virility), and ginseng root (vitality). The state licenses doctors and pharmacists in herbal medicine. ■

Funerals

Everyone, whether resident or tourist, pauses respectfully when a funeral passes. A brass band (sounding more like New Orleans than Nanking) follows a convertible automobile that displays a large photograph of the deceased. This journey allows friends to see the departed one last time, as he or she makes a final visit to favorite places in the neighborhood. ■

Grant Avenue

YOU'RE SURE TO APPEAR IN SOME OTHER VISITOR'S SNAP-shots at Chinatown Gate, the much photographed front door to Chinatown. Also known as the Dragon's Gate, it stands on Grant Avenue, Chinatown's main commercial strip.

Chinatown Gate

🏔 See map p. 71

✉ Grant Ave. at Bush St.

🚉 CC: California, Powell-Hyde, Powell-Mason; Bus: 1, 9X, 15, 30, 41, 45, 83

Chinatown Gate opens toward Union Square and separates two worlds.

CHINATOWN GATE

The gateway was designed by architect Clayton Lee in 1970, with crowning dragons and fish to imitate the ceremonial gates of Chinese villages. Traditionally, the central portal is reserved for persons of high rank to pass through. (Here autos receive this honor, typical of California.) Two flanking portals are guarded by stone *fou* dogs (dragon-like dog figures); the female is on the right (look for the pup under her paw, symbolizing the rejuvenation of life), while the male on the left watches over a pearl whose loss, it is said, would bring catastrophe to the village.

The gate honors principles of *feng shui*, a system of earth divination that aims to align structures in harmony with natural energy forces. The gate faces south, the direction most favorable for an entrance to a building or city.

GRANT AVENUE

This avenue is rich in history. Originally, it was Calle de la Fundación, the main street of the 1830s Mexican settlement of Yerba Buena. Later, as Chinatown's Dupont Street, it was a lair of gamblers and prostitutes. After the 1906 fire, civic leaders hoping to sanitize the street named it for President Ulysses S. Grant. Respectable at last!

The street's plain buildings add flair with Chinese architectural motifs and bright colors. Dragons twine around lampposts, their mouths gripping red lanterns. The streetlights were installed in 1925 as exotic touches when Chinatown began its tourism boom.

Between Bush and Broadway stand many restaurants and shops selling fans, ceramic gods, wind chimes, silk robes, cameras, and other tourist items. Finer stores display imported art pieces and jewelry of gold, jade, and amber. ∎

Color symbolism

To the Chinese, colors have a symbolic meaning, which explains the bright red (happiness and vitality), green (longevity) and yellow (wealth) seen in Chinatown. ∎

Waverly Place

Tin How Temple exemplifies the Street of Painted Balconies.

KNOWN AS THE STREET OF PAINTED BALCONIES—LOOK UP to see why—Waverly Place is sensually exotic. Iron balconies of red, yellow, and green evoke New Orleans' French Quarter … in psychedelic colors. The air is often redolent of temple incense, or the smoky tang of exploded firecrackers. Thundering drums from unseen precincts announce that youth groups are practicing their lion dance.

In early days the two-block street was known as "15 Cents Street"—the cost of a haircut from a Chinese barber. After the 1906 fire, functional brick Edwardian buildings were erected, then given Chinese trimmings. Commercial enterprises generally occupy a building's bottom floor, associations or dwellings fill the middle floors, and temples are on top, closest to heaven.

TIN HOW TEMPLE

You must climb three flights of stairs to reach Tin How Temple, the oldest Chinese temple in the U.S. (founded 1852). This building dates from 1911. The ceiling is hung with lanterns, each dangling a red paper with black calligraphy that represents a member family of the temple. Incense sticks in bronze urns waft aromatic smoke. Folded papers with gold squares are offerings for the deceased.

On the altar resides Tin How, goddess of heaven and sea, who is worshiped by millions of Chinese. The golden figure is supposed to have come from China in 1848. Tin How was born in 960, began meditating at age 11, became a Taoist disciple, and was said to develop the transcendental power of riding the sea to rescue people in distress. As protector of sailors, Tin How has had an important role in San Francisco, because Chinese immigrants had to cross the ocean. She also watches over travelers, actors, writers, and prostitutes—an eclectic group whose common traits make for interesting conjecture.

The carved main altar depicts the life of Confucius. Other temple figures include the three-eyed god Wah Kwong, as well as Madame Golden Lotus and the 18 guardian angels. Outside, more incense sticks waft perfume over Chinatown. ■

Tin How Temple

See map p. 71

125 Waverly Pl.

Bus: 1, 15, 30, 45

Time to go for a wok in Chinatown.

Walk through Chinatown

This walk winds through streets and alleys that reveal Chinatown's public and private personalities.

Begin at the **Chinatown Gate ❶** (see p. 74) and walk up **Grant Avenue ❷**. At California Street enjoy a classic San Francisco view: Chinatown's pagoda roofs, cable cars climbing to Nob Hill, and the Financial District skyscrapers downhill.

Near the corner of Grant and Pine, **St. Mary's Square ❸** features a 1938 statue by Beniamino Bufano depicting Sun Yat-sen (1866–1925), with face and hands of rose granite and a robe of stainless steel. Organizer of the Nationalist Party, Sun raised funds and started a newspaper in San Francisco to foster the 1911 overthrow of China's Manchu Dynasty. He served as first president of the new republic.

Exit the park at California Street, across which you'll see **Dai Choong Low** ("Tower of the Big Bell"), better known as **Old St. Mary's Church ❹** *(660 California St.).* Dedicated in 1854, it was the city's first cathedral and California's largest building, modeled after a Gothic church in Vich, Spain. The foundation granite was quarried in China, and the bricks came around the Horn from New England as ships' ballast. As San Francisco grew, an ocean of sin began to lap against St. Mary's island of Catholic faith. Nearby were opium dens and a red-light district. (Note the Victorian admonishment on the bell tower: "Son Observe the Time and Fly from Evil.") In 1891 a new cathedral was erected in a less notorious area, and the original became Old St. Mary's. The 1906 fire gutted the building, but spared the walls and tower. At the rear of the church are historic photos of Chinatown.

Turn right on Grant and peek into the **Far East Café** *(631 Grant Ave., tel 415/982-3245),* a classic 1920s Chinatown restaurant with tasselled lanterns and carved screens.

At Clay turn right to **Portsmouth Square ❺,** the community living room for crowded Chinatown. Children romp, while elderly men ponder board games. The square has had several historic roles. Laid out in 1839

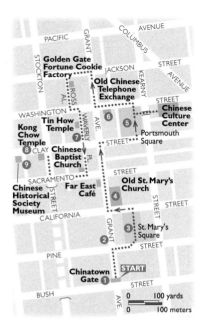

Bright lights advertise Chinatown attractions.

it also became the site of the city's first public school. In the 1860s businesses moved to new commercial districts created as the cove was landfilled, and Chinese people moved in.

On the square's north side a small galleon sails atop a granite base. It is a model of the fictional *Hispaniola* from the novel *Treasure Island*, a monument to its Scottish author, Robert Louis Stevenson, who in 1879 lived nearby and came to the square to watch the passing people and ships with his dark, thoughtful eyes. A statue of the Goddess of Democracy, commemorating the Tian'anmen Square massacre, also stands in this park.

Detour across the bridge to the incongruous gray cement tower of the Holiday Inn, erected without design review in 1971. The third floor shelters modest displays of art and musical instruments at the **Chinese Culture Center** (*750 Kearny St., 3rd floor, tel 415/986-1822, call for tours, www.c-c-c.org, historic $$$; culinary $$$$$, closed Mon.*).

Exiting the square onto Washington Street, head left to the **Old Chinese Telephone Exchange** ⑥ (*743 Washington St.*), a red-and-black pagoda with ornate peaked roofs. Now a bank, it opened in 1909 as the Pacific Telephone and Telegraph exchange. Operators spoke English and five dialects of Chinese. They also had to memorize every customer's phone number, since callers asked for connections by name. (It wasn't polite to refer to a person as a number.)

At Grant Avenue, turn right to **The Ten Ren Tea Company of San Francisco** (*949 Grant Ave., tel 415/362-0656*), which sells

See area map p. 71

► Chinatown Gate

⬌ less than a mile

🕒 2 hours

► Chinese Historical Society Museum

NOT TO BE MISSED

• Grant Avenue
• Portsmouth Square
• Waverly Place
• Tin How Temple

as the plaza of Mexican Yerba Buena, it was located a block west of Yerba Buena Cove (whose shoreline reached today's Montgomery Street). An adobe customhouse processed ships' cargoes. On July 9, 1846, the American flag was first raised over San Francisco by Capt. John B. Montgomery of the U.S.S. *Portsmouth*, the warship for which the square was later named. A memorial marks the spot.

In May 1848, entrepreneur Sam Brannan displayed gold from the American River here and set off the California gold rush. In this wide-open era the square was lined with saloons and gambling houses. Oddly, in 1848

more than 50 tea varieties, with hot samples available. At Jackson Street turn left to Ross Alley, part of a maze of Chinatown back streets whose shadowy atmosphere evokes the bad old days. Nineteenth-century gamblers and prostitutes plied their trades here.

Turn left to the tiny **Golden Gate Fortune Cookie Factory** *(56 Ross Alley, tel 415/781-3956)*, where women pour dough onto small griddles that revolve into an oven. Out come warm, flat cookies, which the ladies fold around paper fortunes. Shopping tip: The factory will insert any message you compose into its cookies.

Follow the alley to Washington and cross the street to **Waverly Place** ❼ (see p. 75), the "Street of Painted Balconies," the location of benevolent associations and temples such as the **Tin How Temple** and the **Norras Temple** *(109 Waverly Pl., 3rd floor)*, whose altar has gilded Buddhas.

Now continue on Waverly Place to the corner of Sacramento Street, where the **Chinese Baptist Church** was built in 1908 of red clinker brick. Turn right on Sacramento,

Grocery shopping is a social ritual.

then right at Stockton to see Chinese grocery items in the windows. Roast suckling pigs hang above trays of chicken feet and bins of *bok choy*.

Across the street you'll see the **Chinese Six Companies** *(843 Stockton St.)*, an umbrella group organized in the 1850s to unite district associations. It is still a business power in Chinatown. The 1908 building is adorned with dragons and fish.

Proceed to the **Kong Chow Temple** ❽ *(855 Stockton St., 4th floor)*. With carved, gilded altars, the temple is devoted to Kuan Ti, a third-century general who read poetry. He watches over soldiers and poets, criminals, and police alike. Turn left on Clay to the **Chinese Historical Society Museum** ❾ *(965 Clay St., tel 415/391-1188, www.chsa.org, closed Mon.)*, which occupies architect Julia Morgan's 1932 Chinatown YMCA, whose brick structure is beautifully integrated with three Chinese towers, decorative tiles, and painted ceiling panels. Exhibits look at Chinese life in San Francisco, and there are changing art shows. ■

Worth Beach is one of the city's most genial districts. It lies between hills that writers and artists discovered long ago.

North Beach, Telegraph Hill, & Russian Hill

Bright lights on Broadway

North Beach, Telegraph Hill, & Russian Hill

IN A CITY OF INTRIGUING NEIGHBORHOODS, NORTH BEACH IS A FAVORITE among San Franciscans themselves. In this sunny valley, you can let your gusto off the leash. Telegraph Hill and Russian Hill rise to either side, with steep streets, huge views, and beguiling houses.

In North Beach the good things—music, art, talk, and especially food—are prized. For this zest for life, we owe the Old World Italians who brought an appreciation of food, wine, and good company. To pretend you're in Italy, just inhale the aromas from trattorias, cafés, bakeries, and coffeehouses. Bask in the warm Mediterranean mood at Caffé Trieste, where the family owners sing opera on Saturday afternoons. To this Italian love of life, North Beach adds a live-and-let-live philosophy inherited from the Beats, who hung out here in the 1950s. Stir in the Asian culture that has pushed in from adjacent Chinatown. The result: a remarkable melting pot of nationalities and lifestyles. In Washington Square Park you might see an Italian baker sharing a bench with a bohemian poet. Meanwhile, on the lawn an elderly Chinese lady goes through the meditative movements of Tai Chi Chuan.

Interestingly, earlier bohemian circles of writers and artists had lived nearby—in the 1890s on Russian Hill, and in the 1920s on Telegraph Hill. Both places offered inspirational views and low rents. On Russian Hill a group calling itself Les Jeunes (The Young) included architect Willis Polk and poet Gelett Burgess (of "I Never Saw a Purple Cow" fame, see p. 35). They met at the home of Catherine Atkinson, who also welcomed visiting writers Mark Twain and Robert Louis Stevenson. A similar salon flourished in the home of poet, editor, and librarian Ina Coolbrith (see p. 100).

In 1952 Jack Kerouac stayed with his friend Neal Cassady on Russian Hill, while he finished *On The Road*. But today few bohemians live on these quiet hills. The houses, cottages, and apartments have largely been taken over by the city's elite and yuppies. The views are still free and

inspiring, though. Wander the tuck box lanes and flights of steep steps on both hills. And don't miss the view from Coit Tower, a Telegraph Hill landmark donated by an eccentric lady who loved firemen. ∎

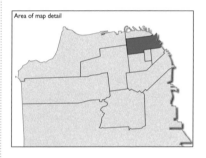

Area of map detail

Diego Rivera's "Making of a Mural" at the San Francisco Art Institute

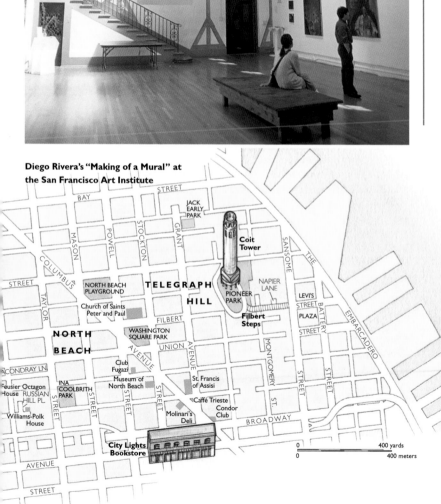

One of North Beach's community living rooms, the North End Café (above). Community life is also evident in the way Italian residents gather in the park to enjoy the sunshine (below).

North Beach

Oddly, North Beach has no beach; by the 1870s the original shore was filled in for industrial use. Today's main street, Columbus Avenue, was laid out in 1872 by cutting a diagonal route between the Financial District and the northern waterfront. The street creates quirky triangular corners and buildings that lend North Beach a touch of Paris.

The neighborhood gained its human character by being close to the port where 1850s immigrants poured in. Streets sang with the languages of Ireland, France, Germany, Chile, Peru, Spain, and Portugal. This was the "Latin Quarter." By the early 1900s, an influx of Italians had transformed the neighborhood into Little Italy.

Beginning in the 1920s, Italians began moving out, either to the Marina District or to farms in rural areas. This left a vacuum in North Beach, creating low rents that attracted a now famous group of bohemians, known as the Beats. They lived on poetry, red wine, bebop jazz, and motormouth conversation fueled by espresso coffee. The Beats scorned authority and conformity, embraced racial and sexual variety, and idealized a vagabond lifestyle on the far-out fringe of society. San Francisco made a perfect roost for them, with its open attitudes and tolerance.

In the evening stroll around North Beach, which comes to life with restaurants, music, and throngs of people—not to mention the heady aromas of garlic, olive oil, and tomato.

CITY LIGHTS BOOKSTORE

"A kind of library where books are sold," says a sign in the window of this pioneering book-store, founded in 1953 by poet Lawrence Ferlinghetti and Peter Martin. The nation's first all-paperback bookshop (it now offers hardcovers, too), City Lights *(261 Columbus Ave., tel 415/362–8193)* is a literary landmark where the Beats used to hang out. You'll feel the presence of novelist Jack Kerouac and poets Gregory Corso, Zen-influenced Gary Snyder, and Allen Ginsberg. In the poetry room upstairs, simple shelves and a funky green linoleum floor seem to match the (involuntary) vow of poverty of the Beats.

Ferlinghetti named the store after a Charlie Chaplin film, as a symbol of the little fellow fighting the big, impersonal world. City Lights

Lawrence Ferlinghetti reads poetry at his City Lights Bookstore.

Publishers has more than a hundred titles in print, including the Pocket Poets Series; one work is Allen Ginsberg's "Howl" (see below). Ferlinghetti's own *A Coney Island of the Mind* is one of America's best-selling poetry books at more than a million copies.

In 1999 Ferlinghetti—who has spent a lifetime thumbing his nose at officialdom—for a time served as poet laureate of San Francisco. As a send-up of corporate ritual, he would hand out poet laureate business cards. ∎

The "Howl" heard 'round the nation

When New York poet Allen Ginsberg moved to North Beach *(1010 Montgomery St.)*, he wrote an extended rant called "Howl" in early 1955. That October, at an old auto-repair shop converted into the Six Gallery *(3119 Fillmore St.)*, he read the poem to a crowd of Beat writers and artists. His delivery was like a free-form jazz improvi-sation, all rhythm and risk: "I saw the best minds of my generation destroyed by madness, starving hysterical naked," he raved. Urged on by Jack Kerouac's shouts of "Go! Go!"

Ginsberg made literary history—particularly when Lawrence Ferlinghetti published the poem in 1956, only to be arrested on obsceni-ty charges. The poem was full of four-letter words, perversions, blasphemies, and generally unsettling or loathsome images. Ginsberg testified that his poem fell in the Hebrew tradition of Old Testament prophets howling in the wilderness. He claimed he was "howling against a crazy civilization." The First Amendment trial ended in acquittal and focused national attention on the Beats. ∎

Broadway offers a
mix of cafés and
strip joints.

Broadway

THE STRETCH OF BROADWAY BETWEEN COLUMBUS AVENUE
and Montgomery Street is known as The Strip. (After all, this is where
entertainers take their clothes off…) A series of nude bars and adult
bookstores carry on, albeit mildly, the traditions of the sinful Barbary
Coast of gold rush days, when brothels, gambling dens, and saloons
filled neighboring Pacific Avenue. Bawdy entertainment spilled over
to Broadway, especially after a cleanup of "Terrific Pacific" following
the 1906 earthquake.

Broadway
- See map pp. 80–81
- Bus: 15, 30, 39, 45

Condor Club
- ✉ 300 Columbus Ave.
- ☎ 415/781-8222

hungry i
- ✉ 546 Broadway
- ☎ 415/362-7763

Carol Doda busted into history in
1964 as a topless dancer at the
Condor Club. Now a retro-style
lounge and dance club, the Condor
still offers a walk down Mammary
Lane: It preserves the piano on
which Carol Doda descended,
gyrating, from the ceiling, and
photos and news stories about the
exotic dancer. The humorously
philosophical Miss Doda once said:
"Anyone can take off their clothes,
but I made them laugh and then I
took off my clothes." The Condor's
bosomy advertising sign was taken
down in 1991.

The **hungry i** (originally located at 599 Jackson St.) was a force in
live entertainment in the late 1950s
and early '60s, when its bare brick
walls resounded with laughs for
new acts, like the Smothers
Brothers, Lenny Bruce, and Bill
Cosby, not to mention Richard
Pryor and Woody Allen. Singers
performing at the club included
Billie Holiday and Barbra Streisand.
The club now presents strip shows,
like many others on the street.
Barkers chant to entice tourists,
sailors, and college boys in.

Your best bet on Broadway is
Enrico's Sidewalk Café (see
p. 252), where you can sit with a
drink or meal and enjoy people-
watching; there is jazz nightly. ■

Washington Square Park

OFTEN CALLED THE HEART OF NORTH BEACH, THIS PARK may also be its green soul. In the shade of cypress and sycamore trees, old Italian men sit on park benches and talk. Of them Lawrence Ferlinghetti wrote: "You have seen them/the ones who feed the pigeons/cutting the stale bread/with their thumbs and pen knives/the ones with old pocket watches/the old ones with gnarled hands and wild eyebrows..." In early morning the sunny lawn attracts Asian practitioners of Tai Chi Chuan. At noontime picnickers appear. The park is a melting pot, arranged in a square.

Washington Square Park
- See map pp. 80–81
- Bus: 15, 30, 39, 45

Church of Sts. Peter & Paul
- 666 Filbert St.
- 415/421-0809
- Bus: 15, 30, 41, 45

Flanking the urban retreat are pale Edwardian buildings and the spires of the Church of Sts. Peter and Paul (which Ferlinghetti called the "marzipan church on the plaza"). The land was reserved as a park in 1847, but in 1872 the southwestern corner was cut off by Columbus Avenue. It now forms a separate triangle with statuary.

In the square's center stands a bronze Benjamin Franklin of 1879. Beneath it, a time capsule to be opened in 2079 contains a bottle of wine, a Ferlinghetti poem, and a pair of Levi's. Another sculpture (1933) depicts volunteer firemen and was funded by a bequest of Lillie Hitchcock Coit (see p. 96).

CHURCH OF STS. PETER & PAUL

A cream-colored Romanesque confection constructed in 1924, the church is especially pretty when illuminated at night. On the facade a line from Dante's *Paradiso*, rendered in mosaic, translates: "The glory of Him who moves all things penetrates and glows throughout the universe." The four Gospel-writers are represented by traditional statues: Matthew (winged man), Mark (lion), Luke (ox), and John (eagle).

On Saturdays the church often buzzes with weddings. Stained-glass windows tint the warm interior, which is packed with statues.

A remarkable 40-foot-high altar resembles an Italian Renaissance city, with spires, domes, and columns of marble and onyx. In October a procession leaves the church for Fisherman's Wharf for the annual blessing of the fishing fleet. ■

The Church of Sts. Peter and Paul is known as the Italian Cathedral.

The Beat generation

The image is part of 1950s cultural history: a black-garbed beatnik wearing a beret, dark glasses, pointy beard, turtleneck, and sandals. He was allergic to work. Or so he appeared to mainstream America.

In the 1950s, most Americans were enjoying peace and prosperity, with new houses, jobs, and families. Along with this came a high level of social conformity. The Beats were disillusioned bohemians who found this conventional behavior intolerably stifling. They distrusted the "American Way of Life" and hated the prevailing complacency about racial problems and nuclear weapons. In North Beach the Beats found a home.

The Beat movement in San Francisco was catalyzed by Allen Ginsberg's 1955 public reading of "Howl" (see p. 83). Jack Kerouac first used the term Beat, meaning that his generation was beaten, weary, in their struggle for individual freedom. Beats wanted to "dig life" and remain in a high state of awareness—perhaps why some sources claim that Beat also relates to the word "beatific."

In 1958, local newspaper columnist Herb Caen invented the word "beatnik" by combining Beat with Sputnik, Russia's recently launched satellite. (Both were "far out," he wrote.) Caen didn't much like the Beats' lifestyle and meant the term to diminish them.

The Beats used a hip lingo derived mostly from blacks and jazz musicians. The terms slowly leaked out to the mainstream culture: cat (man), chick (woman), man (generic address for a cat), cool (good), dig (understand, appreciate), bug (annoy), drag (bore, disappointment), bread (money), blow (play an instrument), fuzz (police), hipster (person in the know), the most (greatest),

pad (apartment), square (conformist), tea (marijuana), wig (mind, brain).

This lingo was staccato poetry, and poetry was paramount in Beat creativity. An older mentor, Kenneth Rexroth, was among the first to read poetry to the accompaniment of jazz. Beats soon gathered in bars and coffeehouses for poetry readings staged while musicians, or perhaps just a bongo drummer, played. Red wine and coffee were the intoxicants of choice, along with marijuana.

In no time the national news media caught on to the movement. Soon busloads of tourists were cruising North Beach, eager to see some genuine beatniks. The unwilling tourist attractions retaliated in 1958 by staging the "Squaresville Tour" through Union Square, marching in sandals and beards and gawking at the squares.

As Beat writers gained fame, wanna-be beatniks poured into North Beach to "dig the scene." Suddenly teenagers all over America wanted to be goateed bongo players. As the tourist boom inflated rents in North Beach by the early 1960s, the Beats moved on—some to Haight-Ashbury, where their bohemianism inspired the emergent hippies. Beat icon Jack Kerouac died of alcoholism in 1969, while living in a Florida tract house. ■

City Lights Bookstore today (top) was a Beat hangout. Legendary Beat writers (below, left to right) Bob Donlin, Neal Cassady, Allen Ginsberg, Robert LaVinge, and Lawrence Ferlinghetti stand outside Ferlinghetti's City Lights Bookstore in 1956.

North Beach cafés

Columbus Avenue

See map pp. 80–81

Bus: 15, 30, 39, 45

Vesuvio Café

✉ 255 Columbus Ave.

☎ 415/362-3370

Tosca Café

✉ 242 Columbus Ave.

☎ 415/391-1244

Caffé Greco

✉ 423 Columbus Ave.

☎ 415/397-6261

Vesuvio Café, an old Beat hangout

COFFEE IS THE LIFEBLOOD AND SOCIAL LUBRICANT OF North Beach. Sample a few cafés; you'll not only catch up on cappuccino but begin to understand the soul of San Francisco.

Across Jack Kerouac Alley from City Lights Bookstore (see p. 83), **Vesuvio Café** is famous for its past as a favorite hangout of Ferlinghetti, Kerouac, Ginsberg, and other Beats. Opened in 1949, the café occupies a post-earthquake building with a fine pressed-metal facade. An outside wall is painted with a poem that reads "When the shadow of the grasshopper/Falls across the trail of the field mouse/On green and slimey grass as a red sun rises/Above the western horizon silhouetting/A gaunt and tautly muscled Indian warrior/Perched with bow and arrow cocked and aimed/Straight at you, it's time for another martini." The Beats liked both wordplay and booze.

The café doesn't serve lunch, but you're welcome to bring your own to accompany a drink. The decor includes photos of writers and paintings by local artists. Upstairs, one seating area is the "John Wilkes Booth," and another is reserved for "Lady Psychiatrists."

OLD & NEW

Something about the red vinyl booths, Italian paintings, and silver espresso machines makes you feel that not much has changed at the **Tosca Café** since it opened in 1919. An unassuming North Beach landmark, Tosca has a jukebox devoted largely to opera. It was a popular hangout for the Beats, especially after beatnik wanna-bes thronged nearby Vesuvio. As at all North Beach cafés, you're welcome to sit and chat, read a good book— or write one. You can order a cappuccino "corrected" with brandy and chocolate.

Busy, busy **Caffé Greco** is a relative newcomer (1988) with calorie-bomb desserts and a variety of coffee drinks. There are tables inside among old European posters, as well as outside on the sidewalk (great for people-watching). Next door is **Caffé Puccini,** whose big windows look onto North Beach street life.

A family-run place that opened in 1956, **Caffé Trieste** is a North Beach favorite and a feast for the

Coffee primer

Espresso Dark-roasted, strong and mellow, brewed by forcing steam through powdered coffee, this coffee is served black.

Cappuccino Espresso topped with frothy steamed milk, or "foam," and powdered chocolate.

Caffé latte Espresso mixed with steamed milk.

Mocha Espresso mixed with chocolate and topped with whipped cream.

Caffé americano American coffee. Add milk for café au lait. ■

Caffé Puccini
✉ 411 Columbus Ave.
☎ 415/989-7033

Caffé Trieste
✉ 601 Vallejo St.
☎ 415/392-6739

Caffé Roma
✉ 526 Columbus Ave.
☎ 415/296-7942

senses, with steaming espresso, friendly chatter, old Italian murals, and, on Saturday afternoons, live opera sung by the owners and a variety of locals.

Caffé Roma specially roasts its own coffee and sells it by the pound, which means you can enjoy it here but also take it home.

Mario's Bohemian Cigar Store Café is a friendly and unpretentious little wedge of a café that lets you plug into the real North Beach. Mario's serves wonderful cappuccino and is legendary for its focaccia sandwiches (with meatball, eggplant, and other delicious and unusual fillings). ■

Mario's Bohemian Cigar Store Café
✉ 566 Columbus Ave.
☎ 415/362-0536

Love what you've done to your hair! A performance of *Beach Blanket Babylon*

More places to visit

CLUB FUGAZI

John Fugazi was a Milanese who made his fortune in America selling hair oil, then went into banking. (His enterprise eventually became part of Transamerica.) He donated this 1912 building of brick and terra-cotta to the Italian community as a meeting hall. The third-floor Italian Heritage Room displays photos. But what draws the crowds is the **Club Fugazi theater,** which stages a send-up of San Francisco called *Beach Blanket Babylon* (see p. 263).

The high-energy, high-camp revue features characters who range from Snow White to Mr. Peanut, and the colossal, zany headdresses are famous. One feathered number supports every city landmark imaginable, including a Chinatown pagoda and the Golden Gate Bridge. The show opened in 1974 and had its roots in "Rent-A-Freak," a service that supplied party hosts with wacky guests in outlandish costumes to add to the fun.

✉ 678 Green St. 🚌 Bus: 15, 30, 39, 45

MOLINARI'S DELI

Delectable whiffs of pesto and mozzarella, homemade ravioli, and air-dried salami fill this classic Italian deli, which has been in business since 1896. Pick up a sandwich, and take it to Washington Square Park (see p. 85) or Vesuvio Café (see p. 88).

✉ 373 Columbus Ave. ☎ 415/421-2337
🚌 Bus: 15, 30, 39, 45

NORTH BEACH MUSEUM

In this small but evocative museum on the U.S. Bank's mezzanine, San Francisco and the early Italian community of North Beach come to life. You'll see photos of Telegraph Hill in 1855 (with no Coit Tower) and a 1914 businessmen's lunch at Fior d'Italia, the nation's oldest Italian restaurant (1886). Artifacts on display include gold-threaded vestments from the Church of Sts. Peter and Paul and a copy of California's first Italian newspaper, the March 1865 *La Parola.* Most arresting, though, are photos of the aftermath of the 1906 earthquake and fire. A shot by W.E. Worden shows men stooped in the rubble to examine safes and retrieve valuables. Representing the Beat era is a handwritten poem, "The Old Italians Dying," by Lawrence Ferlinghetti, whose offbeat calligraphy reveals his artistic skill. (North Beach's resident poet lived in Paris and still produces paintings and lithographs.)

✉ U.S. Bank, 1435 Stockton St. ☎ 415/391-6210 🕐 Closed Sun. 🚌 Bus: 15, 30, 39, 45

ST. FRANCIS OF ASSISI

This pale Gothic church dates from 1860, but the congregation first met in an adobe chapel in 1849, the first American Roman Catholic parish on the West Coast. St. Francis (ca 1182–1226), the city's patron saint, renounced his father's wealth and adopted the ideal of poverty, leaving town regularly to live as a hermit, and returning with illumination to sustain him. He offers a good example for San Franciscans, who live within easy reach of silent places: redwood groves, mountains, and remote shores. ✉ 610 Vallejo St. 🚌 Bus: 15, 30, 39, 45

UPPER GRANT AVENUE

Heading north from Broadway, pubs and off-beat shops inhabit Edwardian buildings topped with apartments. The **Saloon** *(1232 Grant Ave.)* has served beer since 1861 and ranks as the city's oldest continuously operating purveyor of booze; a brothel once flourished upstairs. (Is it any wonder that firefighters saved the building during the 1906 blaze?) In a former life, the bar at 1353 Grant Avenue was a Beat gathering spot called the Coffee Gallery. A few steps off Grant, the **101 Basement** *(513 Green St.)* has 50,000 LP records (unsorted, so it's a treasure hunt), fine vintage stereo gear, and musical instruments. The eccentric **Aria** *(1522 Grant Ave.)* sells eclectica, from architectural remnants to carved saints.

Past Chestnut Street, on the east side of Grant Avenue, steps lead up to **Jack Early Park,** which offers a view from the Bay Bridge to the Golden Gate. Wharves are arrayed below. If Coit Tower is packed with cars and tourists, this makes a good alternative viewpoint. 🗺 Map pp. 80–81 🚌 Bus: 15, 30, 39, 45 ■

Aromatic Molinari's Deli, where locals buy everything from salami to fresh basil

Telegraph Hill

North Beach rises steeply to Telegraph Hill, where suddenly the vista expands to encompass the whole bay. The unobstructed view explains why early San Franciscans climbed the 284-foot hill to look for ships sailing into the Golden Gate. After 1850, arrivals were "telegraphed" to city merchants via a semaphore flag system that gave the hill its name.

The spectacular view also explains why Telegraph Hill accounts for some of today's most desirable real estate. But until the automobile made climbing the hill easier and opened it to the affluent, this was a blue-collar neighborhood housing a succession of immigrants from Chile, Peru, Ireland, and Italy. The 1906 fire torched most of Telegraph Hill's houses, but on the eastern slope Italian residents drenched blankets in red wine and spread them on their roofs to fight the flames.

Coit Tower atop Telegraph Hill

Until 1914 part of the eastern slope was a rock quarry for ships' ballast, landfill, and street paving. (Note the resulting cliff.) In the 1920s, bohemian writers and artists moved onto Telegraph Hill, attracted by the great views and (then) cheap rents. With the building of Coit Tower in 1933, the area became more popular and expensive, finally forcing out the artists.

At the foot of the hill, just before Embarcadero, Levi's Plaza stands on gold rush landfill that includes at least one abandoned ship. ■

Filbert Steps

IN SAN FRANCISCO, STEPS WORK WELL WHERE THE terrain is too steep for a reasonable street. Few stairways anywhere have more charm than this one on the east side of Telegraph Hill.

Filbert Steps

See map pp. 80–81

Bus: 39

The first section leads down Filbert Street from Telegraph Hill Boulevard to Montgomery Street. Here movie buffs may recognize the fine **1936 art deco apartment house** *(1360 Montgomery St.)* as Humphrey Bogart's hideout with Lauren Bacall in *Dark Passage* (1947). Reliefs adorn the building, including a Spanish mariner with a spyglass.

At this point there are two possible detours: You can turn left to the end of Montgomery Street for a look at **Julius' Castle,** a restaurant with a turret and battlements and a romantic view. In earlier days autos used a turntable to reverse direction on the narrow street. You can walk the other way on Montgomery to Alta Street, turning left to **Armistead Maupin's former house** *(60–62 Alta St., private).* The gay author's 1970s *Tales of the City* took place around fictional Barbary Lane, a setting that some say was really nearby Napier Lane (see below); others claim that the model was Russian Hill's Macondray Lane (see p. 100). The end of Alta Street has a vertiginous view.

Below Montgomery the wooden Filbert Steps take you through shady gardens of ferns, vines, and flowers edged with Victorian cottages. Among them, 224 Filbert dates from 1863, while 222 Filbert was once an unsanctioned bar. **Napier Lane** is simply a wooden plank sidewalk, one of the city's last, lined with cottages and apartments from the late 1800s, with lots of cats roaming. You wonder how residents move refrigerators and other heavy objects down the steps to their houses. At the bottom of Filbert, notice the old rock quarry; after the 1906 earthquake, excavation went on here until a few houses slipped into the hole. ■

Filbert Steps has a rustic feel in this busy city.

Coit Tower

ONE OF SAN FRANCISCO'S MOST VISIBLE LANDMARKS, COIT Tower rises above recently renovated Pioneer Park on the summit of Telegraph Hill. In 1876 public-spirited citizens bought the park land for $12,000 in gold coins to preserve it as open space. In the center of the parking plaza stands a 12-foot bronze statue of Christopher Columbus, donated by the city's Italian community.

Coit Tower

- See map pp. 80–81
- Summit of Telegraph Hill, on Telegraph Hill Blvd.
- 415/362-0808
- $ (elevator)
- Bus: 39

The 1933 tower also came about through a generous gift, a $125,000 bequest from Lillie Hitchcock Coit (see p. 96). Arthur Brown, Jr., chief architect of City Hall and the Opera House, won the design competition for the memorial. Brown created a classical fluted column that stands 210 feet tall, with an observation loggia at the top. (Lillie Coit was ardently devoted to the city's fire-fighters, but contrary to popular legend, the cylindrical tower is not meant to resemble the nozzle of a fire hose.)

An elevator and stairs take you to the top, where the view takes in an astounding panorama of city and bay—from Marin County and the Golden Gate to the Bay Bridge and downtown San Francisco. Don't miss this.

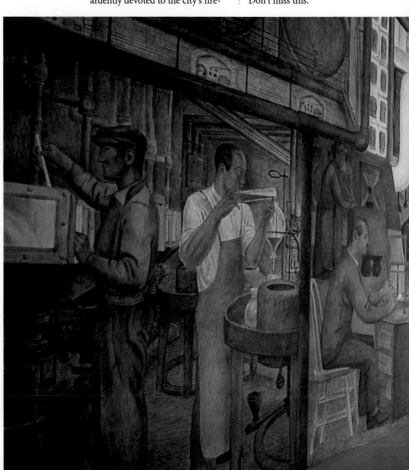

MURALS

The tower lobby is lined with outstanding murals that capture life in California in 1934. They were a pilot program of the Public Works of Art Project (PWAP), a New Deal plan to employ artists during the Great Depression. Working for about $1 an hour, 25 painters and 19 assistants were turned loose on the tower's newly finished blank walls. They revived the art of fresco painting, in which a thin coat of wet plaster is painted with a brush dipped in dry pigments. The work is painstaking: An artist can cover only two square feet a day, and mistakes have to be chipped out.

The frescoes are so similar in style that they appear to have been painted by one artist. The painters achieved this unity by using a stock palette of earth tones and adhering to the style of Mexican muralist Diego Rivera, who liked to overlap two-dimensional figures.

Controversy swirled around the murals, for they depicted not only idealistic scenes of city, factory, and field, but also left-leaning political symbols. In one, a man was reading a Communist newspaper, the *Daily Worker*. Another mural showed a hammer-and-sickle. Such symbols caused particular tension at the time because a bloody strike of longshoremen was in progress, in which two union protesters were shot down. Officials closed the tower until passions subsided. In the end, the hammer-and-sickle were removed.

One of 19 murals inside Coit Tower, painted by a cadre of artists in 1934, that depict life in California

The Christopher Columbus statue donated by Italian Americans in 1957 stands tall beside Coit Tower.

Among the highlights of the murals are "City Life" (Victor Arnautoff), rich in detail: a newspaper stand selling leftist dailies, a banker reading stock market returns, a well-dressed man being robbed at gunpoint while indifferent citizens bustle past, and a cop orchestrating traffic; "California" (Maxine Albro) shows the state's agricultural bounty, with flower growers, a dairy, blossoming almond orchards, and vineyards; "Library" (Bernard Zakheim) depicts a reading room in which one man (modeled on fellow artist John Langley Howard) is reaching for Karl Marx's *Das Kapital;* "Department Store" (Frede Vidar) shows a typical 1930s store with clothes, toys, salespeople, and two women in front of a menu that lists lunch for 25 cents; and "California Industrial Scenes" (John Langley Howard) depicts such enterprises as oil drilling and mining, but also bitterly contrasts the top and bottom levels of technological society: Shabbily dressed migrants are regarded from a limousine by wealthy motorists out for amusement. ∎

Lillie Hitchcock Coit

Lillie Coit wore men's clothes and smoked cigars in an era of petticoats and lace. A loyal supporter of firefighters, she loved to play poker and drink bourbon with them. She also attended every fire in town. (There were plenty in early San Francisco.) Lillie was a beloved San Francisco eccentric.

She was a little girl when her family came to San Francisco in 1851. One day when she was 15 years old she saw the volunteers of Knickerbocker Engine Company No. 5 struggling up Telegraph Hill on the way to extinguish a fire. Impulsively, she tossed down her schoolbooks and ran to a vacant spot on the tow rope, exhorting bystanders: "Come on you men! Everybody pull!" The engine was the first to reach the blaze.

The firefighters made Lillie an honorary member of Engine Company No. 5, and she embroidered a #5 on all her clothes (supposedly including her underwear). The #5 pin that she wore was buried with her.

Lillie married Howard Coit, who held the influential position of caller at the Mining Exchange. Although wealthy, Lillie remained utterly free of snobbishness and was much loved for her wit and spirit. After being widowed, she lived in Europe for years, then returned to San Francisco. When she died in 1924 at age 87, Lillie bequeathed one-third of her wealth to San Francisco "for the purpose of adding to the beauty of the city which I have always loved." That gift built Coit Tower. ∎

Levi's Plaza

THIS IS THE 1982 HEADQUARTERS OF LEVI STRAUSS & CO., built on gold rush landfill and landscaped as a reminder of the company's links with the mining industry in California's canyons.

The staggered design of the complex harmonizes well with the stacked houses on Telegraph Hill behind it, and there is an appealing fountain of Sierra Nevada granite. On the Battery Street side, a 1903 wine warehouse built for the Italian Swiss Colony has been converted into a restaurant.

Levi's jeans were invented in San Francisco and have the city's initials right on their metal rivets. The use of rivets to strengthen pockets was patented by Levi Strauss and Jacob Davis in 1873. Their tough denim pants appealed to miners, who no doubt overloaded the pockets with promising rocks.

A visitor center in the headquarters lobby showcases the company's history, product innovations, and place in popular culture, reflected in decades of TV ads from around the world. ∎

Levi's Plaza & Visitor Center

⬛ See map pp. 80–81

✉ Filbert St. at Sansome St./Battery St., 1155 Battery St.

🚌 Bus: 42, 82X

Locals enjoy sunshine by Levi's Plaza (above), a geometrically designed complex (below).

Russian Hill

At the summit of all residential neighborhoods in San Francisco, serene Russian Hill (294 feet) rises from the margins of North Beach and Fisherman's Wharf to overlook the waterfront, Coit Tower, and the cityscape. Actually, Russian Hill has two summits—Hyde Street at Lombard Street, and Vallejo Street between Taylor Street and Jones Street.

Reportedly, the hill was named for early Russian otter hunters buried on top. Jasper O'Farrell's 1847 survey overlaid the hill with a street grid, including the steepest paved street in the city: Filbert between Leavenworth and Hyde, at a 31.5-percent grade. Other streets looked good on paper but were too steep to pave, so stairs were built, as on Vallejo.

The trudge uphill on routes such as Macondray Lane explains why few people lived here before cable car service came in 1880. But Russian Hill did not become an elite enclave. Residents with more taste than cash fashioned artistic houses and gardens. In 1890 Swedenborgian minister Joseph Worcester built a cottage of unfinished wood and un-Victorian simplicity. Shingled houses followed, giving Russian Hill a distinctive look.

During the last half of the 1800s, Catherine Atkinson opened her house *(1032 Broadway)*

as a literary salon for luminaries such as Mark Twain, Robert Louis Stevenson, and Ambrose Bierce. It was also headquarters for Les Jeunes, the coterie that included Gelett ("Purple Cow") Burgess and Willis Polk, and poet Ina Coolbrith hosted writers' gatherings at 1604 Taylor Street. In bohemian tradition, half a century later Jack Kerouac crashed at Neal Cassady's house at 29 Russell Street and wrote the Beat classic *On The Road,* in which he immortalized the kinetic Cassady as Dean Moriarty.

After the 1906 conflagration—during which one Russian Hill resident sat at a piano in the street playing "Danse Macabre"— the neighborhood was rebuilt. Later, view-obstructing high-rises appeared and protests led to a 1974 moratorium on buildings taller than 40 feet. Nowadays, Russian Hill is quiet and well-kept. Picturesque houses, sharply dropping streets, and bay views make it a popular movie location. ■

Cool place to live: Macondray Lane on Russian Hill

Lombard Street

A CONGA LINE OF CARS SHIMMIES DOWN THE ZIGZAGS OF the "crookedest street in the world," the 1000 block of Lombard. The street makes eight switchbacks as it drops from Hyde to Leavenworth.

Cars negotiate Lombard's zigzags.

The hairpin curves, added in 1922, adjusted the street's original 27 percent grade to 16 percent so cars could descend. Whip out your camera; everyone does. In fact, here lies a problem: Every tourist in San Francisco feels a need to drive on this roller coaster, so cars stack up on the approach. About 750,000 cars make the descent each year.

You can walk down steps that edge the brick-paved street. They have no zigzags, and you'll have time to admire the flower gardens, houses, and apartments lining the street. The Hyde Street intersection at the top of Lombard offers a classic San Francisco view, looking along the cable car tracks to the waterfront and Alcatraz.

At this corner, the house at 1100 Lombard was built for Robert Louis Stevenson's widow, Fannie Osbourne Stevenson. It was designed in Mediterranean style by Willis Polk in 1900. ■

Lombard Street

🅰 See map pp. 80–81

🚃 CC: Powell-Hyde, Powell-Mason; Bus: 30, 41, 45

More places to visit

GREEN STREET

The **Feusier Octagon House** *(1067 Green St.)*, begun in 1859 as a single story, was designed according to the dictates of a popular phrenologist who claimed that octagonal houses promote good health. (See p. 151 for one you can visit.) Merchant Louis Feusier added the second story and mansard roof two decades later. The Tudor Revival former **Engine Company No. 31** *(1088 Green St.)* was built in 1907. Map pp. 80–81 Bus: 30, 45

MACONDRAY LANE

Trees, flowers, and ferns line Macondray Lane, a narrow street that only walkers can explore. Some San Franciscans say that this is the Barbary Lane of Armistead Maupin's *Tales of the City.* A number of houses date from the period after the San Francisco fire; the only pre-1906 survivor is 15–17 Macondray Lane. Map pp. 80–81 Off Jones St., between Green St. and Union St. CC: Powell-Hyde, Powell-Mason; Bus: 30, 41, 45

SAN FRANCISCO ART INSTITUTE

Perched on a hillside, the West's oldest art school (founded 1871) occupies what appears to be a Spanish monastery, designed in 1926 by Bakewell & Brown, around a courtyard.

The **Diego Rivera Gallery** contains a 1931 mural in which the Mexican artist depicted himself painting a mural of American workers. The school café is open to non-students, serving inexpensive food with a million-dollar view. There's also a fine view from the rooftop deck of a 1969 addition of Brutalist concrete. 800 Chestnut St. 415/771-7020 CC: Powell-Hyde, Powell-Mason; Bus: 30

VALLEJO STREET

On **Russian Hill Place** *(off the 1000 block of Vallejo St.)* stands a row of Mediterranean cottages designed by Willis Polk in 1915 with red tile roofs and wrought iron. At the top of the Vallejo Street stairs, the **Williams-Polk House** *(1013–19 Vallejo St., private)* clings to a hillside, showing two stories on Vallejo, but six at the back. In 1892 Willis Polk designed this brown-shingled duplex for the widow of a founder of the San Francisco Art Institute.

The thin sliver of **Ina Coolbrith Park** *(Vallejo St. at Taylor St.)* honors Ina Donna Coolbrith (1841–1928, see below), who in 1919 was named California's first poet laureate. The narrow, manicured park is shaded by pines and has a view of hills, water, and sky. Map pp. 80–81 Bus: 30, 45 ■

Ina Coolbrith

A beloved inspiration to two generations of California writers, Ina Coolbrith attracted admirers such as Mark Twain and Bret Harte, who hinted he would leave his wife for her. Flamboyant poet Joaquin Miller described her as a "daughter of the gods, divinely tall and most divinely fair." Her literary correspondents included Henry Wadsworth Longfellow and Alfred, Lord Tennyson.

Friends called her the "virgin poetess," and none knew that she was once married to an actor. Born Josephine Smith, the niece of Mormon prophet Joseph Smith, she came west in a covered wagon in 1852, the first child to

enter California via the Beckwourth Pass. By age 11 she was a published poet, and in her late twenties she helped Bret Harte edit the *Overland Monthly.*

In 1874 she took a job at the Oakland public library. One day she helped a poorly dressed 12-year-old boy find books. "I loved Ina Coolbrith above all womankind," said the boy, long afterward. "And what I am and what I have done that is good I owe to her." His name was Jack London. Another protégée was modern dancer Isadora Duncan. Ina's long-running literary salon drew many famous and talented writers. ■

Hugely popular Fisherman's Wharf has some nuggets of real interest—don't miss the working docks or the historic ships. It's also the departure point for bay cruises and visits to Alcatraz.

Fisherman's Wharf & Alcatraz

Seafood is a major attraction at Fisherman's Wharf.

Fisherman's Wharf & Alcatraz

ALTHOUGH NOT ACTUALLY REQUIRED TO DO SO BY STATE LAW, JUST ABOUT every tourist in San Francisco goes to Fisherman's Wharf *(www.fishermanswharf.org)*. Each year 11.7 million people—that's more than 30,000 a day—visit this highly commercialized, one-mile stretch of the northern waterfront between Pier 39 and Aquatic Park. They flock here for three main reasons: (1) the water; (2) the irresistible lure of the tacky; and (3) seafood restaurants. Food, shopping, and family attractions make Fisherman's Wharf the most popular tourist tra...um, spot in San Francisco.

To avoid parking problems, take public transportation. The Powell-Mason cable car arrives on the wharf's east end at Bay Street; after touring westward, return to the city center on the Powell-Hyde line from Victorian Park.

The wharf's central section, along Jefferson Street, is a bedlam of shops peddling souvenirs and T-shirts, novelty museums, overpriced art galleries, and street vendors (Psst, how about a Grateful Dead wall plaque?). Street performers work the passing crowd: A singer may compose a rap song about you as you walk by, or a human mannequin stand frozen in position, hoping you'll toss a dollar in his hat.

But if you look past the commercial

hokum, you'll find the *real* Fisherman's Wharf: colorful fishing boats docked after unloading their catches, stalls where vendors steam Dungeness crabs for walkaway seafood cocktails, and a pier with historic sailing ships.

The waterfront's boom began in 1853 at the foot of Powell Street, where Harry Meiggs built 1,600-foot Meiggs Wharf. As a city councilman deep in debt, "Honest Harry" embezzled $365,000 and fled to South America. He built a railroad across the Andes, made an astounding fortune of 100 million dollars, and repaid his obligations in San Francisco.

Around Meiggs Wharf a sawmill and other businesses grew up. Citizens came to enjoy

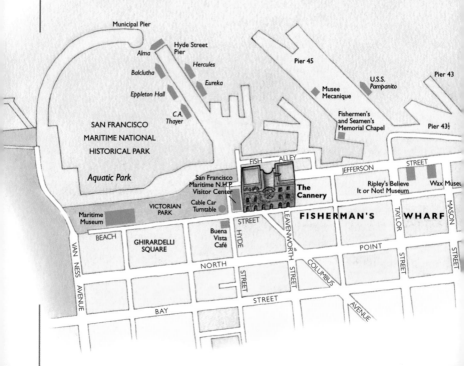

bathhouses and saloons such as Abe Warner's Cobweb Palace, where customers ate crab chowder under a ceiling festooned with spiderwebs. (Superstitious Abe refused to harm spiders.) His menagerie had a monkey that pestered patrons for peanuts and a famous parrot that spoke the nonsense line: "I'll have a rum and gum! What'll you have?" Commercial attractions are nothing new at Fisherman's Wharf.

The waterfront also saw nefarious characters such as Scabhouse Johnny and Three Finger Curtin abducting—or "shanghaiing"—men for involuntary sea duty, usually by giving them knockout drops or a knock on the head. The victims awoke aboard a ship under sail. Captains were desperate because so many sailors arriving in San Francisco ran off to the gold country.

The fishing fleet didn't take up permanent berth at Fisherman's Wharf until 1900. Previously, captains docked at more sheltered wharves jutting from Green, Union, and Filbert Streets. As the waterfront was developed for shipping, the fishing fleet moved to the foot of Taylor Street. Italian immigrants dominated the trade. First had come men from Genoa, who dotted the bay with their feluccas—narrow, 16-foot boats with points at both ends and three-cornered sails. In the 1890s Sicilians took over. As motorized boats and bigger nets later became available, however, the bay and nearby ocean were nearly fished out. By the 1950s San Francisco's fishing fleet was a vestige of what it had been.

But tourism held new promise. Outsiders had long come to the wharf to watch the picturesque scene. Fishermen in blue trousers with colorful sashes sat mending nets with wooden needles. Plump seagulls fluttered above the boats, whose decks were piled high with fish and crabs. Visitors dined at seafood houses such as Alioto's (see p. 253), founded by Sicilian immigrant Nunzio Alioto in 1938 as the wharf's first real restaurant. In 1964 the rehabilitation of the historic Ghirardelli chocolate factory as a complex of shops and restaurants drew more crowds, as did the creation of the similar Pier 39.

Every October visitors enjoy seeing the blessing of the fishing fleet. Beforehand, following Sicilian custom, a portrait of the Madonna del Lume (Mother of Light), the patroness of fishermen, is carried in procession from Sts. Peter and Paul Church in Italian North Beach. The ritual reveals that deep traditions exist just beneath the wharf's commercial hoopla. Across the water and accessible by ferry is Alcatraz Island, best known for the maximum security prison that occupied it between 1934 and 1963. ■

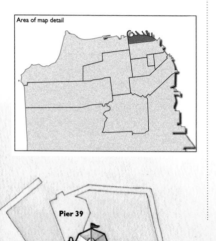

Area of map detail

Pier 39

Pier 41

Aquarium of the Bay

THE

EMBARCADERO

POWELL STREET

STOCKTON STREET

STREET

BAY

STREET

0   200 yards
0   200 meters

Lolling sea lions
are a big draw
at Pier 39.

Pier 39

THIS DEVELOPMENT OF SHOPS, RESTAURANTS, AND amusements is one of San Francisco's top tourist attractions, situated as it is in the heart of Fisherman's Wharf.

Pier 39
www.pier39.com
See map pp.
102–103
Beach St. at the
Embarcadero
415/981-7437
Bus: 15, 39, 42;
Streetcar: F-Line

*The Great San
Francisco
Adventure*
Pier 39
415/956-3456
$$

**Aquarium of the
Bay**
www.aquariumofthebay.com
Pier 39
415/623-5300
$$$

Built on a 1905 cargo pier, this imitation fishing village (1978, Walker and Moody) uses wood salvaged from other piers. Popular attractions here include the **San Francisco Carousel,** with its horses, rocking chariots, 1,800 twinkling lights, and depictions of city landmarks. *The Great San Francisco Adventure* is a wide-screen movie about local history, scenery, and people.

At **Aquarium of the Bay** you're surrounded by ocean creatures of the San Francisco Bay and Northern California as you move along a 300-foot, clear acrylic tunnel through the middle of 707,000 gallons of water in tanks. The aquarium showcases sharks, bay rays, and other undersea denizens from salmon to rock scallops. Informative but pricey.

Some attractions are free. At an **outdoor stage,** you can watch street performers juggle or do magic. ■

Ba-a-a-ark!

Follow your ears to the west side of Pier 39. The noise comes from a colony of California sea lions that took up residence in the adjacent marina in 1990. They loll on docks, pile on top of one another, and generally show off.

On weekends a staffer from the Marine Mammal Interpretive Center (which has displays upstairs on Pier 39) is here to explain that California sea lions (*Zalophus californianus*), unlike seals, have external ear flaps. The blubbery creatures live along the Pacific coast and feed on fish and squid. To breed and give birth, sea lions waddle ashore to form colonies. Males (who may be eight feet long) assemble harems and maintain their territories with displays of barking and head shaking. ■

Bay cruises & more

TO SEE SAN FRANCISCO FROM A FRESH PERSPECTIVE, TAKE a bay cruise. Out on the water you can look back at Fisherman's Wharf and the hilly city, observe the bustling port at work, and see the bay islands up close.

The Red & White Fleet's Golden Gate/Bay Cruise skims along the waterfront with beautiful views of the city skyline, and ventures under the Golden Gate Bridge and near Alcatraz Island. Passengers use headsets for an informative narration (available in six languages).

The Blue & Gold Fleet's Golden Gate Bay Cruise also passes under the Golden Gate Bridge, while also taking in Sausalito in Marin County, Angel Island in the bay, and nearby Alcatraz. It is narrated in English over a loudspeaker. The company also provides ferry services to Sausalito, Tiburon, Alameda/ Oakland, Vallejo, and Angel Island.

U.S.S. PAMPANITO

This 1943 submarine of the Balao class was designed for long-range cruises in the Pacific. During dangerous cat-and-mouse missions in World War II, it sank six Japanese ships and damaged four others, dodging torpedoes and surviving depth charges.

Another problem for the 80 crewmen must have been claustrophobia. The sub operated at a depth of 600 feet. It was so cramped that men slept in the torpedo room. (In addition, imagine 80 men at sea for two and a half months … without a shower.)

A self-guided audio tour, including sound effects, historic recordings, and accounts by *Pampanito* veterans, takes you through small hatches and down narrow companionways and passages. Stops include the galley (look for the Betty Grable pinup picture that symbolized home for U.S. servicemen), engine and control rooms, officers' quarters, and torpedo tubes.

During a battle in the South China Sea, the sub helped sink Japanese ships, not knowing that they carried Australian and British prisoners of war. The *Pampanito* rescued 73 of the POWs. ∎

Red & White Fleet
www.redandwhite.com
- ✉ Pier 43¹/₂
- ☎ 415/673-2900
- 💲 $$$$
- 🚋 CC: Powell-Hyde, Powell-Mason; Bus: 30, 41, 45; Streetcar: F-Line

Blue & Gold Fleet
www.blueandgoldfleet.com
- ✉ Piers 39 & 41
- ☎ 415/705-7555
- 💲 $$$$
- 🚋 CC: Powell-Hyde, Powell-Mason; Bus: 30, 41, 45; Streetcar: F-Line

U.S.S. Pampanito
www.maritime.org/pamphome.shtml
- ✉ Pier 45
- ☎ 415/775-1943
- 💲 $$
- 🚋 CC: Powell-Hyde, Powell-Mason; Bus: 30, 41, 45; Streetcar: F-Line

Alcatraz

Alcatraz

See map pp.
102–103

**Blue & Gold Fleet
ferry & walking
tour**

www.blueandgoldfleet.com

✉ Pier 41

☎ 415/705-5555

$ $$$ (self-guided
day tour) or $$$$
(escorted evening
tour)

ALCATRAZ ISLAND IS "THE ROCK," THE MAXIMUM-SECURITY federal penitentiary that held the superstars of crime—incorrigible bad guys such as Al Capone and George "Machine Gun" Kelly, as well as perverse killer Robert "Birdman" Stroud. From the island, prisoners had a heartbreaking view across the water to carefree San Francisco and freedom, only a mile and a quarter away. The penitentiary is chilling—and not only because of the harsh winds that blow here.

Alcatraz Island has had several lives: fortress, military prison, and federal penitentiary from 1934 to 1963. It was occupied by Native Americans during the 1960s. Today the island is home not to jailbirds but seabirds, including thousands of western gulls.

EARLY DAYS

In 1775, Spanish mariner Juan Manuel de Ayala became the first European to see the 22-acre island. He named it Isla de los Alcatraces, or Island of the Pelicans (although the birds he saw there may have been

cormorants). The island's strategic position near the mouth of San Francisco Bay also made it ideal for a military fort, which was begun in 1853. Next year the Pacific coast's first lighthouse was erected here. Then Alcatraz became a military prison, whose inmates included Confederate sympathizers during the Civil War and Native American captives from the 1870s Indian wars. After the 1906 earthquake flattened San Francisco's jails, civilian prisoners were lodged on the island.

FEDERAL PEN

In 1934 the island was transferred to the new Federal Bureau of Prisons, which wanted to isolate the nation's worst criminal inmates in one maximum-security setting. The country was fighting back against a crime wave brought on by Prohibition, the Great Depression, and the rise of mobsters.

The penitentiary's security measures included barbed wire, guard towers, lights, window bars of "tool-proof" steel, and remote door openers. The final insurance against escape was the surrounding bay, whose cold water and swift currents

Guards and watchtowers kept criminals from escaping, as did swift, cold currents in the bay.

Left: Isolated Alcatraz was the former home of more than 1,500 crooks and gangsters.

(51°F, up to nine knots) were barriers no prisoner was likely to survive.

Alcatraz inmates did dream of escape, of course. But among the 1,545 men incarcerated over the years, only 36 attempted it. All were shot dead, recaptured, or presumed drowned in the frigid bay. In 1939 notorious "Doc" Barker and four other men sawed their way out of their cells. Surprised by guards on

A bridge leads to the visitor center in the old barracks building.

the beach, some surrendered, but Barker ran off into the fog and was cut down by bullets.

In 1962 Frank Morris and brothers John and Clarence Anglin fooled the guards into thinking they were asleep by placing dummy heads in their bunks. (The molded soap-and-concrete heads were thatched with hair pilfered from the prison barber shop.) The convicts broke out and

Lighthouse

Warden's house

Agave Trail

set off across the bay using flimsy lifejackets made of inflated raincoats. No trace was found except for Clarence Anglin's wallet, which washed up on nearby Angel Island. Most likely the men drowned—only to be immortalized in the 1979 Clint Eastwood movie, *Escape from Alcatraz*.

In the last escape attempt, two inmates inflated surgical gloves, filched from the prison hospital, and tried to float across the water. One actually reached San Francisco and collapsed; children summoned police.

In 1963 the high cost of transporting supplies and personnel to the island led to the penitentiary's closure. Six years later the unoccupied island was taken over for 19 months by the "Indians of All

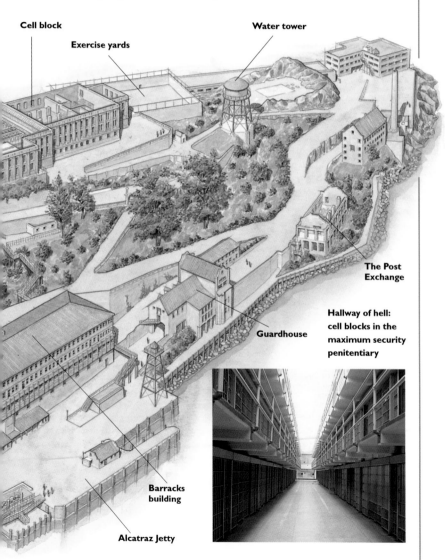

Cell block

Exercise yards

Water tower

The Post Exchange

Hallway of hell: cell blocks in the maximum security penitentiary

Guardhouse

Barracks building

Alcatraz Jetty

Tribes," who claimed ownership of Alcatraz for Native Americans under an 1868 treaty. They departed in 1971, leaving graffiti—"Indian Power"—on the smokestack of the powerhouse.

VISITING ALCATRAZ

Ferries of the Blue & Gold Fleet run to the island. The ticket price includes a recorded cellblock tour narrated in part by former Alcatraz inmates and correctional officers, available in six languages. In summer and on holiday weekends, reserve tickets at least one week in advance. Dress warmly. Evening tours are available.

On-site interpretation includes National Park Service guided walks and an orientation video. For a nature outing, walk the **Agave Trail** just south of the ferry dock. It leads past eucalyptus trees where black-crowned night-herons nest, across a hillside spiked with agaves, and down to views of tide pools and seabirds. The trail goes through a bird sanctuary, and is therefore closed during the nesting season (mid-February to late September).

INSIDE THE BIG HOUSE

In the cellhouse you'll see bleak rows of cells, the D Block (solitary confinement), an elevated gallery where armed guards kept watch, the mess hall (a.k.a. the "Gas Chamber"), and a typical five-by-nine-foot unheated cell.

Inmates were locked in their cells for 16 to 23 hours a day, with a "no talking" rule. To communicate, they either tapped out a sort of Morse code or put their heads in the toilet bowls, covered them with blankets, and spoke through the pipes. Inmates who caused

Notorious prisoners

"Scarface" Al Capone (1899–1947) The 1934 arrival of the notorious gangster made national headlines. Capone installed his family in a nearby hotel and through them ran his criminal organization in Chicago. Mentally disturbed from syphilis, he spent much of his four and a half years here in a hospital isolation cell.

Alvin "Creepy" Karpis (died 1979) A partner of the notorious Ma Barker, Karpis laid waste to the Midwest in a flamboyant spree of robbery and kidnapping between 1931 and 1936. Declared Public Enemy Number One, he spent 26 years on Alcatraz. During his time here, Karpis worked in the prison bakery, where he purloined yeast for making illicit beer.

trouble went to isolation cells, which they left only once a week for a ten-minute shower. Passing time in the recreation yard was a privilege, easily revoked. Two of the prisoners' intramural baseball teams were the Safecrackers and the Bankrobbers. ∎

A typical cell contained one bunk and blanket, a foldout table and chair, a toilet, a sink, and two shelves.

"It looks like Alcatraz got me licked."—Alphonse "Al" Capone

George "Machine Gun" Kelly (1895–1954) Known as the prison's most dangerous inmate, all-around bad guy Kelly was a bootlegger, bank robber, and kidnapper. His trial for abducting a rich Oklahoma oilman was the first under the Lindbergh Law, earning him a life sentence, of which he served 17 years. Kelly became a model prisoner.

Robert Stroud (1890–1963) Known as the Birdman of Alcatraz, Stroud actually was never allowed to keep birds during his 17-year stay. His avian studies took place earlier at Leavenworth penitentiary, where he killed a custodial officer in front of more than 2,000 other inmates. A hostile pervert, Stroud was kept in isolation. ∎

Around Fish Alley

THE HUB OF FISHERMAN'S WHARF IS TAYLOR AND Jefferson Streets, where seafood restaurants overlook colorful fishing boats tied up along the docks below. In a passageway of fish and chowder stalls, cauldrons steam Dungeness crabs that will be cracked for sale by vendors who are characters in themselves. In the early days, fishermen and market laborers came to stalls like these for chowder to eat on the run. Tomaso Castagnola gets credit for adapting the idea to the "walkaway crab cocktail" in 1916. (Dungeness season, when fresh crab is available, runs from mid-November through June.)

Working area

Jefferson St. between Taylor & Hyde Sts.

CC: Powell-Hyde, Powell-Mason; Bus: 30, 41, 45; Streetcar: F-Line

FISHING BOATS

What remains of the city's historic fishing fleet—a mere vestige—is docked to the north of Jefferson Street. An open railing between Taylor and Jones looks onto the Jefferson Street Lagoon, with its Monterey type fishing boats; these resemble the double-pointed feluccas used on the bay by Italian fishermen in the 1800s, but are enlarged and motorized. The color-fully trimmed white hulls create a watercolor effect on the green bay water, like dabs of pigment.

The boats are laden with nets, coiled ropes, reels, plastic buckets, and other tackle, and there's definitely something fishy in the air. Most of the professional activity takes place around dawn, when fishermen unload their catches. The boats bring in squid, sand dabs, sole, sea bass, cod, mackerel, and halibut year round. Crab, salmon, shrimp, and ocean perch are seasonal. The annual catch weighs 20 million pounds.

BEHIND THE SCENES

For a better view, walk to the end of Taylor and go left to the foot of Pier 45. Here you'll see the **Fishermen's and Seamen's Memorial Chapel,** a simple brown wooden structure. Above the door a stained-

Sourdough bread

To accompany your walkaway seafood cocktail or hot clam chowder, pick up some sourdough bread. A good bet is the Boudin Bakery (156 Jefferson St.). In 1849 Frenchman Isidore Boudin baked San Francisco's first sourdough French bread. He used unbleached flour, water, salt, and sourdough starter, or "mother dough." The mother dough that the bakery uses today dates back to Boudin's first loaf. Each day, mother dough from the previous day's baking is added to the batch; this makes the dough rise and "sour" at its own pace, with no need for yeast. Proud San Franciscans say that the microorganisms in the sourdough thrive only in their foggy city and therefore the true product must come from San Francisco. Whatever the truth, crusty sourdough French bread is as San Franciscan as cable cars and the Golden Gate Bridge. ■

glass panel depicts a ship's wheel. In addition to a Sunday Catholic Mass—most fishermen are of Italian descent—services are held that reflect other nationalities and faiths. While you're nearby, have a look at Pier 45, where large fishing vessels tie up. You'll also see hungry sea lions and wheeling gulls.

To explore more of the working area of Fisherman's Wharf, go back to Jefferson Street and walk west; just past Castagnola's, turn right (opposite Jones Street); then turn left along the water, where you'll see more fishing boats. At the end of the block is **Fish Alley,** where catches are landed in the morning. After a peek, turn left up Richard Henry Dana Place to Jefferson Street and a reentry into the commercial hoopla. ■

The fishing fleet, no longer large but still romantically picturesque, docks at the wharf.

Jefferson Street museums

A STRIP ALONG JEFFERSON STREET HAS TWO MUSEUMS designed to be "fun for the whole family." People who like this sort of thing will find this the sort of thing they like.

Jefferson Street

🅜 See map
pp. 102–103

🚌 Bus: 32; Streetcar: F-Line

Ripley's Believe It or Not! Museum
www.ripleysf.com

✉ 175 Jefferson St.

☎ 415/771-6188

💲 $$$

Wax Museum
www.waxmuseum.com

✉ 145 Jefferson St.

☎ 800/439-4305

💲 $$$

Robert Hughes weighed 1,069 pounds at his death at 32. His likeness (above) can be seen at the Wax Museum (right).

Ripley's Believe It or Not! Museum is an "odditorium" of peculiar-but-true displays, based on the famous newspaper cartoon feature begun in 1918 by Robert Ripley. Among the nearly 300 artifacts and re-creations on view are a dinosaur composed of car bumpers, a shrunken human head whose original owner lived in Ecuador, a rotating tunnel for visitors to walk through, a "toast art" portrait of painter Vincent van Gogh made of 63 pieces of toasted bread, dressed grasshoppers playing pool, a wax figure of a Chinese man who had two pupils in each eyeball, and a cable car painstakingly made of 270,836 matchsticks (and 21 pints of glue) by a man with acute arthritis. Cartoonist Ripley himself was an oddity: He owned several luxury automobiles but didn't know how to drive. While drawing, he wore a Chinese bathrobe and let squirrels scamper on his desk.

Muhammad Ali meets John Lennon at the **Wax Museum.** Among the museum's 250 wax likenesses are sports heroes, presidents, religious figures, and movie stars from Marilyn Monroe to Leonardo DiCaprio. Frankenstein lurks in the Chamber of Horrors, while famous paintings are re-created in the Palace of Living Art. ∎

The Cannery

THIS RETAIL AND RESTAURANT COMPLEX WAS A PIONEER in the movement to adapt old industrial buildings to new uses. Originally it was the California Fruit Canners Association plant (1907), which the Del Monte Company made the largest peach-canning facility in the world, producing 200,000 hand-soldered cans each day. The Great Depression closed the plant. In 1968 developers preserved the brick shell and added a new interior for retail shops, with open-air stairways and bridges.

The Cannery
www.thecannery.com

⚑ See map
pp. 102–103

✉ 2801 Leavenworth St.

☎ 415/771-3112

🚋 CC: Powell-Hyde, Powell-Mason; Bus: 30, 47; Streetcar: F-Line

Browse the boutiques on the first level of the restored building for upscale clothing, gifts, and crystal, or seek out the best in world music, Russian crafts, luxury chocolates, teddy bears, and other fun collectibles.

In the courtyard, you can sip a drink while street performers, musicians, jugglers, and comedians do their acts. The top floor offers broad views of San Francisco Bay. Inside **Jack's Cannery Bar** are 17th-century English oak paneling and a carved fireplace taken from a manor house designed by English architect Inigo Jones (1573–1652). The items were bought from William Randolph Hearst's collection.

New at the Cannery is a farmer's market *(Fri., Sat.)* that is modeled on European marketplaces. Under colorful canopies, vendors purvey organic fruits and vegetables, as well as fish, cheeses, and freshly baked breads.

On Sundays an antiques fair, reminiscent of Parisian flea markets, brings vendors selling vintage furniture, paintings, and other upscale items. During summer, there's a free outdoor film festival in the courtyard, whose stage is often used by street entertainers. ■

Exterior of the restored Cannery

Street performers

Like all of Fisherman's Wharf, the Cannery is a showcase for street musicians, jugglers, magicians, mimes, and other entertainers. (Well…are mimes *really* entertaining?) One pavement pioneer of the 1970s was the "Human Jukebox"—basically a large carton that passersby encountered on the sidewalk. When you dropped a quarter in a slot, a disheveled guy holding a trumpet would pop out and play the requested song. It cost extra for "I Left My Heart in San Francisco," because the Human Jukebox was sick of it. ■

Hyde Street Pier

THE ROMANTIC ERA OF SAIL COMES TO LIFE THROUGH historic vessels docked at the wooden Hyde Street Pier. Once a ferry embarkation point, the pier is now part of San Francisco Maritime National Historical Park. The vessels are the crowning glories of the Maritime Museum, whose main building lies two blocks west of the pier at Aquatic Park.

Visitor Center
www.nps.gov/safr
🅰 See map pp. 102–103
✉ 499 Jefferson St. at Hyde, in Argonaut Hotel
☎ 415/447-5000
💳 CC: Powell-Hyde, Powell-Mason; Bus: 15, 30, 41, 45; Streetcar: F-Line

Hyde Street Pier
🅰 See map pp. 102–103
✉ Foot of Hyde St.
☎ 415/447-5000
www.nps.gov/safr
💲 $$ (to board historic vessels)
💳 CC: Powell-Hyde, Powell-Mason; Bus: 15, 30, 41, 45; Streetcar: F-Line

Maritime Museum
www.nps.gov/safr
✉ Aquatic Park, 900 Beach St. at Polk St.
☎ 415/561-7100
💳 CC: Powell-Hyde, Powell-Mason; Bus: 15, 30, 41, 45; Streetcar: F-Line

In the early days of San Francisco, almost everyone and everything came by sea. During the gold rush, sleek windjammers sailed through the Golden Gate carrying hopeful argonauts from the East Coast—a 17,000-mile journey around Cape Horn. (The speed record for a clipper from New York was 89 days, set in 1850.) During the 1870s cargo vessels left San Francisco with wheat for Europe. To cross the bay to points east and north, travelers took ferries—the only transport half a century before the Golden Gate and Bay Bridges were built.

THE *BALCLUTHA*
Among five historical ships for visitors to board, the pier's main attraction is the *Balclutha*, a steel-hulled square-rigger. The bark's proud hull, three masts, and brass fixtures evoke the glory days of the sailing ship. Built in Scotland in 1886, the 301-foot *Balclutha* was designed for cargo. In 17 trips around the Horn, she brought coal and whiskey from Europe and returned with California wheat. From 1902 to 1930 she plied the Alaska salmon trade, carrying fishermen and supplies north and coming back with canned fish. Later roles for the ship were tragicomic. After the *Balclutha* played a bit part in the 1934 movie *Mutiny on the Bounty*, a promoter tarted her up as an ersatz pirate ship to tour the West Coast. Ultimately, the *Balclutha* ended up on the mud flats in

Sausalito, north of the Golden Gate Bridge. In 1954 the San Francisco Maritime Museum rescued her from the scrap heap, and with 13,000 hours of volunteer labor restored the ship.

Peek into the captain's Victorian cabin, with its maple cabinets, liquor bar (suspended from the ceiling), and comfy seating. In contrast, the fo'c'sle had hard wooden bunks for the weary common seamen. Around the ship you'll see nautical gear and historical displays. In the hold a diorama depicts an Alaskan salmon cannery.

OTHER HISTORIC SHIPS
You can't miss the world's largest floating wooden structure—the *Eureka*—an 1890 sidewheel ferry more than 300 feet long. A steam engine four stories high was needed to propel the vessel, which carried up to 120 automobiles and 2,300 commuters between San Francisco and Sausalito. The lower deck displays autos from the 1920s and '30s, when ferries (not bridges) were the commuter's only way to the city.

You can also board the *Alma* (1891), the last San Francisco Bay scow schooner, which carried hay and lumber; and the 1907 steam tugboat *Hercules.* The *Eppleton Hall* is a 1914 English paddle tug, a steam sidewheeler that towed vessels that literally "carried coals to Newcastle."

Away for restoration until early 2006 is the 1895 **C.A. Thayer,** a

schooner that was the West Coast's last commercial sailing ship.

MARITIME MUSEUM AND VISITOR CENTER

Renowned for its Streamline Moderne design, the museum resembles a 1930s luxury liner tied up at Aquatic Park. Nautical elements include "decks" (three tiers), porthole windows, and skylights like hatch covers. It was built by the WPA (Works Projects Administration) as the Aquatic Park Casino (1939), a public bathhouse on a man-made beach. Remaining WPA artwork includes a flowing mural of undersea life (Hilaire Hiler) and carved green slate decorations around the doorway (Sargent Johnson).

The museum brings to life San Francisco's role as a seaport. The nautical treasures include carved figureheads, models of ships under sail and steam power, a whaler's exploding harpoon, scrimshaw (whalebone or ivory carving), the anchor from America's first warship (*Independence*, 1812), and the oldest known photo of San Francisco, an 1849 shot of ships at anchor.

The park's **Visitor Center,** in the brick 1907 Haslett Warehouse, has information and exhibits, including a Fresnel lighthouse lens of brass and polished prisms. ■

Dizzying view from one of the three masts of the *Balclutha*, the flagship of the nautical collection at the Hyde Street Pier

Ghirardelli Square

Ghirardelli Square
www.ghirardellisq.com

See map pp. 102–103

Between Polk & Larkin Sts., Beach St., & North Point

415/775-5500

CC: Powell-Hyde; Bus: 10, 19, 41, 45; Streetcar: F-Line

IN 1964 GHIRARDELLI CHOCOLATE'S HISTORIC FACTORY was revamped as a festival marketplace of shops and restaurants—a design concept that inspired many similar urban restoration projects (such as Boston's Faneuil Hall Marketplace). The multilevel complex has great views of the bay, and scattered plaques offer a self-guided walking tour.

The story began when Domingo Ghirardelli, son of a celebrated chocolatier in Rapallo, Italy, arrived in San Francisco in 1852 and began making chocolate. Most important, he learned how to remove cocoa butter from chocolate and grind the remains into a delicate powder called "broma," used in bakeries and dairies as well as for hot chocolate. By 1885 the company was selling 50,000 pounds of this powdered chocolate annually.

To accommodate the expanding business after Domingo's retirement, in 1893 his sons bought this

Ghirardelli

city block, which included the 1864 Pioneer Woolen Mill, and converted it into a chocolate factory. Working with architect William Mooser II, they added the Mustard Building and others, all surrounding a courtyard where workers could eat lunch on sunny days.

The huge Ghirardelli sign went up in 1915. Measuring 25 feet high and 165 feet long, the sign has radiated a greeting to ships entering San Francisco ever since. (Except during the World War II blackout.)

The picturesque **Clock Tower** (1916) with four faces was inspired by the château at Blois in France. The renovation's landscape archi-

tect, Lawrence Halprin, outlined the tower in white lights, creating a delightful element of San Francisco's nighttime skyline.

In 1962 Ghirardelli Chocolate moved to a new factory, leaving its historic facility threatened with demolition to make room for an apartment development. William Matson Roth, heir to the Matson shipping empire, bought the factory with a vision in mind. Retaining the old brick walls and the wooden floors of the interior, Roth added buildings, fanciful pavilions, and landscaped terraces. The complex has dozens of specialty shops and restaurants. ■

At Ghirardelli Square's Chocolate Manufactory, visitors can sample the *Alcatraz Rock* (a rocky road and vanilla ice cream island set in a bay of whipped cream, armored with a shell of Ghirardelli chocolate and nut rocks).

The timeless Buena Vista Café, home of the first Irish coffee in the U.S.

More places to visit

BUENA VISTA CAFÉ
This is a classic San Francisco saloon, with bay windows and a tile floor. The Edwardian building dates from 1911, but that's not why some citizens consider the Buena Vista a historical site. In 1952 local newspaper columnist Stanton Delaplane returned to the bar from Ireland clutching the recipe for Irish coffee, which the Buena Vista introduced to the U.S. Today the bartender lines up a dozen or more glasses in an assembly line that's fun to watch. In a single glass, Irish coffee provides all four essential food groups: caffeine, alcohol, sugar, and fat. What more could you want?
✉ 2765 Hyde St. ☎ 415/474-5044 🚋 CC: Powell-Hyde, Powell-Mason; Bus: 15, 30, 41, 45; Streetcar: F-Line

MUSÉE MÉCANIQUE
It's like an old-fashioned penny arcade—nearly 200 antique games, fortune-telling machines, strength testers, peep shows, and orchestrions

(automated orchestras). Among mechanized dioramas are a carnival so finely detailed it looks like a movie special-effects miniature, and a farm with 150 moving figures and objects. The games work and are coin operated. Bring quarters!
🗺 Map pp. 102–103 ☎ 415/346-2000, www.museemecanique.com 🚋 CC: Powell-Hyde, Powell-Mason; Bus: 30, 41, 45; Streetcar: F-Line

VICTORIAN PARK
Encompassing more than five acres of tidiness and formality, Victorian Park has old-fashioned streetlights and benches. (You wouldn't dream that the park was created in 1960.) Rest your weary bones here after tramping through Fisherman's Wharf. Take time to enjoy the flowers set against the backdrop of the San Francisco Bay.
🗺 Map pp. 102–103 ✉ Hyde St. and Beach St. 🚋 CC: Powell-Hyde; Bus: 15, 30, 41, 45 ■

West of the Marina District's sailboats and parklands, the coast curves around the San Francisco Headlands. Along the way are historic buildings, architectural wonders, cultural attractions, and rugged coastal scenery.

The Marina & beyond

At the city's old fort

The Marina & beyond

A GRACIOUS AND REMARKABLY UN–CITIFIED PART OF SAN FRANCISCO stretches along the bay from the Marina District westward to the Presidio, passes the Golden Gate, and hugs the shore of the Pacific Ocean.

MARINA DISTRICT

In the Marina District (from Van Ness Avenue to the Presidio, between Lombard Street and the bay), a Mediterranean mood fills the air, with sea breezes, sailboats, and houses painted in pastel colors. The houses and apartments are mostly of Mediterranean revival style, with arches and red-tile roofs.

Unfortunately, they stand on unstable ground—which became obvious during the 1989 earthquake, when a number of buildings sagged or collapsed. They were put up on landfill, originally brought in to prepare the vast site of the 1915 Panama-Pacific International Exposition. Mudflats were filled with earth, sand, and, ironically, rubble from the 1906 earthquake. This gumbo virtually liquefied during the 1989 earthquake.

Highlights of the Marina include the historic Army post at Upper Fort Mason, as well as the museums and theaters at Fort Mason Center. Along Marina Green, dogs are walked, kites flown, and excess pounds jogged off. A jetty encloses the Marina Yacht Harbor. At the end is the wave organ, a scientific sculpture whose submerged pipes gurgle and hum a genuine sea chanty.

A lively neighborhood strip of shopping and nightlife runs along Chestnut Street, west of Fillmore. At the western edge of the Marina stands the last trace of the great 1915 exposition, the Palace of Fine Arts. Behind its rotunda sprawls the nation's original hands-on science museum, the Exploratorium.

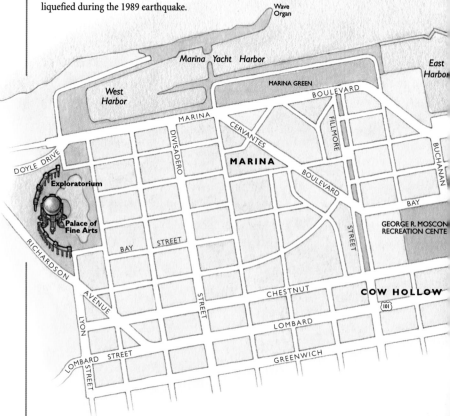

PRESIDIO

The thickly wooded Presidio dates from the Spanish founders of San Francisco, who erected a fort in 1776. Later it became an American military post. Now decommissioned, it constitutes an open-air gallery of American architecture from the mid-1800s on.

Scenic golf course at Lincoln Park

At the edge of the Presidio, the Golden Gate Bridge spans the opening to the bay. An engineering marvel, the 1937 suspension bridge is also a masterpiece of art deco design.

PACIFIC COAST

Follow the shore past the Presidio and you will reach the exclusive residential area of Sea Cliff, sheltered China Beach, and then Lands End, where the Coastal Trail loops across woodlands and bluffs, and down to secluded beaches (beware of incoming tides). The entrance to the Golden Gate is guarded by a red-and-white lighthouse, Mile Rock. The California Palace of the Legion of Honor stands in Lincoln Park. It displays a major collection of European art, and provides a fine backdrop for the Lincoln Park golf course.

Facing the setting sun, the Cliff House continues to purvey food and drink just as it has, in various incarnations, since 1863. Offshore, sea lions loll on the rocks in the sunset glow. ■

Youth Hostel

Fort Mason Center

GOLDEN GATE NATIONAL RECREATION AREA

McDowell Hall

GGNRA Headquarters

GREAT MEADOW

UPPER FORT MASON

LAGUNA

STREET

GOUGH

FRANKLIN

VAN NESS

STREET

STREET

AVENUE

STREET

STREET

101

STREET

STREET

0   200 yards
0   200 meters

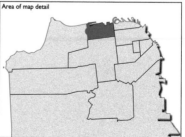

Area of map detail

Fort Mason

Fort Mason

See map pp. 122–23

Marina Blvd. at Laguna St.

Bus: 22, 28, 30, 42, 47, 49

GGNRA headquarters

www.nps.gov/goga

Fort Mason, Bldg. 201

415/561-4700

Fort Mason Center

www.fortmason.org

415/441-3400

Lower Fort Mason, a cultural warehouse with a view

AN OUTPOST OF HISTORY AND CULTURE, FORT MASON occupies 89 acres between Marina Green and Aquatic Park. It has two main areas, Upper Fort Mason and Lower Fort Mason.

UPPER FORT MASON

This section *(enter at Bay and Franklin Sts.)* stands on a bluff above the bay. As a strategic military post, it dates back to the Spanish. In 1797 they installed five brass cannon to protect against invaders in the cove below, but the guns never fired at an enemy.

After California statehood in 1850, the site was declared a U.S. military reservation. But civilian squatters (some quite well-to-do) built houses, and bought and sold property they didn't actually own. Several Gothic revival **squatters' houses** still stand on the east side of Franklin Street.

The area became known as Black Point for a dark cluster of laurel trees on the bluff. During the Civil War, the Union Army ejected the squatters and built Black Point Battery. A portion has been restored, with chest-high brick walls and a 10-inch cannon capable of lobbing a 124-pound shot more than two miles.

An old Civil War clinic is now a youth hostel *(tel 415/771-7277).* **McDowell Hall** (1866) housed army generals and then became the officers' club. The fort was renamed for Col. Richard Mason, California's first military governor, in 1882. After the 1906 earthquake and fire, the point was crowded with the tents of refugees. Military buildings were razed to create the Great Meadow, a pleasant open space now used for picnicking and sunbathing. In 1972 Fort Mason became part of Golden Gate National Recreation Area (see p. 125). The **GGNRA headquarters** is in the old military hospital; it has information on the GGNRA and western national parks.

A four-mile trail, the **Golden Gate Promenade,** runs between Aquatic Park and Fort Point linking the two sections of Fort Mason.

LOWER FORT MASON

On the waterfront *(enter from Marina Blvd. at Buchanan St.),* this was the nerve center of wartime embarkation programs from 1910 to 1963. During World War II, its piers and warehouses operated 24 hours a day, shipping out an unending flow of troops and supplies to the Pacific Theater— more than 1.6 million passengers and 23.5 million tons of cargo.

Warehouses and piers have been transformed into a lively cultural complex, **Fort Mason Center** (see p. 142). Home to 40 nonprofit organizations, it offers activities from art classes to festivals. Pick up a schedule at the **Fort Mason Foundation** *(Bldg. A).* ■

Marina Green

THE MARINA DISTRICT'S COMMUNITY BACKYARD IS MARINA Green, about 10 acres of waterfront promenade laid out between Scott and Webster Streets.

Once a marsh (it was landfilled for the 1915 exposition), Marina Green is a "see-and-be-seen" zone, where affluent young San Franciscans walk their dogs, sunbathe, and jog. The bay views are dramatic, and people of all ages fly colorful kites in the steady breezes.

A jetty encloses the Marina Yacht Harbor, the home of the exclusive St. Francis Yacht Club, designed by Willis Polk. At the end of the jetty is a scientific sculpture called the **wave organ,** whose underwater pipes make vaguely musical sounds as waves roll in. ■

Marina Green

🅰 See map pp. 122–23

🚌 Bus: 22, 28, 30

Stroll or nap at the Marina Green (above), or bike the Golden Gate Promenade (below).

Golden Gate National Recreation Area

Extending in four directions from the Golden Gate, the Golden Gate National Recreation Area (GGNRA) is a group of parks overseen by the National Park Service covering 76,000 acres and containing both natural and historical sites, from redwood groves to old forts. It includes Alcatraz Island, the bay shore (Fort Mason, Crissy Field, Fort Point, the Presidio), the San Francisco Headlands (Baker and China Beaches, Lands End, the Cliff House), and the Pacific shore (Ocean Beach, Fort Funston).

Across the Golden Gate, the GGNRA takes in the Marin Headlands (East Fort Baker; Rodeo, Gerbode, and Tennessee Valleys) and the west Marin coast (Muir Woods, Muir Beach, Stinson Beach, Bolinas Ridge, Olema Valley). ■

Palace of Fine Arts

Palace of Fine Arts
⚠ See map pp.
122–23

✉ 3601 Lyon St. at
Marina Blvd.
🚌 Bus: 22, 28, 30, 41,
43, 45

Palace of Fine Arts

LAST REMINDER OF THE BEAUTIFUL PANAMA-PACIFIC International Exposition of 1915, the Palace of Fine Arts stands reflected in a natural lagoon. Architect Bernard Maybeck wanted the palace to evoke "the mortality of grandeur and the vanity of human wishes. A grand, classical ruin with a cloister enclosing nothing…."

Somehow the architect managed to express a pang of wistful emotion in solid form. Influenced by the drawings of the 18th-century

Italian artist Giovanni Piranesi, he designed an octagonal rotunda with Roman arches and a dome 160 feet high. There were also a massive Corinthian colonnade and an exhibition gallery.

The Palace was never meant to last. Its wood frame was covered with a mixture of burlap fiber and plaster called "staff," which could be molded to any sculptural shape but wasn't enduring, despite a finish that resembled aging travertine marble. San Franciscans loved the Palace so much that when the exposition ended, they insisted that it not be razed like the other buildings. Over time, however, walls cracked and statues tumbled off their columns. In the mid-1960s the Palace was demolished and re-created in concrete and steel. In 1969 the exhibition gallery came back to life as a hands-on science museum, the Exploratorium. ∎

Reflections in a pond mirror the rotunda and peristyle, adding to the romantic air at the Palace of Fine Arts.

Panama-Pacific International Exposition of 1915

This fair ostensibly celebrated the opening of the Panama Canal, but it also trumpeted to the world that San Francisco had risen, glittering, from the rubble of 1906. The exposition was held in today's Marina District, where 635 acres of tidelands were landfilled. Architects and gardeners created a fairy-tale city. Exhibition halls were tinted ivory pink and showed off the graceful beaux arts style on an immense scale. Oregon's pavilion was a Greek temple with redwood logs for columns. The Machinery Hall was so huge that aviator Lincoln Beachey flew an airplane through it. Visitors thronged the Joy Zone, and saw a five-acre working model of the Panama Canal.

The unrivaled centerpiece was the 435-foot-tall Tower of Jewels. One hundred thousand colored glass beads and mirrors sheathed its walls. Nearly 19 million visitors partook of the fair's wonders. ∎

Exploratorium

At the Exploratorium kids and adults alike learn to see the world differently.

THE EXPLORATORIUM HAS BEEN CALLED A MAD SCIENTIST'S penny arcade, a scientific funhouse, and the "best science museum in the world" (by *Scientific American*). This grandfather of hands-on science museums was founded in 1969 by Frank Oppenheimer, whose brother, J. Robert, was the "father of the atomic bomb." If the bomb represents the dark side of science, the Exploratorium is the light side, designed to make the world understandable to everyone. "No one flunks a museum," Oppenheimer once said. More than 600 exhibits have plenty of knobs to twiddle and gears to work. You'll hear laughter and many a "Wow!"—and not just from children. Sixty percent of the annual 3.5 million visitors are adults.

The museum's central theme is human perception, explored through exhibits developed right here. In one, the air is painted with broad brushstrokes of color from the sun; in another, people seem to shrink and grow in a distorted room. The "Pitch Switch" makes your voice sound like that of a squeaky chipmunk. Inside the completely dark **Tactile Dome,** you crawl and feel your way through textured chambers, relying only on your sense of touch. This geodesic dome was designed by August Coppola, brother of filmmaker Francis Ford Coppola.

The Exploratorium engages the creative spirit and the intellect alike. Oppenheimer noted: "Both artists and scientists help us notice and appreciate things in nature that we had learned to ignore or had never been taught to see." ∎

Exploratorium
www.exploratorium.edu
✉ Behind the Palace of Fine Arts
☎ 415/561-0360 or 415/561-0362 (Tactile Dome reservations)
⊕ Closed Mon. except some holidays
$ $$. Free 1st Wed.
🚌 Bus: 22, 28, 30, 41, 43, 45

Presidio

Presidio

www.nps.gov/prsf/home.htm

See map pp.
122–23

Off Lincoln Blvd.

415/561-4323

Bus: 28, 29, 43, 82X

IN SAN FRANCISCO'S NORTHEAST CORNER LIES A 1,491-acre haven of forests, grasslands, and sea cliffs—a miracle, considering how much the rest of the city is built up. You'll find hiking trails, beaches, and some of the most magnificent views in the U.S. The Presidio is also an outdoor museum of 19th-century architecture, with 477 historic structures.

Above the Presidio

The area was first fortified in 1776, after Capt. Juan Bautista de Anza chose it for Spain's military base. A log palisade created a 275-foot square, replaced two years later by solid adobe walls. So began an outpost of empire that never fired a shot in hostility. What remains of the glorious enterprise? Only an adobe wall fragment from the 1791 residence of the comandante, on view inside the present-day U.S. Officers' Club at the Main Post.

After the gold rush made San Francisco an important American city, the United States military reserved the Presidio for itself. A rich California was worth defending. The Army built Fort Point on the ruins of Castillo de San Joaquín, a 1794 Spanish gun battery overlooking the Golden Gate. During the Civil War, the brick fort guarded against Confederates (who never appeared).

In the late 1800s a more developed Presidio housed soldiers of the Indian wars and the Spanish-American War. It sheltered 16,000 refugees after

Marin Headlands

Baker Beach

China Beach   GGNRA

LINCOLN

BOULEVARD

SEA CLIFF

Lands End   GOLDEN GATE NATIONAL RECREATION AREA

Mile Rock

DEL MAR

California Palace of the Legion of Honor

LINCOLN

EL CAMINO

LINCOLN PARK GOLF COURSE

U.S.S. San Francisco Memorial

PARK

34TH

28TH

25TH

21ST

Point Lobos

Sutro Baths (ruins)

POINT LOBOS AVENUE

GEARY   BOULEVARD

Seal Rocks

SUTRO HEIGHTS PARK

48TH   41ST   AVE   STREET   RICHMOND   AVENUE   AVENUE

AVENUE   ANZA   AVE

Cliff House

Fort Funston

BALBOA   STREET

the 1906 earthquake, and trained soldiers for World War I. During World War II, it was Western Defense Command headquarters. When decommissioned in 1994, the Presidio was the headquarters of the Sixth U.S. Army. ("The best duty station, bar none, in the United States Army," said one major.) Today the Presidio is part of the Golden Gate National Recreation Area.

MAIN POST

Begin at the **Visitor Center,** located in the 1934 Officers' Club, to learn about points of interest and Presidio history, see videos and special exhibitions, and browse a small bookstore. From here you can explore the historical attractions around the heart of the Presidio.

At the southeast corner of the Main Post, along Funston Avenue, stands a row of **officers' quarters**—Victorian houses built to a cookie-cutter plan during the Civil War. Originally they faced

Visitor Center

✉ Officers' Club (Bldg. 50) on Moraga Ave.

☎ 415/561-4323

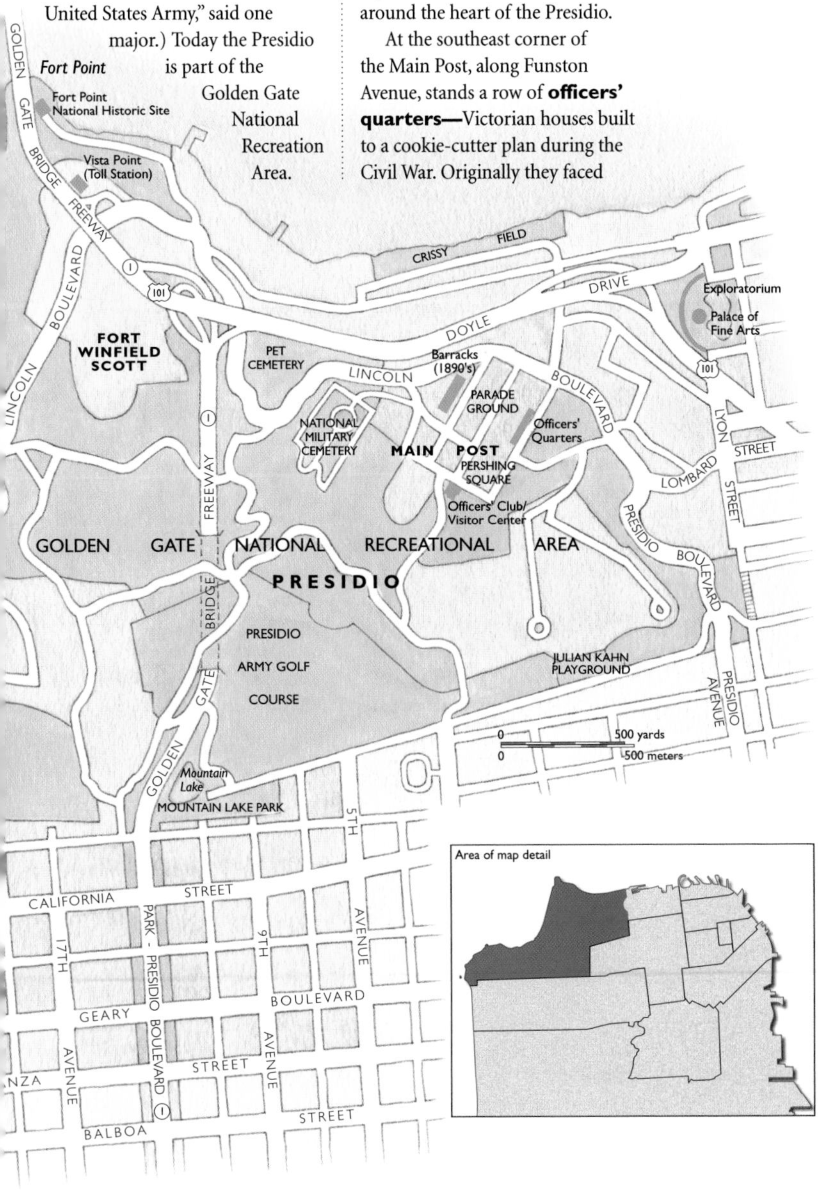

Fort Point
Fort Point National Historic Site
Vista Point (Toll Station)

CRISSY FIELD
DRIVE
Exploratorium
Palace of Fine Arts

FORT WINFIELD SCOTT
PET CEMETERY
LINCOLN
DOYLE
Barracks (1890's)
BOULEVARD
LYON STREET

NATIONAL MILITARY CEMETERY
PARADE GROUND
MAIN POST
Officers' Quarters
LOMBARD STREET

PERSHING SQUARE
Officers' Club/ Visitor Center
PRESIDIO BOULEVARD

GOLDEN GATE NATIONAL RECREATIONAL AREA

PRESIDIO

PRESIDIO ARMY GOLF COURSE
JULIAN KAHN PLAYGROUND
PRESIDIO AVENUE

0   500 yards
0   500 meters

Mountain Lake
MOUNTAIN LAKE PARK
5TH

Area of map detail

CALIFORNIA STREET
PARK PRESIDIO BOULEVARD
9TH AVENUE
GEARY BOULEVARD
17TH AVENUE
NZA AVENUE
STREET
BALBOA STREET

National Military Cemetery
✉ Lincoln Blvd. at Sheridan Ave.

Pet Cemetery
✉ Off Lincoln Blvd. on McDowell Ave.

Crissy Field
www.crissyfield.org
☎ 415/561-4323

Gulf of the Farallones National Marine Sanctuary Visitor Center
www.farallones.org
✉ West Crissy Field, near Mason St. & Fort Point
☎ 415/561-6625
🕐 Closed Mon.–Tues.

the other direction, but in 1878 the porches were moved to show a more pleasing face to the street. At Funston Avenue and Presidio Boulevard stand several Victorians that combine both Stick and Queen Anne styles (see p. 45), such as horizontal siding combined with fish-scale shingles. They were built in 1885 for higher ranking officers.

At **Pershing Square,** archaeologists discovered the foundations of the old Spanish fort, and a plaque marks the northwest corner of the adobe quandrangle. Also here are two late 1600s bronze cannon, emblazoned with the Spanish royal shield. The square's flagstaff marks where Brigadier General John J. Pershing's house stood, until a fire killed his wife and daughters in 1915. Pershing commanded the American Expeditionary Force in Europe during World War I. North of the flagpole stands a white 1863 Army blockhouse in whose west wall is lodged a cannonball.

Enlisted men's barracks stand along the north end of Graham Street. They were built after the Civil War, when the Army increased the size of a company from 75 to 100 men and more housing was needed.

Across the main parade ground —now a parking lot, but eventually to become a seven-acre greensward —stand five identical barracks of the 1890s that distinguish the first extensive use of brick among the Presidio's buildings, a symbol that the U.S. Army was there to stay. Each soldier had a bed, a footlocker, and zero privacy. But what a location!

NATIONAL MILITARY CEMETERY
Headstones date back as far as the Civil War in what was originally the post burial ground, and then in

1884 was declared a national military cemetery. Among notables is Brigadier General Frederick Funston, who won the Congressional Medal of Honor for bravery in the Philippines in 1899 and kept order in San Francisco after the 1906 earthquake. Also here is Pauline Cushman Fryer, an 1860s actress who spied for the Union Army while touring the South.

The nearby **Pet Cemetery** was the burial plot for guard dogs of the K-9 corps and later for pets of Presidio families.

CRISSY FIELD
A former marsh that was landfilled for the 1915 Panama-Pacific International Exposition, this bay-side stretch of land served as an Army airfield from 1919 to 1963. The National Park Service has transformed the asphalt expanse into a wild, open 100-acre shoreline park, with restored dunes, a tidal marsh, and a waterfront promenade that's popular with walkers, joggers, and baby-strolling parents. Crissy's old grass airfield has been restored, offering a huge lawn for recreation. An 1890 Coast Guard station houses the **Gulf of the Farallones National Marine Sanctuary Visitor Center,** which gives details on the 1,255-square-mile sanctuary that stretches north of the Golden Gate; there's a large ocean mural and a touch tank.

FORT WINFIELD SCOTT
When coastal defense batteries were installed along the San Francisco Headlands, Fort Scott housed the artillerymen. Ranged in a horseshoe, the fort's barracks (1910–15) are of uniform mission revival style, with white walls, arched porticos, and red-tile roofs—quite a departure from the usual Army look, but fitting for this "post within a post." The

coastal defense batteries, built in the 1890s to guard the Golden Gate, lie along the Coastal Trail between Fort Point and Baker Beach *(access from Lincoln Blvd.)*. They never fired a hostile shot. From the bluffs you'll see the Golden Gate and Marin Headlands.

FORT POINT

Known as the "Gibraltar of the West," this four-tiered fort was erected between 1853 and 1861 to defend the Golden Gate. Granite and more than eight million bricks were used to create walls up to seven feet thick. Fort Point contains 90 casemates, or gun rooms, but by the mid-1880s the guns were out of date and the fort was soon virtually abandoned. Today the structure is appreciated as a classic pre-Civil War fortress and a fine example of the mason's craft.

Inside the sally port on the ground floor you'll find a visitor center (guided, headphone, and self-guided tours), a theater (17-minute historical movie), and the former powder room with walls 15 feet thick. Around the open courtyard rise three levels of brick arches. The second floor housed officers, but enlisted men had to climb to the third floor. On the water side, casemates sheltered up to 102 guns at the fort's greatest strength.

Also intriguing is Fort Point's location under a vaulting steel arch of the Golden Gate Bridge. This design saved the fort from demolition for the bridge's southern anchorage. There's a memorable view of the bridge and bay from the fort's rooftop or the seawall—not to mention the sight of surfers racing across huge waves that roll through the Golden Gate.

BAKER BEACH

The city's most popular beach has picnic areas, dunes, and a view of the Golden Gate Bridge. On the bluff stands **Battery Chamberlain** (1904), with its six-inch "disappearing" rifle, whose carriage folds down behind a wall to vanish from enemy view; rangers give weekend demonstrations. Warning: Do not swim, due to riptides. On the northern stretch of sand, you may spy the species *Homo sapiens* in its natural state.

NATURAL LIFE

The urban forest of the Presidio numbers more than 200,000 pine, cypress, and eucalyptus trees. Woods and shoreline are home to more than 170 species of birds, from California quail to bald eagles. On the Pacific shore you might see anything from wee snails in tide pools to 90-foot blue whales passing offshore. ■

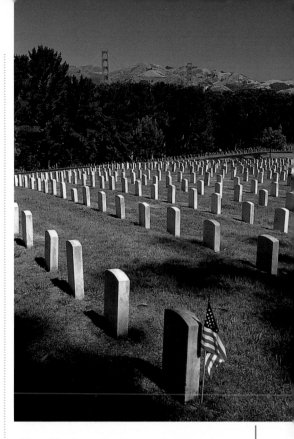

At the 28-acre National Military Cemetery

Fort Point
www.nps.gov/fopo
✉ Off Lincoln Blvd.
☎ 415/556-1693
🕐 Closed Mon.–Thurs.

Baker Beach
✉ Off Lincoln Blvd. at Bowley St.

Golden Gate Bridge

Above and right:
The famous bridge
spans the Golden
Gate, a mile-wide
gap inexplicably
missed by
explorers Cabrillo
and Drake.

Golden Gate
Bridge
www.goldengatebridge.org

🅰 See map pp.
128–29

🚌 Bus: 28, 29, 76

THE GOLDEN GATE BRIDGE SPANS THE OPENING TO THE
San Francisco Bay and links San Francisco with Marin County. Is
it science or art? One can regard the bridge as a milestone of
engineering. Or as an art deco masterpiece, a reddish orange sculpture set against the blue water and green headlands.

The Golden Gate is a suspension
bridge. The basic design: Towers
at each end support cables, from
which the roadway is suspended.
This simple idea dates from before
the Iron Age, when people used
bamboo and vines as cables. As
early as A.D. 65, the Chinese erected
a 250-foot-long iron chain suspension bridge over a river.

For sheer scale, the Golden Gate
Bridge boggles the mind. Its length,

including approaches, is 8,981 feet.
The main span, at 4,200 feet, was
the world's longest until 1964,
when it was edged out by New
York's Verrazano Narrows Bridge at
4,260 feet. The two side spans
measure 1,125 feet each.

Two art deco towers rise 746 feet
(191 feet taller than the Washington
Monument), about 48 stories.
Together, the towers weigh more
than 88 million pounds. The pier

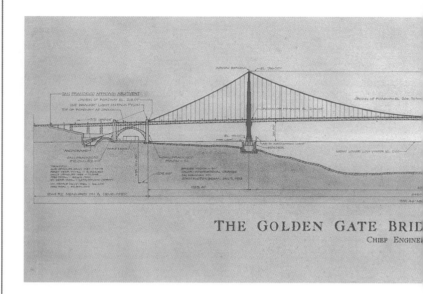

THE GOLDEN GATE BRID
CHIEF ENGINE

Counting the part under water, the bridge's tallest tower rises nearly as high as the Transamerica Pyramid.

The bridge from every angle

For great views on the San Francisco side:

Vista Point & visitor center (off Lincoln Blvd. or US 101) At the toll station, as well as the view: schlock souvenirs, Strauss statue, cable cross-section.

Fort Point (off Lincoln Blvd.) A view from below, along the seawall.

Lands End (U.S.S. *San Francisco* Memorial parking lot, off El Camino Del Mar) The bridge from the west.

On the Marin side:

Vista point (off US 101 north) It stands against the green Presidio.

East Fort Baker (US 101 north to Alexander Ave. exit; at Bunker Rd. follow signs to Bay Area Discovery Museum) Spectacular view from a cove below the bridge.

Conzelman Road (US 101 north to Alexander Ave. exit; left at Bunker Rd., left on McCullough Rd., left on Conzelman Rd.) Great prospect from the Marin Headlands. ■

for the south tower had to be constructed a quarter-mile offshore, on a foundation 110 feet below water level. Workmen built an oval concrete fender as long as a football field. Water was evacuated and the pier sunk inside. The fender, with conduits added to let sea water circulate, was left in place to cushion the pier against tides.

The bridge's two cables thread over the towers and anchor at each end to massive blocks of concrete. Each anchorage can withstand a pull of 63 million pounds from the cables. The cables weigh 11,000 tons apiece. Each is 36⅜ inches in diameter and contains 27,572 wires. The total length of wire adds up to 80,000 miles, enough to twine around the equator three times.

In a strong wind or earthquake, the bridge's center span is designed to handle 27.7 feet of sway (or

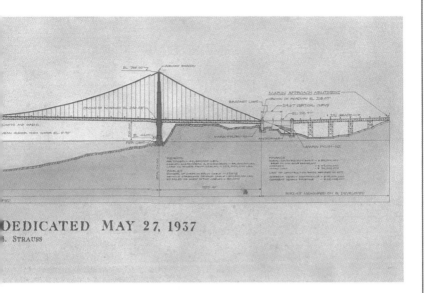

DEDICATED MAY 27, 1937

J. STRAUSS

"transverse deflection"). The roadway has a mean clearance above the water of 220 feet.

The bridge has been painted continuously since opening day in 1937. The first coat took 60,000 gallons of paint. The bridge's distinctive color is International Orange, but is more accurately vermilion, a vivid reddish orange. The hue was suggested by consulting architect Irving Morrow as an alternative to the usual dull engineer's gray. Morrow's vision for lighting the bridge was finally realized on its 50th anniversary in 1987, with the mounting of 48 high-pressure sodium lamps. The desired effect was achieved—that the towers seem to fade gradually into the sky.

Chief engineer Joseph Strauss had to create a structure that could stand up to 60-mile-an-hour tidal surges, ocean waves, buffeting winds, fog, even earthquakes. He also had to overcome opposition by the Southern Pacific Railroad, whose ferries would lose profits. Construction (1933–37) cost 35 million dollars and provided jobs for thousands of workers during the Great Depression. Accidents killed 11 men, a number that might have been larger had not Strauss insisted on strict safety measures, including nets, during construction. Since the bridge opened, ironically, more than 1,000 suicides have jumped from it.

To comprehend the scale of the bridge, walk across. Look down at the water, a dizzying 220 feet below. Bring a jacket against the wind, and choose a quiet traffic hour, such as Sunday morning. ∎

The bridge's non-stop traffic streams to and from Marin County.

San Francisco Headlands

See maps pp. 122–23 & 128–29

Bus: 18

THE SAN FRANCISCO HEADLANDS STRETCH WEST AND south around the coast from Baker Beach. This is a rugged corner of ocean bluffs and tangled vegetation.

Chinese immigrants were reputedly smuggled ashore at China Beach.

A civilized touch as you approach the headlands from the Presidio is the neighborhood of **Sea Cliff** (*off El Camino Del Mar at 25th–27th Aves.*). It is unique among residential neighborhoods because it fronts the ocean. (Otherwise, the city's Pacific shoreline is devoted to parks and public beaches.) Many houses are 1920s Mediterranean style and have ocean views.

The sandy cove at **China Beach** (*end of Seacliff Ave.*) was named for Chinese fishermen who once anchored their junks and camped here. Sheltered from the wind, this is a good spot for

Lincoln Park golf course overlooks the city.

sunbathing, a picnic, or a chilly swim. (Be wary of unpredictable surf conditions.) On clear days you can see Mount Tamalpais and Point Reyes in Marin County.

LANDS END

Edging the coastline between Sea Cliff and the Cliff House, this wild swath contains a tame section, **Lincoln Park.** This was a cemetery area until John McLaren (of Golden Gate Park, see p. 156) laid out the plantings. It has a golf course (1909) with views so spectacular that even a pro would be distracted. The **California Palace of the Legion of Honor** (see p. 137) exhibits a treasure trove of European art.

The **Coastal Trail** (*accessible from the palace or the Merrie Way parking lot*) threads the headlands, looping among cypress trees, fields, and steep bluffs, with expansive views of the strait. You can descend to **Lands End Beach**. Part of the trail follows the old roadbed of the 1880s Ferries & Cliff House Railroad, which brought the seaside as close as a nickel's ride.

Walk the trail, or drive, to the **vista point** and **U.S.S. San Francisco Memorial** (*off El Camino Del Mar*). This World War II cruiser took 45 hits in the Battle of Guadalcanal, and its shell-pierced bridge serves as a monument. Offshore, treacherous rocks have wrecked many ships. Parts of some unlucky vessels can be spied from the Coastal Trail. Farther south are the **Cliff House, Sutro Heights,** and **Sutro Baths** (see pp. 140–41). ∎

California Palace of the Legion of Honor

THE SOCIALLY MINDED ALMA DE BRETTEVILLE SPRECKELS persuaded her sugar-baron husband to reproduce the French pavilion from the 1915 Panama-Pacific International Exposition as an art museum. (The pavilion was itself modeled on the 1782 Palais de la Légion d'Honneur in Paris.) Then the philanthropic Mrs. Spreckels filled the colonnaded wings of the museum with treasures, including more than 80 pieces of Rodin sculpture in bronze, marble, terracotta, and plaster. Many were acquired directly from the artist in his studio, including an early cast of "The Thinker" (1904).

Rodin's classic bronze "The Thinker" puzzles things out in front of a classical colonnade.

California Palace of the Legion of Honor
www.thinker.org/legion
✉ Lincoln Park, near 34th Ave. & Clement St.
☎ 415/863-3330
🕐 Closed Mon.
💲 $$. Free Tues.
🚌 Bus: 1, 18, 38
Note: Traveling exhibits that formerly went to the de Young (see pp. 165–67) will come here until that museum reopens in 2005.

The museum, which honors California's dead in World War I, was designed in 1924 by George Applegarth and expanded below ground in 1994. To view the galleries in order, start to the left of the main entrance.

Medieval Art (exhibited in galleries 1, 2, & 3) opens a view into the Europe of monasteries and cathedrals during the thousand years after Rome fell in the fifth century. The art, meant to evoke the glory of God, ranges from a French Limoges reliquary of blue enamel (ca 1200) to an alabaster carving of Jesus reprimanding Adam and Eve (Spain, 14th century). Styles include the flattened, stiff Romanesque (11–12th century) and the more naturalistic Gothic (12–16th century). In secular art you'll see early tapestries and a 15th-century Spanish ceiling.

During the Renaissance (galleries 4 & 5), mankind and the self gradually took center stage. Look for early Renaissance works by Fra Angelico and other Italian painters. High Renaissance art (Titian, Tintoretto) was realistic in style, but evolved into the artifice of mannerism, of which an example is El Greco's "St. John the Baptist" (ca 1600), which elongates the gaunt figure to mystical effect.

The "father of modern sculpture," Auguste Rodin (galleries 8, 10 & 12), brought new psychological depth and sensual passion to renderings of the human figure. Do see "The Kiss" (1886) and reduced casts of figures from "The Burghers of Calais" (1886), which were often cited as the sculptor's greatest work.

The 17th-century Dutch and Flemish collection (Galleries 14 & 15) includes a portrait of sea captain Joris de Caulleri (1632) by a 26-year-old Rembrandt, along with works by Van Dyck and Rubens.

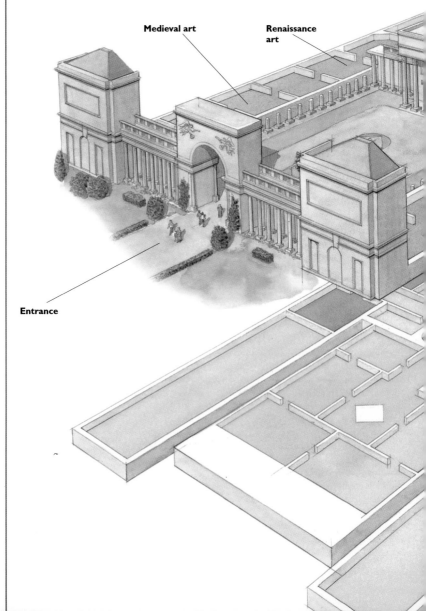

Medieval art

Renaissance art

Entrance

In the 19th-century European galleries (17 &18), rapid social change is reflected in the evolution from Romanticism (Gericault's equestrian portrait of Charles V, 1814) to Social Realism (Manet's "At the Milliner's," 1881) to Impressionism and novel styles such as Pointillism (Seurat's "The Eiffel Tower," 1889).

Challenging new ideas of form and content began to emerge in 20th-century Europe (gallery 19). Don't miss Monet's "Waterlilies" (ca 1914–17), a late work that turns a natural scene into a nearly abstract array of color. Also be sure to see Picasso's "Still life with Skull, Leeks, and Vase" (1945), a World War II work painted in occupied Paris. ■

Auguste Rodin sculpture

Many of the museum's Rodin pieces were acquired directly from the artist.

17th-century Dutch & Flemish art

19th-century European art

20th-century European art

Various art displays

Florence Gould Theatre

Constance & Henry Bowles Porcelain Gallery

Achenbach Foundation for graphic arts

Special exhibition galleries

Other areas

The spacious interior allows visitors to enjoy an unobstructed view of the exhibits.

Cliff House, Sutro Heights, & Sutro Baths

Cliff House
www.cliffhouse.com
✉ 1090 Point Lobos Ave.
☎ 415/386-3330
🚌 Bus: 18, 38

FOR 150 YEARS, SAN FRANCISCANS HAVE BEEN HEADING west for a day at the beach. To serve them, the Cliff House rose in 1863. It wasn't much to look at, but its location drew U.S. presidents and the carriage trade, including the Stanfords and Hearsts. Later it became a shadier haunt for men's gambling and general debauchery.

Sutro Heights Park
✉ Enter at 48th Ave. & Point Lobos Ave.

Two stone lions guard the entrance to Sutro Heights.

In 1881 Adolph Sutro appeared on the scene. A Comstock (see p. 27) millionaire who owned one-twelfth of San Francisco's land, he purchased the Cliff House and fell in love with the view from the bluff above it—which he promptly bought. There he built his home, Sutro Heights, and employed ten gardeners to transform the sandy acres with roses, tapestry gardens, exotic trees, and hundreds of European statues "to educate and enlighten" the populace, who were

free to roam. His own guests ranged from President Benjamin Harrison to Oscar Wilde. The gardens, now **Sutro Heights Park,** are cared for by the GGNRA.

To deliver the public to his seaside attractions, Sutro built a railroad whose fare was just a nickel. After an 1894 fire destroyed the Cliff House, Sutro rebuilt in style. His eight-story French château had turrets, panoramic windows, and an observation tower. A much loved spot for dining, dancing, and

entertainment, it too burned in 1907. A neoclassical Cliff House was put up in 1909 by Sutro's daughter. It survived the Great Depression and two world wars, but later was remodeled several times before the National Park Service acquired it in 1977.

In 2004 a complete renovation created a fourth incarnation of the Cliff House, designed to bring back the character and dignity of the 1909 neoclassical structure, while also adding a new wing inspired by the architecture of the old Sutro Baths. The dining room offers dramatic views of Ocean Beach, Seal Rock, and the rolling hills of Marin County.

A short walk north of the Cliff House you'll find the remnants of **Sutro Baths,** a public swimming house that was a marvel of artistic detail and engineering ingenuity. Sutro spent $250,000 to build the three-acre baths, which opened in 1886. Visitors swam in six saltwater "swimming ponds," the largest 300 feet long, kept at various temperatures by steam heat. Under two acres of arching glass, swimmers frolicked on springboards, trapezes, and toboggan slides.

A freshwater pool was supplied by an ever flowing spring. A laundry washed rental bathing suits (20,000 daily) and towels (40,000). Three restaurants seated 1,000 people at a time. Among other attractions were artwork, cabinets of ancient Egyptian artifacts, and an amphitheater that seated 3,700 people for stage shows. Guests paid only a dime to enter, 25 cents to swim. The baths' revenues didn't meet expenses, though, and in 1937 Sutro's heirs converted the large tank into a skating rink. A fire destroyed the baths in the 1960s. ∎

The magnificent scale of Sutro Baths is difficult to imagine today.

Religious statuary in the Mexican Museum at Fort Mason

More places to visit

FORT MASON CENTER

The center's theaters include the **Cowell Theater** (*Pier 2, tel 415/441-3687, plays, dance, music*); **Magic Theater** (*Bldg. D, tel 415/441-8822, works by Sam Shepard, emerging playwrights*); **Young Performers Theater** (*Bldg. C, tel 415/346-5550, children and professional actors working together*); and **Bay Area Theater Sports** (*Bldg. B, tel 415/474-8935, improvisations, workshops*).

You can also visit museums, which present changing exhibits. These include: **San Francisco Museum of Craft & Folk Art** (*Bldg. A, tel 415/775-0991, historical and contemporary crafts from diverse cultures*); **Museo Italo-Americano** (*Bldg. C, tel 415/673-2200, Italian and Italian-American artists*); **San Francisco African-American**

At the Museum of Craft & Folk Art

Historical & Cultural Society (*Bldg. C, tel 415/441-0640, culture, arts, and crafts*); and the **Mexican Museum** (*Bldg. D, tel 415/202-9700, Mexican and Latino arts. Note: Moves to Yerba Buena Center at the end of 2006*). The **National Maritime Museum Library** (*Bldg. E, tel 415/561-7080*) focuses on sail and steam vessels from the gold rush through post-World War II, with historical documents, photos, plans, and periodicals. **Greens** vegetarian restaurant (see p. 253) is also situated here. For information on Fort Mason see p. 124.

✉ Lower Fort Mason, Marina Blvd. at Laguna St. 🚌 Bus: 22, 28, 30, 42, 47, 49

PRESIDIO GOLF COURSE

This 6,477-yard, par 72 public golf course is located in the heart of San Francisco. When it was built in 1895, on what was then a U.S. Army Post, it was open to military personnel and members of a small private club only. The military post at the Presidio closed in 1995, and its ownership was transferred to the National Park Service, which opened the golf course to the public.

The only 18-hole golf course located on National Park Service land (although managed by a private company), it has a clubhouse whose Presidio Café is open to the non-golf-playing public.

✉ 300 Finley Rd. ☎ 415/561-4653 (golf), 415/561-4600 (café), www.presidiogolf.com 🚌 Bus: 28, 29, 41, 43, 45 ∎

Stroll among luxury mansions and apartment blocks in the elevated district of Pacific Heights. Japantown lies on its southern fringe.

Pacific Heights & Japantown

The Japanese community comes together for the Cherry Blossom Festival.

Pacific Heights & Japantown

SAN FRANCISCO HAS NO BETTER ADDRESS THAN PACIFIC HEIGHTS, WHICH offers everything an elite residential neighborhood should: First, a preeminent perch—a high ridge running between Van Ness and the Presidio (and bounded by California and Green). Second, beautifully designed and built houses and apartments. Third, million-dollar views (in some cases, many millions).

The area developed as transit did. The advent of cable cars created the first wave of building in the 1870s. Mansions lined Van Ness Avenue, which was laid out as the city's widest street (125 feet) for this very purpose. In the 1880s fine Victorians rose near two neighborhood parks, Lafayette and Alta Plaza, and others followed, appearing across the heights like pop-up pictures in a storybook. Often rows of houses were constructed to similar plans by speculative builders. Owners chose decorative trim and gingerbread from millwork catalogs to individualize their homes. During the 1906 earthquake and fire, Brigadier General Frederick Funston had the houses on the east side of Van Ness dynamited to create a firebreak, successfully blocking the fire from marching westward across the city. Van Ness later became a commercial thoroughfare.

Pacific Heights' stock as an elite enclave rose higher after 1906, when wealthy families whose houses had burned on Nob Hill came to build lavish homes. You'll see everything

from Italian villas to grand piles of brick and stone, often with well-tended gardens or landscaped terraces. In the 1920s and '30s, apartment

Elite Pacific Heights

buildings replaced many large old houses in the eastern section of Pacific Heights. Along the south side of the Presidio, more rows of magnificent houses fill Presidio Heights. A highlight of this neighborhood is the simple but profound Swedenborgian Church, a true retreat from city life.

Between Pacific Heights and the Marina lies Cow Hollow, a former dairy-farm area that became a Victorian residential neighbor-hood. In the 1950s, shops and restaurants began to occupy old-fashioned houses along the main thoroughfare. The architecture was largely saved, but in some cases preservation crosses the line into studied quaintness.

South of Pacific Heights, the cultural hub of San Francisco's Japanese-American

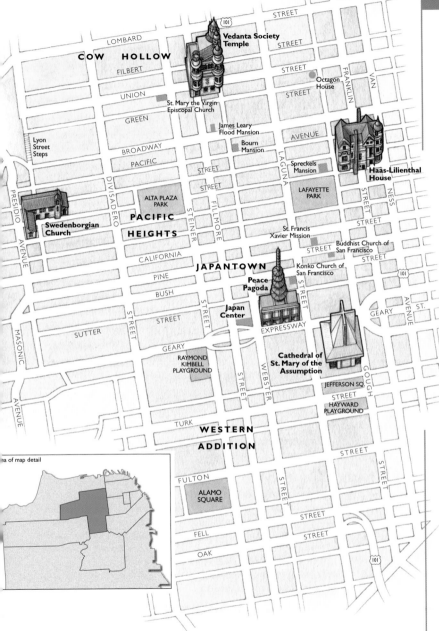

Vedanta Society
Temple

STREET

LOMBARD

COW HOLLOW

FILBERT

STREET

Octagon
House

UNION

St. Mary the Virgin
Episcopal Church

GREEN

James Leary
Flood Mansion

AVENUE

Bourn
Mansion

Lyon
Street
Steps

BROADWAY

PACIFIC

Spreckels
Mansion

Haas-Lilienthal
House

STREET

STREET

ALTA PLAZA
PARK

LAFAYETTE
PARK

PRESIDIO AVENUE

Swedenborgian
Church

PACIFIC

HEIGHTS

St. Francis
Xavier Mission

STREET

Buddhist Church of
San Francisco

CALIFORNIA

JAPANTOWN

Konko Church of
San Francisco

PINE

Peace
Pagoda

BUSH

Japan
Center

MASONIC

SUTTER

STREET

GEARY

EXPRESSWAY

GEARY

RAYMOND
KIMBELL
PLAYGROUND

Cathedral of
St. Mary of the
Assumption

JEFFERSON SQ.

STREET

AVENUE

TURK

WESTERN

HAYWARD
PLAYGROUND

ADDITION

ea of map detail

STREET

FULTON

ALAMO
SQUARE

STREET

FELL

STREET

OAK

STREET

community, Nihonmachi (Japantown),
occupies part of the city's Western Addition.
It was once more expansive, but Japantown
virtually emptied during World War II as
Japanese residents (two-thirds of them U.S.
citizens) were relocated to internment camps.

In the 1960s, urban renewal razed many
blocks of Victorians in what had become a
slum, forcing 4,000 households to relocate.
The Japan Center was constructed, as were
temples and churches, making the district a
cultural focus for Japanese Americans. ■

Grand houses

IN MOST CASES YOU CAN ONLY GAZE AT THE SPLENDID homes of Pacific Heights from the outside, but their architectural extravagance makes them well worth the look.

Haas-Lilienthal house

www.sfheritage.org

✉ 2007 Franklin St.

☎ 415/441-3000

🕐 Tours Wed., Sat.–Sun. (call for times)

💲 $$

🚌 Bus: 1, 12, 19, 27, 47, 49

HAAS-LILIENTHAL HOUSE

The Haas-Lilienthal house is one that you can visit. This stately gray residence of peaked gables, bay windows, and a corner tower blends Queen Anne and Stick styles. The 1886 house was lived in by two generations of the same family until 1972, and now serves as a Victorian house museum and head-quarters of the preservationist San Francisco Architectural Heritage organization. The house is a sur-vivor: Many Victorians were lost in the 1906 fire, and of those that remained, most in this area of eastern Pacific Heights were demolished to erect apartments.

Designed by Peter Schmidt, the three-story house was built for William Haas, a German Jewish immigrant who started work as a wholesale grocer and ended as a director of Wells Fargo Bank. (His youngest daughter married Samuel Lilienthal.) The 24-room house, with 11,500 square feet, shows how an upper-middle class mercantile family aspired to live. The interior glows with polished woods. The master bathroom boasts newfangled devices such as a gas jet to heat hair-curling irons. Parlors, the dining room, and a bedroom are furnished in varying styles of the half century after the house was built.

SPRECKELS MANSION

Do you mean to say that *your* house doesn't take up a whole city block, look like the Parthenon, and have 26 bathrooms? Few houses could match the palatial French baroque Spreckels mansion *(2080 Washington St., private)* built in 1913 for Adolph Spreckels (son of sugar king Claus Spreckels) and his wife, Alma de Bretteville Spreckels. The architect was George Applegarth (designer of the California Palace of the Legion of Honor, which the couple donated to the city). Today, beyond the mansion's Ionic columns lies the sanctum of best-selling novelist Danielle Steel. In the entry court-yard you'll see ranks of luxury auto-mobiles, perhaps belonging to some of the author's many children.

FLOOD MANSIONS

In 1912 the son of a Comstock silver king used his bottomless pockets to build the **James Leary Flood Mansion** *(2222 Broadway, private),* now part of the Schools of the Sacred Heart. Architects Bliss & Faville designed the Italian Renaissance pile, sheathing it in Tennessee marble around a steel frame engineered to resist earth-quakes. To imagine the Flood lifestyle, look through the front door, down a marble-clad hall that stretches nearly 150 feet, and to a window at the end, which frames a grand piano.

Flood and his wife lived in an earlier **Flood Mansion** *(2120 Broadway, private,* designed by Julius Krafft in 1901), after the 1906 earthquake gutted their mansion on Nob Hill (now the Pacific Union Club) and before they moved to the new mansion described above. Flood's sister, Cora Jane ("Miss Jennie"), remained in the stately house until 1924. Four years later it

was converted into the Sarah Dix Hamlin School.

The 24-room Edwardian mansion has a classical symmetry imposed by Ionic columns, pilasters, and pedimented windows. Granite steps watched by gray marble lions (known to students as Leo and Leona) lead to a mosaic-and-marble vestibule. Beyond that lies a two-story central hall paneled in golden oak and topped with an art-glass canopy measuring 26 feet across. Among remarkable rooms are the solarium (now the student cafeteria) with its mosaic-tile floor, and the Chinese Room with its bamboo ceiling, red lacquer, and green silk walls—one of the few remaining examples of a decorating conceit once popular among wealthy San Franciscans. ∎

Showing the exuberance of San Francisco's Victorian age, the Haas–Lilienthal house is an architectural confection, as ornamental as a wedding cake.

The Lyon Street Steps help walkers negotiate the steep hills of Pacific Heights—and offer a million-dollar view.

Two views & a street

Three Pacific Heights experiences: Walking the Lyon Street Steps *(Broadway to Green St.)* gives a colorful view of the Palace of Fine Arts' red-orange dome, the blue bay, and green Marin County—just what you'd see from the window of a Pacific Heights mansion. Another fine view is the cityscape from the summit of Alta Plaza Park. To sample the neighborhood's tony but unstuffy public life, hit Fillmore Street *(south from Jackson St.)* for shopping and dining. ■

Presidio Heights

JUST WEST OF PACIFIC HEIGHTS, THIS NEIGHBORHOOD also has rows of splendid houses built by the ultra-rich, but its two striking and unusual religious buildings provide a pleasing contrast of style and mood.

Fine, large residences lie along Pacific, Jackson, and Washington Streets. Bernard Maybeck designed the **Roos House** (*3500 Jackson St.*), with dark half-timbering and heavy flower boxes. The elite **Presidio Terrace** neighborhood (*off Arguello Blvd. near Washington St.*) has residences by Bakewell & Brown (No. 15), George Applegarth (No. 34), and Julia Morgan (No. 36). This well-manicured loop street was being developed as early as 1905. The upscale Presidio Heights community does its shopping, dining, and moviegoing along a quiet, appealing section of Sacramento Street (*between Lyon and Spruce Sts.*) that has very much a neighborhood feeling.

TEMPLE EMANU-EL

Inspired by Hagia Sophia in Istanbul, Temple Emanu-El was designed in 1926 by Bakewell & Brown for a congregation of San Francisco's successful Jewish community. Jewish immigrants arrived with the gold rush and did well in the burgeoning city. This congregation dates from 1850. The temple's main designer, Arthur Brown, Jr., was also the architect of the War Memorial Opera House, City Hall, and Coit Tower. The most powerful feature of the temple, its Byzantine dome, soars to a height of 150 feet and is sheathed in red terra-cotta tiles. Another major element, the cloistered courtyard, was inspired by the buildings of the 1915 Panama-Pacific International Exposition, which were joined by similar courtyards and covered walks with open colonnades. Plants named in the Bible have been put in the courtyard, including date and olive trees.

In the vestibule, the ceiling is painted to look like a star-studded sky. The 1,700-seat temple has no supporting columns, and the dome creates a lofty, uplifting feeling. The commanding Ark, which contains the Torah, lies in an ornate gilded cloisonné box under a green marble canopy. In 1973 stained-glass windows were added, designed by Mark Adams to represent the natural elements of fire (on the east, or bay, side) and water (to the west).

SWEDENBORGIAN CHURCH

An architectural gem, the 1895 Swedenborgian Church has been called the "church of the simple life." The church's theological foundations come from Emanuel Swedenborg (1688–1772). A Swedish scientist turned mystic, he perceived that all life is spiritual and that all things in creation reveal the divine. His ideas influenced American transcendentalist Ralph Waldo Emerson. Twentieth-century Zen scholar D.T. Suzuki called Swedenborg the "Buddha of the North," and some of his meditative practices resembled yoga.

The church was planned by theologian and architecture critic Joseph Worcester, who designed California's first full-fledged arts and crafts house in the 1870s. A. Page Brown guided the project, while Bernard Maybeck helped design the interior. The church is

Temple Emanu-El
- ✉ Arguello Blvd. at Lake St.
- ☎ 415/751-2535
- 🚌 Bus: 3, 12, 22, 24

Swedenborgian Church
www.sfswedenborgian.org
- ✉ 2107 Lyon St. at Washington St.
- ☎ 415/346-6466
- 🚌 Bus: 3, 12, 22, 24

The timbered interior of the Swedenborgian Church creates a mood of serenity and calm

one of San Francisco's most popular wedding sites.

Visitors enter a walled garden to find what appears to be an Italian village church of simple stucco and oven-fired brick. Inside, the church evokes a rustic forest lodge, or perhaps a sacred grove. Beams of madrone wood are still covered in their natural bark. A fireplace fills the room with warmth and the scent of woodsmoke. The congregation sits on comfortable maple chairs with rush seats, rather than hard pews. (These chairs inspired Gustav Stickley in creating his craftsman style furniture.) Four pastoral murals by William Keith depict the seasons of northern California and reveal an appreciation of the subtleties and mystery of nature ■

Cow Hollow

DAIRY FARMS ONCE DOTTED THIS HOLLOW BELOW THE ridge of Pacific Heights, but it was the stink from the attendant slaughterhouses, meat-packing houses, and leather tanneries of the late 1800s that gave the valley its nickname. At last neighboring citizens convinced the city to shut down these polluting businesses and landfill the hollow, which became a residential area.

In the 1950s antique dealers and interior designers moved into the Victorian houses on Union Street, and were followed by more shops, restaurants, and bars. Today **Union Street** *(Steiner St. to Van Ness Ave.)* is a boutique boomtown. Designer clothes, expensive baubles for the home, fashion eyeglasses, jewelry—it's all here. Strolling down Union is a popular way to pass an early evening or weekend afternoon.

At Steiner and Union stands the redwood-shingled **St. Mary the Virgin Episcopal Church.** Resembling a church on a country lane, it has a garden courtyard that shelters an original spring where early dairy herds drank.

Look downhill from Union on Webster Street to see the old **Vedanta Society Temple.** Built in 1905, it blends a basically Edwardian building with an East Indian balcony arcade, red onion domes, and other exotica. The eclectic mix of decorative elements is intended to reflect the Vedanta idea that all religions aim at realizing the same one god. Vedanta is a branch of Hinduism.

At **2040 Union** the 1873 Victorian house and barn of Cow Hollow's first dairy farmer (the appropriately named James Cudworth) have metamorphosed into retail and restaurant space.

Are people healthier if they live in an eight-sided building? Some people believed so when the **Octagon House** was built in

1861. Perhaps the theory arose because a house with more sides lets in more fresh air and light. It turns out that when an octagonal house is divided into square rooms, it leaves triangles that make good closets (and water closets). The house, now home to the National Society of Colonial Dames of America in California, displays furniture and decorative arts of the colonial and federal periods, as well as the signatures of Thomas Jefferson, Benjamin Franklin, and others whose names appear on the Declaration of Independence. ■

Cow Hollow

- See map pp. 144–45
- Bus: 22, 41, 45

St. Mary the Virgin Episcopal Church

- ✉ 2325 Union St.
- ☎ 415/921-3665
- 🕐 Closed Sun.

Vedanta Society Temple

- ✉ 2323 Vallejo St.
- ☎ 415/922-2323
- 🕐 Closed during services

Octagon House

- ✉ 2645 Gough St.
- ☎ 415/441-7512
- 🕐 Open 2nd Sun., 2nd & 4th Thurs.

Octagon House

Japantown

A Japanese tradition, the Cherry Blossom Festival parade features authentic kimonos.

A CULTURAL CENTER FOR THE JAPANESE-AMERICAN community (but not a residential hub like Chinatown), Japantown has two major sections: Japan Center and the Buchanan (or Nihonmachi) Mall.

Anchored by the Miyako Hotel and the AMC Kabuki 8 movie theaters, the **Japan Center** was built in 1968 during urban renewal. The five-acre complex looks blandly modern, so don't come expecting anything like the gorgeous old Japanese city of Kyoto. However, it has all the sushi and tempura you can eat, shops filled with Japanese arts and household goods, and entertainment. The year's big event is the Cherry Blossom Festival *(April),* featuring a parade and the

music, dancing, and foods of Japan. The **Peace Pagoda** rises more than 100 feet from a concrete plaza, with five round, copper-clad roofs topped with a spire of nine rings supporting a golden ball that is an emblem of virtue.

Nearby **Buchanan** or **Nihonmachi Mall** *(Buchanan St. between Sutter and Post Sts.)* is a cobbled walking street lined with stucco-and-wood buildings scaled to seem like a Japanese village. Sculptor Ruth Asawa created the two fountains and benches.

CHURCHES & TEMPLES

The 1984 **Sokoji-Soto Zen Buddhist Temple** reflects Zen practice, with a simple interior and cushions for sitting *zazen,* or engaging in Zen meditation. The altar, though, is rich, with a golden figure of Shakyamuni Buddha.

The beliefs of the **Konko Church of San Francisco** revolve around the Principle Parent of the Universe, who combines aspects of mother earth and father heaven. The church, based on but independent from Shinto, has its roots in religious truths revealed to a Japanese farmer who survived a major illness in 1859. On the church's wooden altar offerings are placed that range from flowers to canned goods, soft drinks, and beer, in appreciation to the Principle Parent for the things that sustain human life. Above the altar a golden disk symbolizes divine light. (Konko means "golden light.")

You must climb to the second floor of a plain 1938 building to

Interior of the
Konko Church of
San Francisco

**Sokoji-Soto Zen
Buddhist Temple**
- ✉ 1691 Laguna St.
- ☎ 415/346-7540
- 🕐 Closed Mon.

**Konko Church of
San Francisco**
- ✉ 1909 Bush St.
- ☎ 415/931-0453

**Buddhist Church
of San Francisco**
- ✉ 1881 Pine St.
- ☎ 415/776-3158
- 🕐 Call for appt.

reach the **Buddhist Church of San Francisco,** whose rooftop *stupa*, or dome, holds reputed relics of the Buddha. In the worship hall are peacock screens and a gilded altar, combined with such western touches as pews and an organ.

Mission architecture melds with Japanese hallmarks (upturned eaves, green-tile roof) at **St. Francis Xavier Church** *(1801 Octavia St.).* ∎

St. Mary's Cathedral

JUST SOUTH OF JAPANTOWN, THE CITY'S THIRD CATHOLIC cathedral (Belluschi, Nervi, McSweeney, Ryan & Lee), built between 1967 and 1970, is like no other building in the city.

**St. Mary's
Cathedral**
- ✉ 1111 Gough St.
- ☎ 415/567-2020

Following a geometric design known as a hyperbolic paraboloid, the reinforced concrete structure curves upward from the four corners, meeting in a cross 190 feet above. Sheathed in Italian marble, the structure rests on corner pylons that can support ten million pounds of pressure, yet are just two feet in circumference at their narrowest point. (They extend 90 feet into bedrock.) Huge corner windows open the church to the city.

Inside, visitors see four seams of stained glass, each 138 feet long and 6 feet wide, that sweep to the top of the cupola. The colors of the faceted glass symbolically represent the four elements of creation: earth (green), air (yellow), water (blue),

and fire (red). As they join high overhead, the four windows create a golden cross.

The cathedral's altar is one massive, ten-ton piece of Botticino marble. Hanging 75 feet above it by golden wires, a baldachino of triangular aluminum rods scintillates with reflected light, symbolizing the channel of love and grace from God. The sculpture, created over three years (1967–70) by Richard Lippold, is 15 stories tall and weighs one ton.

Another remarkable feature is the 4,842-pipe organ, whose sound can fill the vast cathedral. Made by Ruffatti Brothers of Padua, Italy, it has a solid-state console installed high on a concrete pedestal. ∎

Enjoy a Japanese bathing experience at Kabuki Hot Springs.

More places to visit

ALTA PLAZA PARK
This park is used mostly by nearby residents who come to play tennis or to give their kids and dogs some playtime. Alta Plaza gives you a chance to see how the other one percent live—the wealthy of Pacific Heights.

🅜 Map pp. 144–45 ✉ Bet. Clay, Steiner, Jackson, and Scott Sts. 🚍 Bus: 1, 3, 12, 22, 24

KABUKI SPRINGS & SPA
One block west of Japantown is a traditional spa, equipped with hot tubs, sauna, steam room, and communal baths. Luxurious treatments such as a shiatsu massage and scrub are available by appointment.

✉ 1750 Geary Blvd. ☎ 415/922-6000
🚍 Bus: 2, 3, 4, 22, 38

LAFAYETTE PARK
Join local dog-walkers at this park, whose 12 acres climb from open lawns to a knoll shaded by trees. At 378 feet, this is the height of Pacific Heights and offers views of the city and bay.

The hilltop was set aside for a park in 1855, but not improved with plantings until 1910. At the peak once stood the 1867 mansion of Samuel Holladay, a lawyer who found a loophole in city ordinances that let him grab this prime real estate—park or no park.

🅜 Map pp. 144–145 ✉ Enter at Sacramento and Octavia 🚍 Bus: 1, 12

OTHER GRAND HOUSES
Grand residences can be seen all over the neighborhood, especially as you approach the Presidio along **Jackson Street, Pacific Avenue,** and **Broadway.** Across from terraced Alta Plaza Park stands the former **Music and Arts Institute** (*2622 Jackson St.*). Designed by Willis Polk as his first San Francisco project in 1894, the stone residence looks like a classical villa in Tuscany. Another Polk design, the baronial **Bourn Mansion** (*2550 Webster St.*) is an 1896 Georgian Revival town house with a restrained facade of rough, burned-looking (or "clinker") brick. Ornately carved stonework frames a central window, beneath which lies the unassuming entry. Its owner, William Bowers Bourn, parlayed a gold rush fortune into other enterprises. In addition to this mansion, he also built the Filoli estate on the peninsula (see p. 210) and what are now the Christian Brothers Greystone Cellars in Napa Valley.

🅜 Map pp. 144–45 🚍 Bus: 3, 12, 22, 24 ∎

Flower power first bloomed in the area surrounding the fabled crossroads of Haight and Ashbury Streets. Close by are the real floral delights and museums of Golden Gate Park.

Haight-Ashbury & Golden Gate Park

Haight-Ashbury mural detail

Haight-Ashbury & Golden Gate Park

WEST OF DOWNTOWN, HAIGHT-ASHBURY AND GOLDEN GATE PARK WERE
once bleak sand dunes partly occupied by squatters. Yet in 1868, when the city acquired
the land, a local newspaper hooted that the purchase was a white elephant, a sprawl of
sand dunes where constant winds would prevent anything from growing. Once the park
was established, its environs became desirable, and so Haight-Ashbury began its history
as a respectable Victorian neighborhood.

It was the decline of the neighborhood, and
the cheap rents that resulted from it, that
brought first the Beats and then the hippies to
this area. "The Haight" remains the city's most
countercultural neighborhood, packed with
tattooed urban youth and wanna-be hippies.
Tourists dip into ersatz "head shops" (see pp.
162–63) to buy psychedelic posters and bong
pipes as though they were sacred relics of the
1967 "Summer of Love."

In 1887 Hall's successor arrived at Golden
Gate Park, the legendary John McLaren, a
Scot who had worked at Edinburgh's Royal
Botanical Gardens. Known as "Uncle John," he
was determined, crusty, and much loved. He
spent nearly 56 years creating groves, lakes,
and flower gardens, meanwhile taming windy
dunes and windier politicians who had
designs on the park.

Golden Gate Park ranks as
one of America's finest urban
landscapes and its largest
developed city park—1,017
acres in a rectangle stretching
from Stanyan Street to Ocean
Beach. Residents think of the
park as their backyard, which
makes sense in the West's most
densely populated city, where
yards (if they exist) are minimal.
In the park they soothe frayed
city nerves with a balm of
green leaves. They stroll through
rhododendron dells and picnic
in meadows, enjoy sports from
Frisbee-tossing to tennis, and visit
fine museums.

The site of the park was part of
the "Outside Lands"—trackless sand
dunes the city obtained after a legal
wrangle with squatters. In 1871
new park superintendent William
Hammond Hall began planting
beach grass, barley, and wild lupine
to stabilize the soil against the wind.
Within a few years, trees and flowers
flourished along an eight-block carriage
approach to the park (the Panhandle)
and in the park's eastern section.

In 1894 the California Midwinter Fair was staged here to publicize San Francisco's Mediterranean climate. The fair site became the Music Concourse, hub of the park's museums. Today as many as 100,000 people from all over San Francisco enjoy the park on a sunny Sunday, just as in the late 1960s it attracted flocks of hippies from nearby Haight-Ashbury to groove at free concerts and "tribal" celebrations. ■

Area of map detail

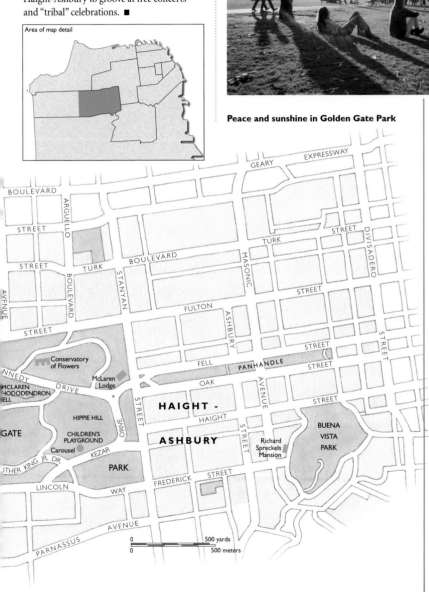

Peace and sunshine in Golden Gate Park

Haight-Ashbury

In the popular mind "Haight-Ashbury" means flower children, tripping along in tie-dyed clothes and flashing the peace sign through clouds of suspicious-smelling smoke. (Some nicknamed the neighborhood the "Hashbury.") Centered around Haight and Ashbury Streets, it was home to bands that invented psychedelic rock, including Jefferson Airplane and the Grateful Dead.

It wasn't always this way. In the 1880s the Haight was a resort district near Golden Gate Park. People rode the Haight Street cable car to an 1895 amusement park, the Chutes, to ride a gondola down a 300-foot slide into a lake. Victorian houses rose on the flats near the Panhandle and on fancier Ashbury Heights. Growth boomed after the 1906 earthquake, as the neighborhood was undamaged.

With the Great Depression, the Haight declined and Victorian houses were divided into flats. By the 1950s low rents attracted poor blacks and Beats driven from North Beach. The mid-sixties brought the flower children, mind-altering drugs, and "free love." By the end of the decade, though, the love had gone out of the Haight with an influx of hard drugs, criminals, and the mentally

"Spare change"

A few lines that young panhandlers on Haight Street have used on passersby:

(1) "Spare change for alcohol?"

(2) "Got any money so I can buy a sailboat?"

(3) "Hey, how about a $15,000 loan for five years at ten percent?"

(4) "I need a ticket to Indonesia so I can work for Nike for $33 a week."

(5) Hand-lettered cardboard sign: "Need Change 4 Weed."

(6) When turned down: "*@#! You're ruining my day, man! My whole *@#! life!" ■

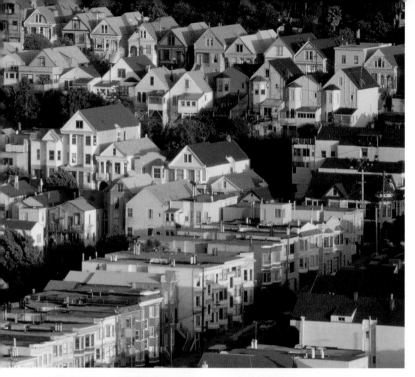

The Haight: Restored Victorians (top) and Haight Street's funky shops (above and right)

unbalanced. The neighborhood became a psychedelic ghetto.

Remarkably, the neighborhood made a comeback as gays and young professionals restored Victorian houses with financial incentives from the city. More than 1,100 Victorians survive, mostly Queen Annes (see p. 45) with elaborate gingerbread and towers.

On Haight Street, visitors must adjust to the throng of panhandlers, skateboarders, neo-hippies, bikers, and gray-haired flower children. But the street has interesting shops, good cheap restaurants, and blast-from-the-past encounters with black-light posters and scented candles to waft you back to the sixties. ∎

Haight-Ashbury walk

This walk looks at the contemporary street scene of Haight-Ashbury, and offers flashbacks to the hippie era. It also takes in fine Victorian houses from the turn of the century.

Start at Haight and Stanyan Streets. Behind you in Golden Gate Park is **Hippie Hill,** where the "tribes" (see pp. 162–63) gathered in the Sixties. A few decades later it became an encampment for homeless people, where aimless youth and street dwellers coexisted until they were moved on in 1997.

Walk east on **Haight Street,** and you'll meet the locals, including perhaps a rainbow-garbed, headband-wearing, drum-beating hippie who was born years after the Summer of Love; teenage girls with eyes far too streetwise; a couple dressed entirely in black, with at least two dozen body piercings between them; a left-over 1960s flower child looking through pin-wheel eyes at something the rest of us can't see; and many panhandlers (see p. 158).

Haight Street is chockablock with shops. You can buy retro or trendy clothes, "healing crystals," books, hippie regalia, and psychedelic posters (especially of departed rock stars: Jimi Hendrix, Jerry Garcia, Jim Morrison). Along your way, look at **1779–83 Haight,** the commercial zone's oldest building (1893); **1775 Haight,** site of the Diggers' free crash pad (see pp. 162–63); and **1677–81 Haight,** a 1904 building in Parisian style.

The **Red Victorian** ❶ (see p. 255) is a 1904 hotel that proprietor Sami Sunchild runs as a shrine to the Summer of Love. Some rooms feature 1960s posters and beads, and the toilet tank in one bathroom has live gold-fish inside. ("This is the dawning of the Age of Aquarius…"?) At **1660 Haight,** the art nouveau facade of the 1911 Superba Theater now fronts Wasteland, a vintage clothing store. The **Haight-Ashbury Free Medical Clinic** ❷ *(Clayton St.)* was opened in 1967 by a crusading doctor to provide no-cost help for bad LSD trips, drug abuse, venereal diseases, and other health problems of the hippie lifestyle.

On Haight between Cole and Clayton Streets, the Chutes amusement park once attracted the public with a waterslide, zoo, theater, and other attractions. At **1535 Haight**

stood the Psychedelic Shop, opened in 1966 as the world's first "head shop" (see pp. 162–63). At Haight and Ashbury, which gave its name to the neighborhood, turn left. Walk two blocks to Oak Street and the **Panhandle** ❸, an eight-block swath of greenery laid out in the 1870s as a carriage entrance to Golden Gate Park. Here the social elite of San Francisco rode and showed off their finest clothes. After the 1906 earthquake and fire, 30,000 displaced people lived in the Panhandle in tents and refugee cottages. Nowadays it's a park, where you should look past the seediness to recognize the Panhandle as a living museum of trees. Among them are the earliest ones planted in the effort to fashion Golden Gate Park from windblown dunes. Look for eucalyptuses and cypresses, Chinese ginkgoes and Greek olives, Moroccan cedars and California sequoias. Note: Avoid this area at night.

Turn right on Oak, and walk along the Panhandle to Masonic. Turn right and return to Haight. The building on the northeast corner housed the 1967 "Drogstore" café, a hippie gathering spot. A pharmacy previously occupied the building, but city officials wouldn't let the café keep the name "Drugstore" because of its counterculture connotations.

Turn left on Haight, noting **Bound Together** *(1369 Haight St.)*, a longtime anarchist bookstore. At Lyon Street, you can detour left to **No. 122,** where rocker Janis Joplin once lived. (A renter, she was evicted—not for sex, drugs, or loud rock 'n' roll, but for keeping a dog against the rules.)

At Haight and Lyon, go into **Buena Vista Park** ❹ and climb the path to the right. (Note: The park has had a reputation as a gay pickup spot, and transients sometimes sleep in the bushes.) Foresting of this 36-acre park began in the 1880s, when schoolchildren planted seedlings given by philanthropist Adolph Sutro. Around 1910 John McLaren (of Golden Gate Park) planted pines and cypresses, eucalyptuses, and a small redwood grove. Today the trees partially screen the "good view" for which Buena Vista Park was given its name. In the 1930s the WPA built retaining walls and drainage ditches of granite and marble salvaged from former cemeteries; look for faint inscriptions on headstone fragments.

Explore the park, then descend to the perimeter at **Buena Vista Avenue West** and head uphill. This street shows off residential styles from Tudor and Queen Anne to modernist. The 1897 **Richard Spreckels Mansion** ❺ (*737 Buena Vista Ave. W.*) was built for a nephew of sugar king Claus Spreckels. Grand marble stairs lead to a columned porch, and there are fanlights above the windows. Reputedly, tenants have included writers Jack London and Ambrose Bierce.

At Java Street, turn right and walk the short block to Masonic Avenue. You can detour uphill to see a shingled house designed by Bernard Maybeck (*1526 Masonic Ave.*). Walking downhill, you'll find a row of 1891 **Eastlake Victorians** ❻ (*1322–42 Masonic Ave.*). At Waller see a row of 1896 **gabled houses** ❼ (*1315–1335 Waller St.*) that are among the most finely ornamented in San Francisco. Going west on Waller, detour south to a row of 1890s Queen Annes that include the old **Grateful Dead house** ❽ (*710 Ashbury St.*), where the band was busted for drugs in 1967. Or turn right on Ashbury and return to Haight. ■

The Haight-Ashbury Free Medical Clinic still provides care for the neighborhood's indigent population.

See area map pp. 156–57
Haight and Stanyan Sts.
1.5 miles
2 hours
Haight St.
Bus: 6, 7, 33, 37, 43, 66, 71; Streetcar: N Line

NOT TO BE MISSED
- Street life on Haight St.
- The Panhandle
- Buena Vista Avenue West
- Gabled houses on Waller St.

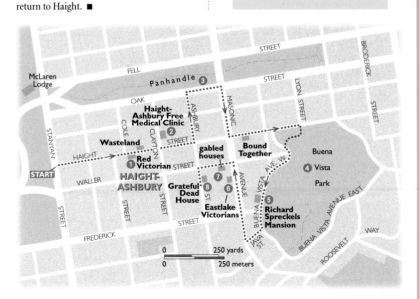

Hippies: the love generation

Before they shook all of America, the seismic social shocks of the hippie era took place in San Francisco. Repelled by established authority and the "system," hippies adopted ideals of community, peace, and love. Early on, theatrical anarchists called the Diggers espoused the idea that goods should be free, so they opened a store in Haight-Ashbury where no money changed hands and customers donated as well as took.

The Haight was already home to some relocated 1950s Beats, whose bohemianism was infectious. It was the Beats who coined the term "hippie," meaning junior-grade hipster. The word first hit print in a September 1965 story in the *San Francisco Examiner*.

In Haight-Ashbury, roomy Victorian houses were available at low rent. Some rock bands, like Jefferson Airplane, moved in together as communal "families." Boys grew long hair, girls donned Victorian lace and velvet from thrift shops. All wore "love beads" from India, perfumed themselves with patchouli oil, and experimented with new lifestyles and art forms. Bands such as the Grateful Dead played freewheeling improvisations. To advertise rock concerts, posters vibrated with psychedelic colors and bulbous lettering, a new style of graphic art.

Hippie life revolved around idealism and music, with a touch of Eastern mysticism—but also around marijuana, LSD, and other mind-altering drugs, as well as a new sexual liberation. In fact, "Sex, Dope, and Cheap Thrills" was the suppressed full title of a famous album by Janis Joplin. Its cover was drawn by San Francisco underground cartoonist R. Crumb, whose *Zap Comix* portrayed hippie lust and drugs with artistic glee.

LSD (a.k.a. "acid") had come on the scene in 1965 via novelist Ken Kesey, who encountered it as a volunteer in experiments at Stanford University. With his Merry Pranksters, Kesey staged multimedia LSD happenings, whose handbills asked: "Can You Pass the Acid Test?" But by October 1966, California prohibited LSD, making hippies into outlaws. The same month, the Psychedelic

Hippie in "love beads"

Shop opened on Haight Street, selling hippie accoutrements and pot-smoking paraphernalia. It was the world's first "head shop."

In January 1967 tens of thousands of flower children converged on the polo field at Golden Gate Park for the "Human Be-In/Gathering of the Tribes," an event featuring Jefferson Airplane, poet Allen Ginsberg, and Harvard-professor-turned-acid-guru Timothy Leary. This was probably the biggest event of the hippie subculture until Woodstock.

Strangely, it was San Francisco's police chief who first called hippies the "Love Generation." The national media took note, and *Time* magazine declared the Haight the "vibrant epicenter of America's hippie movement." The attention attracted hordes of footloose youth, who turned Haight-Ashbury into such a freak show that the Gray Line actually ran a bus tour there called the "Hippie Hop."

The idea of the 1967 "Summer of Love"—an invitation to the world to share the good vibes—was popular with Haight-Ashbury merchants. The Diggers, however, wanted to keep the neighborhood out of the limelight and objected to the commercialism of vendors who sold "Love Burgers" and the like.

Top: Ken Kesey's Merry Pranksters decorate their bus for an LSD happening. Above: Allen Ginsberg addresses the 1967 Human Be-In, with hippie accompanists.

The Summer of Love attracted sincere seekers and "plastic hippies" alike, along with drifters, the mentally disturbed, drug pushers, and violent criminals. Good vibes turned bad. In October the Diggers held a "Death of Hippie" march to the Haight's Buena Vista Park. In the early 1970s cheap heroin poured into the neighborhood, bringing addiction, street crime, violence, and death. The Love Generation was over, and the hippie movement was dead.

Nonetheless, good things survived: American society became more tolerant of nonconformity. (In San Francisco this was reflected in open acceptance of gays.) Where there is acceptance, the original hippie spirit of "peace and love" lives on. ∎

Children play by the park's music concourse.

Golden Gate Park East

Not every city boasts a playground three miles long and half a mile wide. But that's Golden Gate Park. It has about 20 access points along its perimeter, while two main roads thread its length: John F. Kennedy Drive and Martin Luther King Jr. Drive. (On Sundays and most holidays, Kennedy Drive is closed to cars between Kezar and Transverse Drives.) This half of the park boasts some of the city's major museums.

Get information and maps at park headquarters, inside the east entrance *(Fell St. at Stanyan St.)*. It occupies **McLaren Lodge** *(John F. Kennedy Dr. at Stanyan St., tel 415/831-2700, closed Sat.–Sun.)* designed in 1897 by Edward R. Swain. This handsome Moorish-Gothic building with coarse sandstone walls and red tile roofs was home to longtime superintendent John McLaren. A visitor center is located in the western section of the park (see p. 177).

A free shuttle *(May–Oct. weekends & holidays)* runs from McLaren Lodge to Ocean Beach at the park's west end, making stops along the way at 15 attractions. Route maps are available at the park and on the Internet *(www.goldengatepark concourse.org)*.

Sights listed below run from east to west. The **Children's Playground** was the nation's first public playground (1888). Nearby you'll see the painted horses, camels,

and dragons of the beautifully restored 1912 Herschell-Spillman carousel. The **Conservatory of Flowers** (see p. 165) is a Victorian glass palace of tropical plants. Farther west sprawls the **John McLaren Rhododendron Dell,** where spring blossoms set off a statue of superintendent McLaren—who, ironically, despised statues as intruders on nature and often screened them behind foliage.

The nearby Music Concourse is formally landscaped with English plane trees (much like sycamores) and fountains and bordered by museums: the M. H. de Young (see pp. 166–68, *reopens summer 2005)* and the California Academy of Sciences (see pp. 169–71, *reopens 2008).* At one end stands the **Spreckels Temple of Music** (1899), a bandstand of Italian Renaissance style donated by Claus Spreckels. Built of Colusa sandstone, with reliefs carved by Robert Aitken, it is home to the nation's oldest municipal band. ∎

Conservatory of Flowers

THE OLDEST EXISTING CONSERVATORY IN THE WESTERN Hemisphere is a living museum of tropical plants, ranging from palms and orchids to slightly unsettling carnivorous varieties.

The most visited place in Golden Gate Park, the greenhouse was put up in 1879 after being purchased as a kit from the heirs of wealthy businessman James Lick, who died before it could be erected at his Santa Clara Valley estate. Today the conservatory displays 1,500 plant species from more than 50 countries, including the world's best public collection of Dracula orchids.

It was closed from 1995 to 2003 for a $25 million rehabilitation to repair damage from a 100 mph windstorm, the worst in park history. Today the conservatory envelops visitors in San Francisco "flower power"—a colorful, almost hallucinogenic trip to the cloud forests of Costa Rica, the steamy heart of the Congo, and the lush islands of the Philippines, all under one immense glass roof.

There are five galleries. Under the dome in the Lowland Tropics gallery, a light rain falls on a canopy of palms and the colossal leaves of a century-old Imperial Philodendron. Also on view are cycads, a type of plant that predated the dinosaurs, and modern commercial plants such as chocolate, coffee, and vanilla. Sweet fragrances fill the air.

The air cools in the east wing's Highland Tropics section, where orchids grow on the bark of gnarled trees among ferns and creeping vines. Cases resembling Victorian armoires hold valuable orchid specimens. The Aquatic Plants gallery enfolds you with the sound of water and the sight of giant lilies and floating flowers. (One water lily variety has leaves that can grow to six feet across and support the weight of a small child.)

The west wing holds the potted plant gallery, with seasonal floral displays, and a gallery for special exhibits. ∎

Conservatory of Flowers
www.conservatoryofflowers.org

See map pp. 156–57

JFK Drive, Golden Gate Park

415/666-7001

Closed Mon.

$$

Bus: 5, 7, 21, 33, 44, 71; Streetcar: N Line

An avenue of flowers leads to the Victorian-era Conservatory of Flowers.

M.H. de Young Memorial Museum

M.H. de Young Memorial Museum

www.thinker.org/deyoung

See map pp. 156–57

75 Tea Garden Dr., Golden Gate Park

415/863-3330

Closed for extensive renovations; reopens late summer 2005

Bus: 5, 21, 38, 44, 71; Streetcar: N

THE OLDEST PUBLIC MUSEUM IN SAN FRANCISCO HOLDS the West Coast's most comprehensive survey of American paintings. To replace the original building, which was earthquake damaged, a new state-of-the art structure will open in late summer 2005. Meanwhile, parts of the collection may be seen in touring exhibitions.

It started with M. H. de Young, the publisher of the *San Francisco Chronicle*, who helped the city acquire the Fine Arts building from the 1894 California Midwinter Fair as a museum. De Young established his own program of acquisitions—none too skillfully at first. His taste for the curious and ornamental was reflected in armor, paintings, objects from the South Pacific, an Egyptian mummy, birds' eggs, handcuffs, and even reproductions. One of his early acquisitions, John Vanderlyn's 1807 painting "Caius Marius amid the Ruins of Carthage," which won a gold medal at the Paris Salon in 1808, formed the nucleus for the collection of American art.

The museum moved into a Spanish plateresque building in 1919. By the 1930s it had refocused on fine and decorative art. In 1932 the museum held the "Group f.64" show of Bay Area photographers—among them Edward Weston and Ansel Adams (see p. 40).

Major gifts brought the museum a number of European works. When the M. H. de Young merged with the California Palace of the Legion of Honor (see p. 137–39) in 1972 as the Fine Arts Museums of San Francisco, European works went to the Palace. In 1979 John D. Rockefeller III donated more than 100 works of American art, propelling the M. H. de Young into the big leagues. Other donations included the H. McCoy Jones collection of rugs, carpets, and embroideries from the Near East and Central Asia, and the Wagner collection of Teotihuacan murals from Mexico. The major focuses are:

AMERICAN PAINTING

More than 200 paintings in the collection offer a survey of American art from colonial days through the mid-20th century. The museum's earliest painting is "The Mason Children" (1670), which depicts three upper-class Boston youngsters. (Note the numbers above their heads, indicating their ages.) Noteworthy portrait artists include the self-taught John Singleton

Architectural rendering of the new M. H. de Young

Copley ("Mary Turner Sargent," 1763), Gilbert Stuart (famous for his portrait of George Washington), John Singer Sargent, the most sought-after portrait artist at the turn of the 20th century ("A Dinner Table at Night," ca 1880), Robert Henri ("O in Black with Scarf," 1910), and Mary Cassatt, associated with the French Impressionists and here represented by an 1889 portrait of her mother in beige and black.

The museum hangs landscapes by Albert Bierstadt ("California Spring," 1875), the Hudson River school's Frederic Edwin Church ("Rainy Season in the Tropics," 1866), and William Keith, who painted the western out-of-doors.

Less purposefully majestic, genre paintings portray daily life. A highlight is George Caleb Bingham's "Boatmen on the Missouri" (1846), which depicts three raftsmen, one wearing a broken top hat, who sell wood to passing steamboats. The men are painted in bold patches of color, with the misty landscape subtly painted behind. This was one of the first views of frontier life to appeal to viewers on the East Coast. Other genre works include Winslow Homer's "The Bright Side" (1865) and Thomas Anschutz's masterwork, "The Ironworkers' Noontime" (1880).

Regionalist art is represented by Grant Wood in "Dinner for Threshers" (1934), which presents a farmhouse at mealtime in a cutaway view of multiple rooms. The panoramic painting looks strikingly modern, yet also harks back to Italian Renaissance triptychs. John Langley Howard's "Embarcadero and Clay" (1935) gives a view of San Francisco with vintage cars and a hotel.

Raphaelle Peale's small "Blackberries" (1813) is one of the earliest American still lifes. A gallery of trompe l'oeil still lifes presents the uncannily realistic "The Trumpeter Swan" (1900) by Alexander Pope, and William M. Harnett's "After the Hunt" (1885), depicting an iron-hinged door hung with a rifle, powder horn, and game.

The de Young's acclaimed American art collection, comprising more than 200 paintings spanning colonial times through the 20th century, includes George Caleb Bingham's "Boatmen on the Missouri" (1846).

John Frederick Peto's "The Cup We All Race" (1900) is almost holographic in its representation of reality … or unreality.

Early 20th-century paintings include the immense purple blossoms of Georgia O'Keeffe's "Petunias" (1925). Look also for mid-20th-century works by Richard Diebenkorn ("Seated Woman," 1965) and Bay Area artists such as Wayne Thiebaud, whose "Three Machines" (1963) pictures colorful gumball machines.

The sculpture collection includes William Wetmore Story's "King Saul" (1882) and Frederic Remington's "The Bronco Buster" (1895), a bronze with details characteristic of the artist's paintings.

DECORATIVE ARTS

An Adams-style George III dining room, a federal parlor from an 1805 Massachusetts home, Joseph Dufour wallpaper, a 1780 high chest made in Philadelphia, silverwork by Paul Revere, and Shaker chairs all trace early work in America.

The Arts and Crafts movement of the early 20th century is represented by a Stickley oak sideboard with hammered metal fixtures, and by Frank Lloyd Wright's "Tree of Life Window" (1904), his finest from the prairie school period, with a stylized tree motif in clear, colored, and iridescent glass. Also on view is a Greene and Greene side chair of mahogany with ebony, copper, pewter, coral, and mother of pearl.

This kneeling warrior vessel of red clay can be found in the museum's Art of the Americas collection.

TEXTILES

Pieces are rotated from a collection of rugs, carpets, and embroideries from the Near East and Central Asia, including the finest holdings of Anatolian *kilims* outside Turkey. Kilims are flat-woven wool textiles used as floor coverings, wall hangings, and bed coverings, with geometric designs in rich, brilliant colors. Other highlights are *suzanis*, dowry embroideries from Samarkand, Bokhara, and Tashkent.

OCEANIC ART

Oceanic art pieces from the 1894 California Midwinter Fair became part of the museum's charter collection. Among them is a Maori canoe prow from New Zealand (19th century), made of wood and shell. Also notable: a roll of feather money from the Nindu island of Santa Cruz, a rare navigation figure from the Caroline Islands of Micronesia, and a 10-foot housepost from the Iatmul culture of Papua New Guinea.

AFRICAN ART

Sub-Saharan Africa is represented in such pieces as a power figure from the Congo and carved granary doors from Mali. A helmet mask made by the Fang people of Gabon, painted with white kaolin, was used to initiate members of the Ngil society, a sort of tribal "police." Luba figures from Zaire were among the earliest African sculptures to inspire modern artists.

ART OF THE AMERICAS

Fine pieces cover the period from 1200 B.C. to the 16th century. They include stunning Teotihuacan murals and a mouth mask (around A.D. 200–600) of hammered gold with red cinnabar, made by the Nazca culture of Peru. Northern Peru's Moche civilization (400 B.C.–A.D. 600) produced ceramic vessels decorated with surprisingly naturalistic and expressive figures. From Mexico, Colima ceramic animals and figures were funerary objects meant to escort the dead into the afterlife. Aztec, Olmec, and Maya works are also on view. From British Columbia comes a cedar Tsimshian totem pole (late 19th century), carved and painted to represent a bald eagle, killer whale, bear, and fish. ∎

California Academy of Sciences

THE FIRST SCIENTIFIC INSTITUTION IN THE WEST (1853), the academy has moved to a temporary home *(875 Howard St., south of Market Street)* until the 2008 opening of its dramatic new facility in Golden Gate Park. The country's only combined aquarium, planetarium, and natural history museum, the academy's new facility will transcend the traditional way of organizing science exhibits—separate halls for different branches of science or geographical areas —by integrating exhibitions to convey the interconnectedness of the living world.

In fact, the new academy will make nature part of its very structure, with a "living roof" where native plants grow and an undulating shape that suggests "hills" in the natural landscape around it. The facility has been designed by

Pritzker Prize-winning architect Renzo Piano to bring visitors an eye-opening experience of the natural world. In a multilevel rain forest section, visitors will take a vertical journey from the forest floor to the upper canopy, as they

A lizard from Brazil is one of 281,000 specimens in the Academy's Herpotology Department.

California Academy of Sciences

www.calacademy.org

✉ Temporary home until 2008: 875 Howard St. See p. 190

☎ 415/750-7145

$ $$.

Turtles (above) and Army ants (below) are some of the critters at the California Academy of Sciences.

wander among the unique plants, insects, reptiles, and amphibians that live there. The new **Steinhart Aquarium** will showcase a 225,000-gallon living coral reef habitat, while the new **Morrison Planetarium** will offer a trip to the edges of space and time, look back at the beginnings of the universe and reveal the latest cosmic discoveries.

BEGINNINGS

The academy has come a long way from its start after the California gold rush, when a group of naturalists met each week in a small office in San Francisco to present scientific papers. The early academy grew into a museum of birds, animals, and "curiosities" (extinct dodo, woolly mammoth) and in 1916 relocated to Golden Gate Park. Today it holds more than 18 million examples of plants, animals, fossils, and artifacts for scholarly study.

TEMPORARY HOME

At its temporary home downtown, the academy brings the natural world into an urban setting. Some

5,400 creatures from the academy's Steinhart Aquarium have been moved here, including seahorses, turtles, poison dart frogs, and Methuselah, a 65-year-old lungfish (a species that can breathe air). The aquarium exhibit's design brings the backstage apparatus to the front, allowing visitors to see mechanisms that sense the temperature and salinity of the tank water. A living coral reef tank next to the stairs lets visitors peer into different levels as they ascend to see a rainbow of reef fish (harlequin tusk fish, yellow tangs) and even a giant clam.

Natural history displays include Snake Alley; a naturalist center where visitors participate in hands-on scientific activities; and "Astrobiology: Life in the Extreme," which looks at organisms that manage to survive in harsh conditions such as hydrothermal vents and deserts. ■

The new California Academy of Sciences, scheduled for completion in 2008, will include a planetarium, garden roof, and bubble-shaped, four-level rain forest, as shown in this model.

**Relax with
tea and fortune
cookies among
blossoming trees.**

Japanese Tea Garden

ON AN UNCROWDED DAY IN THIS GARDEN OF CHERRY trees, ponds, and bonsai trees, you might feel you've been wafted to a quiet corner of the old Japanese city of Kyoto. In Japanese tradition, the garden captures the spirit of nature in a limited space. Its serenity is stylized, an expression of high art.

The nation's oldest Japanese garden began as part of the 1894 California Midwinter Fair. It was proposed by Asian art dealer George Turner Marsh, who admired gardens in Japan, and it was overseen for three decades by gardener Makoto Hagiwara. From 1895 until 1942 he and his family lived in the garden, caring for and enhancing its plantings and features. Visit in March, when the cherries blossom, or autumn, when ginkgo trees blaze yellow.

In Japanese gardens, many plants have symbolic meanings: Pines, often twisted and sculpted with time, represent dignified old age. (Black pines are considered masculine, red pines feminine.) The chrysanthemum is the symbol of Japan's Imperial House.

You enter the five-acre garden through a ceremonial gate of Japanese Hinoki cypress, traditionally used for temples. Winding paths give changing views of the foliage.

The **Moon Bridge** arches high over a pond, its reflection completing a circle, like a full moon. The garden's five-roofed **pagoda** was built for the 1915 Panama-Pacific International Exposition. Nearby is the green bronze **Peace Lantern,** a 9,000-pound symbol of friendship funded by schoolchildren in Japan to commemorate the 1951 U.S.–Japanese peace treaty.

At the popular **tea pavilion,** waitresses in floral silk kimonos serve fragrant tea and fortune cookies. The cookies were introduced here by Makoto Hagiwara in 1909, and were later taken over by Chinese restaurateurs. Nearby sits a bronze **Buddha** that weighs a ton and a half. Cast in Japan in 1790, it is called Amazarashi-No-Hotoke ("The Buddha That Sits Throughout Sunny and Rainy Weather Without a Shelter").

There is also a small **Zen garden,** a meditative space originally designed to aid monks in their search for enlightenment. Japanese landscape architect Nagao Sakurai designed this example in 1953. ■

Japanese Tea Garden

▲ See map pp. 156–57

✉ Hagiwara Tea Garden Dr., Golden Gate Park

☎ 415/752-1171

$ $; free admission 8:30–9:30 a.m. & last hour of day

⏰ Tours available May–Oct. Sat.–Mon. & Wed. at 2 p.m.; rest of year Sun. & Wed. only

🚌 Bus: 5, 44, 71; Streetcar: N Line

Strybing Arboretum & Botanical Gardens

www.strybing.org

- See map pp. 156–157
- 9th Ave. at Lincoln Way, Golden Gate Park
- 415/661-1316
- Call for tours
- Bus: 44, 71; Streetcar: N

Strybing Arboretum & Botanical Gardens

AS AN URBAN OASIS OR AN OUTDOOR CLASSROOM FOR plant lovers, this spot can't be beat. Here the gardening possibilities of San Francisco's Mediterranean climate are gloriously displayed on 55 acres planted with more than 7,000 varieties of rare and unusual species from around the world. Both the arboretum and botanical gardens came about in 1940 through a bequest from philanthropist Helene Strybing.

Arranged around a central lawn are geographic and specialized collections from places as varied as a California meadow and an Asian cloud forest. Among the highlights is the **Cape Province garden,** representing South Africa's Cape of Good Hope, one of the world's go-go areas for botanical species. Among them are proteas (which look like science-fiction plants from Venus) and brilliant orange aloes. The **Australian garden** shows off such unusual plants as the kangaroo paw, with its clusters of yellow, green, and red blossoms. Plants from Chile include lilies in hot colors and winter's bark, a sacred tree used for healing. In the **California** area stands a grove of redwood trees more than 100 years old. At the Japanese **Moon-Viewing Garden,** a pond reflects maple trees by day and the moon by night. In the **New World Cloud Forest** are colorful passion vines, and tree daisies with remarkably large leaves.

Inhale deeply at the **Garden of Fragrance,** whose aromatic plants include rosemary, salvia, and lavender. The garden was designed for blind and visually impaired visitors, with plants chosen for their scents or textures. Birds flock to this warm area of the gardens, so the bronze statue of St. Francis is appropriate. Planting beds are edged with stones from a 12th-century monastery purchased in Spain by William Randolph Hearst.

The garden's 18,000-volume **Helen Crocker Russell Library of Horticulture** provides help with plant research and presents botanical art exhibits. ■

Kids and geese alike enjoy the botanical gardens.

Jewel on the shore: the Chinese Moon Pavilion at Stow Lake

Golden Gate Park West

West of the museum complex, Golden Gate Park stretches toward the ocean. The carefully reclaimed and landscaped area devotes itself to outdoor recreation and enjoyment, with man-made features simulating idyllic rural settings.

A pleasant place to stroll or go boating is **Stow Lake,** which was created in 1893 as a reservoir. It holds 15 million gallons of water and feeds directly into the park's irrigation system. The lake encircles **Strawberry Hill,** a woodsy island that rises 425 feet and is the highest point in the park. (When the park was first being planted, the hill was known as "The Island" because it was the only area of vegetation in a sea of sand. Now it's a true island, surrounded by water.) You can rent paddleboats, rowboats, or even small powerboats. Two bridges take you to the hill's nearly 1-mile perimeter path, where you can stroll and talk back to the quacking ducks. You'll come upon the **Chinese Moon Pavilion,** donated in 1981 by San Francisco's sister city, Taipei. Octagonal, with red columns and a green-tile roof, the pavilion is intended for people to rest and contemplate nature (including the moon). Nearby **Huntington Falls,** financed

by railroad baron Collis P. Huntington in the 1890s, cascades 100 feet.

If you decide to walk up Strawberry Hill, you'll find California quail running across your path. Look for New Zealand tea trees, which have white flowers in spring; this species is widely used to reclaim sandy areas. The hilltop is usually peaceful and quiet, a place to get above it all, with wonderful views of the park, city, and bay.

North of the lake, the carved sandstone **Prayer Book Cross** was modeled on a Celtic cross on the Scottish island of Iona. Below it, **Rainbow Falls** tumbles down a cliff. When the falls were created in the 1930s, hidden colored lights made rainbows appear in the spray.

Alongside tranquil Lloyd Lake, the **Portals of the Past** is a neoclassic colonnade that in a former life was the entry to the Towne mansion on Nob Hill. The **stables** are located next

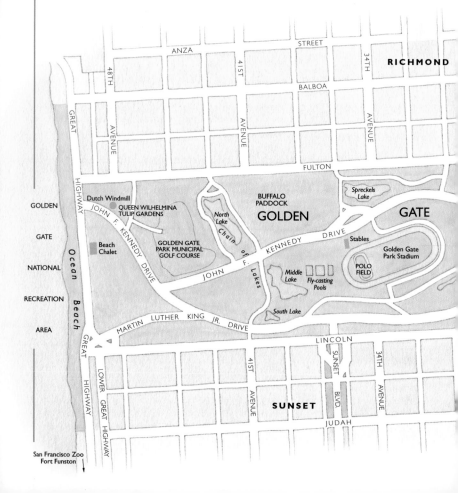

Golden Gate Park West

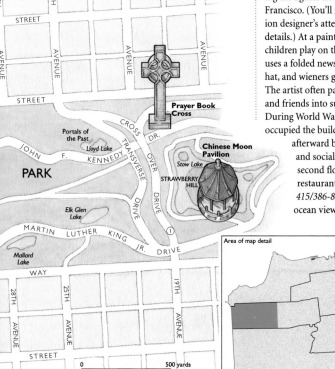 Also see map pp. 156–57

Beach Chalet Visitor Center

✉ 1000 Great Hwy.

☎ 415/751-2766

🚌 Bus: 5

Among the largest North American land animals, buffalo (properly, bison) symbolize the American West.

to the old polo field, a stadium now used for track and field sports. Nearby **Spreckels Lake** is popular with model boat enthusiasts. The park's recreational areas also include fly-casting pools, a dressage ring, and a par-3 golf course.

Don't miss the **Buffalo Paddock,** home to a small herd of shaggy American bison. The park's first bison were brought from Montana in 1890. At the western edge, the **Queen Wilhelmina Tulip Garden** blooms with 10,000 tulip bulbs in February and March. The adjacent **Dutch Windmill** once pumped 30,000 gallons of water hourly to irrigate the park. Built in 1903, the shingled windmill

has spars that measure 102 feet—plenty big enough to catch winds off the Pacific Ocean.

The **Beach Chalet** is located on the Great Highway that fronts the park and the ocean. Inside, a **visitor center** sells park information and maps. The Spanish colonial building was the last design (1925) of architect Willis Polk, with a restaurant on the upper floor and changing rooms downstairs. In the early 1930s two sisters opened a tearoom on the first floor, carefully screening off their oriental carpets from the sandy-footed bathers.

Then in 1936 French artist Lucien Labaudt—a fashion designer who costumed San Francisco's high society—began painting the unadorned walls of the first floor with murals depicting the lighter side of life in San Francisco. (You'll notice the fashion designer's attention to clothing details.) At a painted Baker Beach, children play on the sand, a woman uses a folded newspaper for a sun hat, and wieners grill over a fire. The artist often painted his wife and friends into such scenes. During World War II, the Army occupied the building, which afterward became a bar and social hall. Today the second floor houses a restaurant/brew pub *(Tel 415/386-8439)* with an ocean view. ■

ANZA

STREET

STREET

PARK

Portals of the Past

Lloyd Lake

JOHN   F.   KENNEDY

Elk Glen Lake

MARTIN LUTHER KING JR. DRIVE

Mallard Lake

WAY

STREET

Prayer Book Cross

CROSS

TRANSVERSE

OVER

DRIVE

DRIVE

DR.

Chinese Moon Pavilion

Stow Lake

STRAWBERRY HILL

Area of map detail

0   500 yards
0   500 meters

Places to visit south of the park

FORT FUNSTON

Fort Funston is a coastal parkland of bluffs and sand at the south end of Ocean Beach, and is part of the GGNRA (see p. 125). Among hang gliders, this ranks as one of the nation's top spots for ridge soaring (season: late March–Oct.), thanks to steady ocean winds and dunes as high as 200 feet. A hillside deck gives a spectacular view. Bank swallows nest on the northern cliffs (April–July). On the beach, look for sand dollars and shells.

The fort is named for Frederick Funston, the army general in charge of relief efforts after the 1906 earthquake and fire. The fort's Battery Davis (1938) had two 16-inch guns capable of shooting shells 25 miles. It was the first coastal gun battery to be protected in a casemate, or fortified enclosure. (With advances in military aircraft, batteries on open ground became easy targets.) Nike missiles guarded the coast from the 1950s until the fort closed in 1963. Today the barracks house an environmental education center—a real instance of beating swords into ploughshares.
⊠ Off Skyline Blvd. (Calif. 35) 0.25 mile south of John Muir Dr. ☎ 415/239-2366
🚍 Bus: 18

OCEAN BEACH

San Francisco's longest beach runs south from the Cliff House (see pp. 140–41) along the edge of the **Sunset District,** a neatly ordered residential neighborhood that was once a sand dune wilderness. The beach is part of the Golden Gate National Recreation Area (GGNRA, see p. 125) and makes for good strolling, but the water is dangerous; rip currents have swept people away even in shallow water.

Many ships foundered along Ocean Beach, and for residents, scavenging was a recreation. At a wreck near the Cliff House in 1887, about 50,000 people came to pick up souvenirs. Off Ortega Street, look for the hull ribs of an 1878 shipwreck, the *King Phillip.*
☎ 415/239-2366 🚍 Bus: 5, 18, 23, 31, 38, 48, 71; Streetcar: L, N Lines

SAN FRANCISCO ZOO

Located near the south end of Ocean Beach, the zoo devotes itself to conservation. Lemurs frolic in a forest where visitors observe them at treetop level. Penguins play in a pool, while koalas snooze in a eucalyptus grove. Chimps and orangutans roam the Great Ape Forest. An African savanna is home to giraffes, zebras, eland, and ostriches—all viewable from platforms and, via a tunnel, from the middle of the habitat itself. Other zoo denizens range from tarantulas to lions. (Big-cat feeding time is 2 p.m. daily, except Mon.)
⊠ Sloat Blvd. off Great Hwy. ☎ 415/753-7080, www.sfzoo.org 💲 $$ 🚍 Bus: 18, 23; Streetcar: L Line ∎

A hang-glider takes off at Fort Funston bluffs, a popular launch site.

The Civic Center is the seat of government and home of well-established arts venues. Just south, the old industrial district of SoMa has been transformed by a lively arts scene and a major development project.

Civic Center & SoMa

At the San Francisco Museum of Modern Art

Civic Center & SoMa

THESE NEIGHBORING DISTRICTS SHOW DIFFERENT BUT VITAL ASPECTS OF San Francisco's personality. The seat of government, the Civic Center assembles what is perhaps the nation's finest collection of beaux arts buildings, with the City Hall as an urban palace. In contrast, the neighborhood South of Market (whence SoMa), bounded by Market, the Embarcadero, and Berry Street, was always designated an industrial zone, with broad streets and large blocks laid out in the 1847 street grid drafted by Jasper O'Farrell.

When the 1906 earthquake and fire smudged out much of San Francisco, it offered a golden opportunity to institute the Burnham Plan (see p. 31), a design for a lovelier city. Only the City Hall was achieved at first. As government dragged its heels, businesses and residences were rebuilt along the old street pattern. Later the Civic Center was built up further, but the overall plan for the city was unrealized.

Somewhere for the children to escape

The original city hall, built with shoddy materials under an earlier corrupt city government, tumbled in the earthquake like a house of cards. In 1915 the productive administration of Mayor James "Sunny Jim" Rolph, Jr., built a new City Hall, and the opera house, symphony hall, and other public buildings followed. Today, the Civic Center is an active government hub, a beacon of culture, and a focal point for the arts, as its acquisition of the immense Asian Art Museum demonstrates.

Surprisingly, the wealthy lived in industrial SoMa, sipping their tea in mansions on Rincon Hill and town houses around South Park. But the development of the cable car in the 1870s lured the rich away to Nob Hill. This left the district to workers' families and to

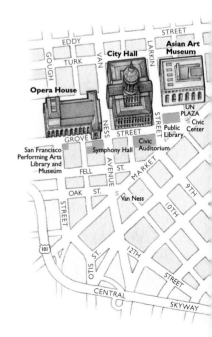

warehouses, factories, sawmills, ironworks, and wharves.

After the 1906 earthquake and fire, cheap hotels and rooming houses appeared, mostly occupied by old-age pensioners and day laborers, and by the vagrants and alcoholics of skid row. In 1936 houses on Rincon Hill were removed for the approach to the Bay Bridge. By the mid-1950s, the city made plans to demolish some of the district for urban renewal projects. When developers tried to move hundreds of residents out of the area in 1967, however, an injunction and lawsuits tied up the development for a decade. Finally, low-cost housing was included as part of the vast Yerba Buena Gardens plan. The Moscone Center opened for conventions in 1981.

In the 1980s an alternative art scene thrived in SoMa as painters, musicians, and dancers converted warehouse spaces into studios and homes, resulting in the opening of small

galleries and the adoption of seedy dives as arty hangouts. When Yerba Buena Gardens opened in 1993 and the new San Francisco Museum of Modern Art in 1995, the cultural die was cast. Now this part of the district is filling with upscale hotels, a business zone dubbed Multimedia Gulch, condominiums, galleries, restaurants, designer-label outlet stores, and nightlife. ■

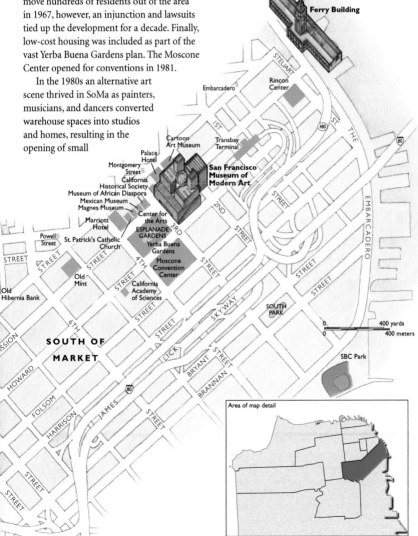

Around the Civic Center

CIVIC CENTER PLAZA, WHICH STRETCHES EAST OF CITY Hall, has been restored to its original appearance with a long lawn and rows of English plane trees. The plaza serves as a platform for political protests, as it holds tens of thousands of people.

Bill Graham Civic Auditorium
- ✉ 99 Grove St.
- ☎ 415/974-4060
- 🚌 Bus: 5, 19, 21, 26, 42, 47; Streetcar: J, K, L, M, N; BART: Civic Center

San Francisco Main Public Library
- http://sfpl.lib.ca.us
- ✉ 100 Larkin St.
- ☎ 415/557-4400
- 🕐 Closed Fri. & Sun. a.m. Tours offered; call for hours
- 🚌 Bus: 5, 19, 21, 26, 42, 47; Streetcar: J, K, L, M, N; BART: Civic Center

San Francisco Performing Arts Library & Museum
- www.sfpalm.org
- ✉ 401 Van Ness Ave., 4th fl.
- ☎ 415/255-4800
- 🕐 Library closed Sun.–Tues.; museum closed Sun.–Mon.
- 🚌 BART: Civic Center

On the south side of the plaza, **Bill Graham Civic Auditorium,** designed by Arthur Brown, Jr., in 1915, was built for the Panama-Pacific International Exposition. It is now a top performance venue.

To the east of the plaza are the **Asian Art Museum** (occupying the redesigned beaux arts Old Library Building; see pp. 185–88) and the stunning **San Francisco Main Public Library** by Pei Cobb Freed & Partners, completed in 1995. The library's plaza facade gives a postmodern twist to beaux arts architectural conventions, yet relates to the nearby historic structures by using granite from the same quarry. The back, though, is contemporary, deconstructionist, and angular.

Between the library buildings, on Fulton Street, stands the 1894 **Pioneer Monument** by Frank Happersberger. Sculptures depict a Spanish friar with an Indian convert, and gold miners striking pay dirt, while bronze panels portray California figures such as Padre Junìpero Serra and John Sutter.

Just to the east, nondescript **United Nations Plaza** commemorates the 1945 drafting of the United Nations Charter at the War Memorial Opera House and its signing at the Veterans Building. Columns carry the names of UN member nations. This spot is brightened on Wednesday and Sunday mornings by a **farmers' market.**

Considered one of the city's loveliest buildings, the **Old Hibernia Bank** (*Jones St. at McAllister St., near Market St., not open to the public*) is a beaux arts jewel designed in 1892 by local architect Albert Pissis. The granite structure's classical elements include Corinthian columns and a dome at the corner entrance. The banking hall boasts elaborate plasterwork, marble, and stained glass, but the building is a police station. (The **Tenderloin District,** an

area of crime, prostitution, and homelessness, begins at Jones and spreads eastward toward Mason. Use caution, and avoid it at night.)

To the west of Civic Center Plaza and City Hall, across Van Ness, stand two nearly identical beaux arts buildings designed in 1932 by Arthur Brown, Jr. Both honor World War I soldiers. On the right, the **Veterans Building** plays host to small concerts and lectures in the Herbst Theater.

If you have footlight fever, go upstairs to the **San Francisco Performing Arts Library and Museum** to see books, posters, and playbills tracing the city's love affair with the theatrical arts, which first blossomed during the 1850s.

On the left stands the **War Memorial Opera House** (see p. 263), whose 3,100 seats fill up for San Francisco's celebrated opera and ballet companies. This was the nation's first opera house to be financed by a municipality.

Just south on Van Ness at Grove is the curving glass and granite of the 1980 **Louise M. Davies Symphony Hall** (see p. 263), by Skidmore, Owings & Merrill. In addition to housing the city's exceptional symphony orchestra, the hall boasts a computer-assisted organ with 9,235 pipes. ∎

Veterans Building

✉ 401 Van Ness Ave.

☎ 415/621–6600

🕐 Closed Sat.–Sun.; tours Mon.

🚍 Bus: 5, 19, 21, 42, 47; Streetcar: J, K, L, M, N

The City Hall was carefully restored after the 1989 earthquake.

City Hall

WHEN THE 1989 EARTHQUAKE DAMAGED CITY HALL, SAN Francisco spent 300 million dollars on seismic retrofitting and refurbishing. Once again the building gleams like a municipal temple, all granite and marble and gilded ironwork. Filling two city blocks, this is the world's largest building that doesn't touch the ground: its foundations rest on "base isolators," huge metal and rubber discs designed to absorb the shock of an earthquake.

Lavishly restored, the four-story City Hall resembles a classical temple.

City Hall

🗺 See map pp. 180–81

✉ Polk St. between Grove St. & McAllister St. Go to Van Ness Ave. entrance for tours.

☎ 415/554-6023

🕐 Closed Sun. Tours Mon.–Fri. 10 a.m., 12 & 2 p.m., Sat. 12:30 p.m., but check ahead

🚌 Bus: 5, 9, 19, 21, 47, 49; BART: Civic Center

Built in 1915, the edifice has two colonnaded wings linked by a copper-domed rotunda. The dome resembles that of St. Peter's in the Vatican and soars 307 feet 6 inches, which is taller than the U.S. Capitol in Washington by about 40 feet—a fact that Mayor Rolph (see p. 184) delighted in pointing out. With the advent of such a building, San Francisco announced that it was no longer a mere frontier town, but the great port of the West Coast and a capital of the Pacific Rim.

The City Hall's French Renaissance Revival design by Arthur Brown, Jr., was influenced by his studies in Paris at the École des Beaux-Arts. It incorporates classical elements such as Doric columns and sculptured pediments; the figures above the Polk Street entrance, carved by Henri Crenier, represent California's agriculture and riches (on the left) and navigational skills (right). They also symbolize San Francisco's role as link between the riches of California and the mercantile needs of the rest of the world.

Inside the central rotunda gleams a marble floor, while glass lanterns glow in ornate iron fixtures. Fancy plasterwork abounds. The rotunda rises through all four stories to a ring of Corinthian columns and the lofty dome (which is in fact three nesting domes). Ceremonial occasions (such as inaugurations, vote announcements, and lyings-in-state) are staged on the landing of the monumental staircase.

Up the stairs, the Board of Supervisors' chamber is so beautiful that it almost makes you want to be a politician! Oak-paneled walls glow beneath an ornate Spanish ceiling of pale blue-green and gold. Computer terminals at the supervisors' seats look anachronistic, but installing modern electronics was an integral part of the building's refurbishment.

In the upstairs mayor's offices in 1978, ex-supervisor Dan White shot and killed Mayor George Moscone and Supervisor Harvey Milk, the nation's first openly gay official. ∎

Asian Art Museum

WITH 15,000 OBJECTS SPANNING 6,000 YEARS OF HISTORY and more than 40 Asian countries, this is the largest museum in the United States devoted exclusively to Asian art. The museum began in 1966 as a means of displaying a vast collection donated by Avery Brundage (1887–1975), a Chicago industrialist. Brundage also served as president of the International Olympic Committee (and himself competed in the 1912 Olympics decathlon). With an interest in Asian art piqued by his travels, he began collecting in the 1920s.

Asian Art Museum
www.asianart.org
- See map pp. 180–81
- 200 Larkin St.
- 415/581-3500
- Closed Mon.
- $$. Free 1st Tues.
- Bus: 5, 19, 21, 26, 47; BART Civic Center

The museum's galleries, which display some 2,500 objects from the collection and introduce all of Asia's major cultures, emphasize three themes: the development of Buddhism; trade and cultural exchange by pilgrims, travelers, and armies; and local beliefs and practices. Visitors encounter the galleries in this order:

INDIA

India is represented by works of art that range from temple sculptures to miniature paintings, from wood carvings to calligraphic scrolls.

Religious statuary in many media (bronze, wood, stone, clay) highlight the collection. A carved schist Bodhisattva Maitreya (second to third century) represents an enlightened being, called a bodhisattva; this example came from Gandhara, an area influenced by Greco-Roman styles through foreign contact dating to Alexander the Great. A south Indian carved stone Ganesha (13th century) depicts the Hindus' elephant-headed god of wisdom and wealth. A gallery is devoted to Sikh art, the only such exhibit in the Western Hemisphere.

PERSIAN WORLD/ WEST ASIA

Art on display from this region (Iran, Iraq, Afghanistan, Turkmenistan, Uzbekistan) begins with Neolithic ceramics (stags, mythical creatures) and ranges through intensely colored Islamic ceramics, jewelry, architectural adornments, bronzes, miniature paintings, jade vessels, and illuminated manuscripts.

SOUTHEAST ASIA

These galleries hold objects from Thailand, Cambodia, Burma, Laos, Vietnam, Indonesia, Malaysia, and the Philippines. From Thailand come ceramics and a notable collection of paintings, as well as a large and varied collection of Thai and island-nation *krises* (daggers), many elaborately decorated or jeweled, so they are at once lovely and menacing. One particularly beautiful object in the collection is a gold repoussé dedicatory plaque (perhaps eighth or ninth century) from a Cambodian Hindu temple—a place thought to be the gods' domain on Earth and symbolic of a microcosm of the universe. Angkor Wat is represented by many stone and bronze objects. Shiva and Uma (11th century) are examples of the refined sculptures that the Khmer people of the kingdom of Angkor created to decorate temples. Khmer worshipers combined their own religion with elements of both Hinduism and Buddhism. Also on view: textiles, jewelry, ceramics, terra-cotta objects, and paintings.

A 7th–8th century bronze of Mahakaruna Lokeshvara from Thailand

An 18th-century representation of the Buddhist deity Simhavaktra Dakini stands in the museum's Himalaya and Tibetan Buddhist World gallery.

HIMALAYA/TIBETAN BUDDHIST WORLD

From Tibet come rare scrolls from the Shalu and Ngor monasteries. A thunderbolt and bell of gilt metal (15th century) are ritual objects used in Tibetan Buddhist prayers and rituals. A lacquered wood figure, "Simhavaktra Dakini" (18th century), depicts a dancing, lion-faced female guardian of Vajrayana Buddhism who guides mortals on the proper path and can clear away obstacles such as pride and ego. In Tibet's Tantric Buddhism, ritual objects of human bone are used as reminders that life is brief, death inevitable.

Works from Nepal include colorful cotton mandalas (mystical diagrams to aid meditation) and Buddhist sculptures.

CHINA

As the main focus of the museum's founding donor, Avery Brundage, the Chinese arts are strongly represented with bronzes, ceramics, calligraphy, sculpture, and painting. Of historical importance are Neolithic oracle bones that record ritual events and represent China's first written language. Also significant is China's oldest lacquer vessel that has a maker's mark (A.D. 1).

A collection of nearly 300 Chinese ritual bronzes, some nearly 3,000 years old, is considered the best outside Asia. The earliest known Chinese Buddha (A.D. 338), a highlight of the collection, is a seated figure of gilt bronze, with eyes and nose that look quite Chinese, indicating an evolution of the Indian style that dominated China's

(A.D. 618–907) depicts a camel in three-color *sancai* glaze. The Tang dynasty developed porcelain, a hard white translucent ceramic made by firing a pure clay and then glazing it. China's first blue-and-white porcelain appeared early in the Ming dynasty (A.D. 1368–1644).

The collection also includes fan painting, and calligraphy on paper from the Ming dynasty. Hanging scrolls use varied textures and tones of ink to evoke exquisite landscapes of mist-shrouded mountains, foliage, and water.

Popular with museum visitors are objects made of jade, a mineral whose qualities Confucius (551–479 B.C.) likened to those of a true gentleman: "Its polish and brilliancy represent the white of purity. Its perfect compactness and extreme hardness represent the sureness of intelligence. Its angles, which do not cut although they seem sharp, represent justice.... Its interior flaws, always revealing themselves through its transparency, call to mind sincerity. Its iridescent brightness represents heaven."

Among the collection's more than 200 jade pieces, one standout is a late Neolithic *cong* (3100–2200 B.C.), a short tube that is square on the outside and round on the inside; it was probably used in rituals to worship the Earth. A rare *bi* disk (2500 B.C.) has a round shape with a central hole and symbolizes the sky.

The collection is rich in Qing dynasty (1644–1911) jades with auspicious meanings. These include a 19th-century openwork carving of the "Three Plenties" represented as fruits: a Buddha's-hand *citron* (blessings), a peach (longevity), and a pomegranate (fertility, symbolized by its seeds). A modern tour de force is an incense burner with ten musicians intricately carved in

early Buddhist art. Buddhism spread at the close of the Han dynasty (A.D. 220), penetrating a 2,000-year-old Chinese culture that considered itself superior to foreign ideas and that had a state religious cult based on Confucianism. Buddhism was attractive during the era's warfare and famine because it offered all people an end to the cycle of suffering.

Bronze ritual vessels from the Shang dynasty (1122–1028 B.C.) include an appealing rhinoceros whose naturalistic shape cleverly suits its function as a wine container. Ceramics range from a Neolithic earthenware jug with a roof-shaped top (2500–1500 B.C.) to pieces from the Song dynasty (A.D. 960–1279) glazed in green celadon. A tomb figurine from the Tang dynasty translucent white jade, an object created for the foreign trade in the 1930s.

Also in the collection: paintings and calligraphic works, textiles, and objects made of cloisonné, ivory, bamboo, glass, and horn.

KOREA

The oldest objects in the collection, which is the finest outside Korea, are two Bronze Age slate daggers (600 and 500 B.C.). Other important pieces include bronze Buddhas, earthenware and stoneware vessels, and hanging scrolls.

A duck-shaped earthenware vessel, probably made for ritual or burial purposes, represents the Three Kingdoms (57 B.C.- A.D. 668), a period famous for earthenware and stoneware in imaginative forms.

This Japanese robe, decorated with a floating pattern of butterflies and pampas grasses, was worn by a male actor in the title role of the Noh play "Butterfly" (Kocho).

The Unified Silla Kingdom (A.D. 668-935) presided over the golden age of Buddhist art. Its capital, Kyongju, was described as having Buddhist temples as numerous as the stars of heaven and pagodas lined up like flying geese. A large eighth-century gilt bronze figure of Amitabha Buddha—the Buddha of eternal life and boundless light—is notably fine.

The devoutly Buddhist Koryo dynasty (A.D. 935-1392) produced rich paintings, such as the 14th-century "Buddha Amitabha with the Eight Great Bodhisattvas," while the ensuing Choson dynasty (A.D. 1392-1910) embraced stern neo-Confucianism. The "Portrait of Sosan Taesa" (late 16th century), painted in ink and colors on silk, depicts an elegantly dressed monk who taught the unity of Confucianism, Buddhism, and Taoism.

The collection also includes paintings of various styles—courtly, scholarly, Buddhist, folk—as well as lacquerware and textiles.

JAPAN

No U.S. museum offers a broader survey of Japanese art, including bronze ritual bells, gilded wood Buddhas, dry lacquer figures, glazed stoneware, porcelain, hanging scrolls, rare painted screens, and netsuke carvings.

The earthenware "Standing Warrior" (sixth century), wearing a tunic, puffy pantaloons, and a helmet, was a burial object meant to show off the high economic and social position of the deceased. Among glazed stoneware, look for the tea bowl with dragon medallions (mid-17th century) by Nonomura Ninsei, one of the first potters to mark his works with his own seal. This large bowl would keep tea warm longer for guests in winter, and it is partly glazed black like a winter night. Another ceramic highlight is the glazed stoneware "Bottle with Splashes of Glaze" (1960s) by Kanjiro Kawai, whose early technical experiments quickly won him artistic fame. Later he turned to this *mingei* style that revived traditional handicrafts and employed basic decorating techniques from village potters. In describing how he used a brush to splash three glazes on this bottle, Kawai said he felt as if he was "assisted by an invisible power other than myself."

Notable among the museum's screens is "The Path Through Mount Utsu" (18th century), portraying a scene from *The Tales of Ise*, a tenth-century poetic narrative that unfolds around a romantic journey. A collection of bamboo baskets is the largest and finest outside Japan. ∎

Yerba Buena Gardens

YERBA BUENA GARDENS IS AN EVOLVING SOMA NEIGHBOR-
hood. A massive two-billion-dollar redevelopment project was
overlaid on an existing neighborhood whose residents ranged from
blue collar to skid row. It was a place of $7-a-week transient hotels
and cheap bars. Now increasingly white collar, Yerba Buena Gardens
includes the San Francisco Museum of Modern Art (SFMoMA),
Moscone Center, Yerba Buena Center for the Arts, the Children's
Center, museums, luxury hotels, residential units, and stores.

Fronting Mission between Third
and Fourth, the Yerba Buena Center
is built (although the casual visitor
wouldn't know it) atop the underground Moscone Center. An oval
garden of grass and trees called the
Esplanade draws strollers and
picnickers. Because the Moscone
Center's roof couldn't support
heavy soil and turf, there are blocks
of styrofoam beneath the surface of
the lawn. Unfortunately, the "garden"
and its plaza are all too obviously
man-made, as if each blade of grass
and tree was laid out with calipers
by office-bound urban planners.

Enter the gardens along Mission
between Third and Fourth Streets,
and you will see a **memorial to
Rev. Martin Luther King, Jr.,**
consisting of a broad artificial
waterfall and grotto, where quota-
tions from the civil rights leader
are chiseled into granite and glass
panels: "We will not be satisfied
until justice rolls down like water
and righteousness like a mighty
stream." A promenade and cafés
line a terrace above the waterfall.

On the northeastern side of the
complex stands the **Center for
the Arts** (701 Mission St., tel
415/978-2787, tours first Thurs. 6
p.m., closed Mon.), conceived as a
more adventurous setting than
SFMoMA for the art community. Its
Galleries & Forum Building
($$ for galleries, free first Tues.),
designed in 1993 by Fumihiko Maki,
looks like a well-engineered factory,

sheathed in glass and ribbed
aluminum. From inside, the
windows frame carefully chosen
views, in the manner of "borrowed
scenery" in traditional Japanese
architecture. Exhibits focus on local
artists and ethnic groups. At the
adjacent **Center for the Arts
Theater** (700 Howard St., tel
415/978-2787), designed in 1993 by
James Stewart Polshek, industrial-

**Yerba Buena
Gardens**
www.yerbabuenaarts.org

🔼 See map pp.
180–81

✉ Bounded by Market,
Harrison, 2nd, & 5th
Sts.

☎ 415/541-0312 to
arrange tours

🚍 Bus: 9, 12, 14, 15,
30, 38, 45, 76;
BART: Embarcadero,
Montgomery, Powell
St.

**"Justice rolls
down like water"
in memorial to
Rev. Martin
Luther King, Jr.**

California Academy of Sciences

✉ Temporary location until 2008: 875 Howard St.

☎ 415/750-7145

looking exposed beams and lighting hardware make it seem as if you're sitting backstage.

Also built on top of Moscone Center, the **Children's Center** at Yerba Buena Gardens has an indoor, NHL-size ice-skating rink *(Tel 415/820-3521)*, a bowling alley *(Tel 415/820-3521)*, and a multimedia art studio called Zeum *(Tel 415/820-3351, www.zeum.org)*, where kids can try stop-motion clay

Neon art piece at the Yerba Buena Center for the Arts, which presents contemporary and daring works

animation and computer creativity (they can bring the results home with them on video). On the 1906 **Looff Carousel** *(4th St. at Howard St.)*, originally from Playland-At-The-Beach, 62 brightly painted wooden giraffes, bejeweled horses, and other animals whirl in a glass pavilion illuminated at night. Drop by the temporary home of the **California Academy of Sciences** (see pp. 169–71) to see thousands of water creatures relocated from the Steinhart Aquarium along with other natural history displays.

Several museums and other sights are located in (or will soon relocate to) the Yerba Buena Gardens neighborhood, including

the **Cartoon Art Museum** *(655 Mission St., tel 415/227-8666, www.cartoonart.org, closed Mon., $$)*. Its shows are often drawn from an 11,000-piece permanent collection that includes original art from newspapers, comic books, and animated films.

Redbrick **St. Patrick's Catholic Church** *(756 Mission St.)* dates from 1909; the interior glows with marble from Connemara, Ireland, and stained-glass windows on Celtic themes. In the background looms the **Marriott Hotel** (1989), a controversial, glitzy building that apparently got lost on the way to Las Vegas.

The **California Historical Society** *(678 Mission St., tel 415/357-1848, www.calhist.org, closed Sun.–Thurs., $)* mounts exhibitions from its collections, including paintings by Albert Bierstadt and William Keith; furniture, silver, and costumes; photographs documenting California history; and letters from gold miners.

The **Contemporary Jewish Museum** *(121 Steuart St., tel 415/591-8800, www.thecjm.org, closed Fri.–Sat., $)* has changing exhibitions that look at contemporary Jewish life through art. The museum moves to a new home in 2005, a 1909 Pacific Gas & Electric brick substation designed by Willis Polk.

New to the area: The **Museum of the African Diaspora** *(90 New Montgomery St. in St. Regis Museum Tower, tel 415/358-7200, www.musemoftheafricandiaspora.org, closed Sun.–Tues., $)*, open in summer 2005, looks at the journeys and achievements of Africa-descended people around the world. In late 2006 the **Mexican Museum** (now at Fort Mason Center; see p. 142) takes up residence in a Pueblo-style building on Mission Street. ∎

Like a modern sculpture in the cityscape, SFMoMA assembles itself from basic geometric shapes.

San Francisco Museum of Modern Art

OF ALL THE MUSEUM'S EXHIBITS, THE FINEST MAY BE THE museum itself. Swiss architect Mario Botta's powerful design is a mass of geometric forms. A brick facade steps back from the street in three huge, windowless blocks. On top rises a central cylinder finished in bands of black and silvery gray granite.

The tower is sliced off at an angle to create a skylight, larger than the western rose window of Notre Dame in Paris. Light pours through into a central atrium. A staircase provides access to the upper stories, and a steel catwalk crosses beneath the skylight 75 feet above the floor.

Of course, not everyone likes the museum's design. The late columnist Herb Caen apologized for saying the skylight looked like the funnel on an ocean liner. "The building looks more like a giant toaster extruding a cheese Danish," he amended. Art critic Robert

San Francisco Museum of Modern Art
www.sfmoma.org
🅼 See map pp. 180–81
✉ 151 Third St.
☎ 415/357-4000
🕐 Closed Wed.
💲 $$. Free 1st Tues.
🚌 Bus: 5, 9, 12, 14, 15, 30, 38, 45

The spacious galleries where the works hang (top) are complemented by the thought-provoking design of the building that houses them (above).

Hughes of *Time* magazine asked, "Why a whole ground floor without any place to hang a picture or put a sculpture?"

The second floor is devoted to exhibits from the museum's permanent collection and the third floor to photographs and other works on paper. The top two floors show temporary exhibitions and large-scale contemporary art from the museum's collection.

The museum dates back to 1935 when it was housed in the War Memorial Veterans Building in the Civic Center. In the 1940s it gave Jackson Pollock his first major solo show and acquired his early master-piece, "Guardians of the Secret" (1943). The museum also exhibited work by other charter members of the Abstract Expressionist movement—Arshile Gorky, Clyfford Still, Mark Rothko, and Robert Motherwell—when they were art-world nobodies. Over the years the museum continued to expand its holdings, in 1995 moving to this new building with 50,000 square feet of gallery space.

HIGHLIGHTS

SFMoMA has amassed 18,000 works of 20th-century art, so pieces are rotated in and out of the galleries, although certain "star" works are likely to be on view almost all the time.

In the second-floor galleries are paintings and sculpture. Early modernism is represented by Cézanne, Brancusi, Gris, Picasso, and Matisse, whose "Femme au Chapeau" ("Woman with the Hat," 1905) is the museum's most renowned picture. It is a classic example of Fauvism, an early 20th-century French style of vivid colors and strong, often distorted, forms.

Also represented are modernist Mexican painting (Rivera, Tamayo),

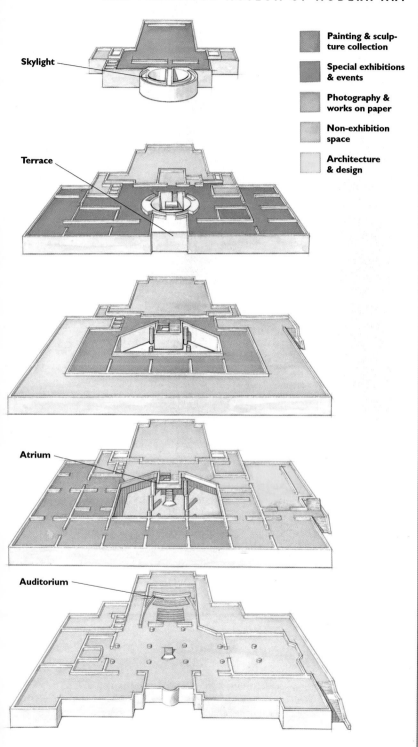

Skylight

Painting & sculpture collection

Special exhibitions & events

Photography & works on paper

Non-exhibition space

Architecture & design

Terrace

Atrium

Auditorium

The exhibits compete with the window views at SFMoMA.

tires; the resulting 22-foot-long tire print is shown unrolled like a Japanese scroll.

The museum owns René Magritte's "Les Valeurs Personelles" ("Personal Values," 1952), one of the artist's masterpieces, and Piet Mondrian's unfinished "New York City III" (1942–44), which still shows the colored tape strips the artist used to refine the placement of his vertical and horizontal lines before painting them in oil.

Andy Warhol's "Red Liz" (1963) is an early portrait of Elizabeth Taylor in lavender, black, and turquoise set against a red background. Also on the second floor are rotating exhibits focused on architecture, furniture, and product and graphic design, with pieces by Bernard Maybeck, Willis Polk, Frank Lloyd Wright, and Frank Gehry. Highlights include an entire conference room designed by the revolutionary Charles and Ray Eames, as well as more than 400 rock 'n' roll posters.

On the third floor are examples from the museum's collection of 10,000-plus photographs, beginning with the 1840s and representing each of the major developments and movements from 19th-century photographers to contemporary artists. You may see images by Alfred Stieglitz, Edward Weston, Ansel Adams, and European avant-gardists of the 1920s and '30s, as well as conceptual work by Duane Michaels and manipulated images by Ray Metzker. A collection of films, videos, and computer work is also here, representing the electronic art media.

The fourth and fifth floors are designed to showcase larger pieces. These are mostly contemporary works, whether experimental installations or selected works from the museum's permanent collection unsuitable for display elsewhere. ∎

abstract expressionism (you'll probably see "Guardians of the Secret" here), Bay Area figurative art (Joan Brown's 1964 "Noel in the Kitchen"), funk, and contemporary art (Warhol, Polke, Koons).

The museum's recent major acquisitions include Robert Rauschenberg's "Erased De Kooning Drawing" (1953), in which he tried to expunge the other artist's drawing and, symbolically, the practices of abstract expressionism. Rauschenberg's conceptual "Automobile Tire Print" (1953) was produced by having his friend, composer John Cage, drive a Model A Ford over art paper as he continually re-inked one of the

Ferry Building & around

RENOVATED IN 2003 AS A PUBLIC FOOD MARKET, THE VENerable Ferry Building centers around a 660-foot-long skylit nave that evokes the market halls of Europe. It is lined with food shops, cafés, and restaurants, and there are outdoor markets. After restoration of its brick arches and marble floors, it is easy to picture the days when the Ferry Building was the world's second busiest transit terminal.

Always a romantic symbol of San Francisco, the 1898 **Ferry Building** by Arthur Page Brown is still a lovely sight, especially when lighted at night. Its 235-foot clock tower, designed by Willis Polk, survived the 1906 and 1989 earthquakes, although its four clocks stopped each time. But ferry service couldn't survive the building of the bay's bridges in the 1930s. Today, though, ferry use is on the rise again, with 12,000 commuters every weekday traveling from Marin and the East Bay. Behind the Ferry Building is a 1988 bronze **sculpture of Mahatma Gandhi.**

NOTABLE BUILDINGS
One Market (at Steuart St.) blends the 1916 redbrick beaux arts facade of the Southern Pacific Railroad headquarters by Bliss & Favelle with office towers.
Rincon Center (101 Spear St.) incorporates the Moderne 1940 Rincon Annex Post Office; inside, bold 1940s murals by Anton Refregier depict San Francisco's colorful past.
   The **Pacific Telephone and Telegraph Building** (140 New Montgomery St.) brought New York sophistication to the city in 1925. The lobby has black marble walls with a Chinese red plaster ceiling, ornamented with Asian designs. The **Pacific Bell Museum** traces the history of telecommunications, from the city's first phone book and old switchboards to satellite technology. Highlights include telephones dating from the 1910s through the 1970s, glass insulators used on telephone pole lines (now highly collectible), and a photo-and-artifact exhibit on the old Chinatown telephone office, including one of the red dresses worn by the operators, who had to memorize every patron's name because the Chinese didn't like being reduced to numbers. ■

Ferry Building
www.ferrybuildingmarket
place.com
✉ Foot of Market St.
🕐 Tours Sat., Sun.,
Tues. at noon
through City Guides,
www.sfcityguides.org
🚌 Bus: 1, 14, 32;
Streetcar: F, J, K,
L, M, N; BART:
Embarcadero

Pacific Bell Museum
✉ 140 New Mont-
gomery St.
☎ 415/542-0182
🕐 Closed Fri.–Mon.

The newly renovated Ferry Building sparkles at night.

More places to visit

BAY BRIDGE
Forever playing second banana to the graceful span across the Golden Gate, the Bay Bridge opened in 1936 as the world's longest steel structure. The 70-million-dollar bridge extends 8.4 miles—about 4.25 miles over water, the rest in approaches—seven times longer than its golden rival.

Its two sections meet in mid-bay at Yerba Buena Island, where cars pass through a tunnel. The spans join at an immense concrete anchorage reaching 220 feet below the bay.

Each day 250,000 cars cross the bridge on two decks, the westbound traffic on top paying a toll but enjoying a fine view. The 1989 earthquake caused a section of the upper deck to collapse onto the lower, killing one person. It took workers only a month to restore the bridge to service.
✉ No pedestrians

The Giants have a new SoMa stadium.

OLD UNITED STATES MINT
The old mint was built in 1874, when the city's original mint couldn't process all the wealth of Nevada's Comstock Lode. (At one point this mint also held about 30 percent of U.S. gold reserves.) The mint is a neoclassic building with a solid granite foundation and Doric columns. The mint stamped out vast numbers of silver dollars that bore the "S" mint mark

(for San Francisco). Today numismatists prize these dollars for their beauty and their associations with the Nevada silver bonanza and old San Francisco. The mint building survived the 1906 fire, thanks to employees who helped wield a firehose, thus rescuing 200 million dollars in silver and gold from a meltdown. The mint went out of service in 1937 and has been declared a National Historic Landmark.
✉ 88 5th St. 🕐 Not open to the public
🚌 Bus: 14, 26, 27; Streetcar: J, K, L, N

SOUTH PARK
Established by Englishman George Gordon in 1855, South Park was modeled on parkside developments in London; each resident of the original town houses set around the long oval park had a key to the gate. After the neighborhood lost its cachet in the early 1870s, cheap rooming houses and machine shops moved in. In 1876 Jack London was born at Third and Brannan, an event commemorated by a plaque on the corner bank building.

Still industrial, the neighborhood has seen an influx of designers and galleries, restaurants and bars. Much new energy has come as fans throng **SBC Park,** the San Francisco Giants' state-of-the-art baseball stadium on the bay at the south margin of the Embarcadero.
✉ King & Third Sts., by China Basin
☎ 510/762-2277 (Giants tickets), http://sanfrancisco.giants.mlb.com

TREASURE ISLAND
Connected to Yerba Buena Island by a causeway, this 400-acre island was created for the 1939 Golden Gate International Exposition. The city later planned to build an airport here, but the Navy took it over for training during World War II. The naval station closed in 1997. Recently several hangars were converted to movie sound stages.

Hotly debated suggestions for the island's development include an amusement park, a women's prison, and affordable housing. One problem for developers: Treasure Island has sunk five feet, and at high tide some sections are under water.
✉ Off Bay Bridge at Treasure Island/Yerba Buena Island exit 🕐 Not open to the public ■

These highly distinctive districts both have a zest that makes them worth visiting. The Mission is the main Hispanic quarter; Castro is the city's gay capital.

The Mission & Castro Districts

The sign for the Castro Theater

The Mission & Castro Districts

LOCATED NEITHER CLOSE TO THE BAY'S BLUE WATERS NOR HIGH ON panoramic hills, these southern districts of San Francisco have been a sort of backwater, largely bypassed by tourism. Genuine, vital, down to earth, these neighborhoods *feel* like neighborhoods, and are worth checking out.

Colorful but down at the heel, the Mission District *(bounded approximately by 14th St., Potrero Ave., 25th St., & Church St.)* has San Francisco's greatest concentration of Hispanic residents, mainly from Mexico and Central America. Perhaps it's no coincidence that people from hot countries ended up in the city's warmest neighborhood, where hills block the fog. On the streets (particularly 24th Street) you'll smell south-of-the-border foods cooking at *taquerías*, see small markets that sell tropical fruits, chilis, and dried beans, and hear salsa music blasting out of the shops and shoppers gossiping in Spanish.

The Mission neighborhood's Hispanic roots go back to 1776, when Padre Francisco Palou first celebrated Mass beneath a brush shelter in this wide, sheltered valley. In 1791 the Franciscan fathers (using Indian labor) completed Mission Dolores, the district's namesake. After the mission was secularized in the 1830s, *Californio* ranchers grazed cattle in the valley.

After the gold rush, immigrants from Germany and Scandinavia settled here, followed by Italians and Irish. (Soon the neighborhood, then known as the "Mish," had its own Brooklynese accent.) A return to Hispanic roots began in the 1920s, with the arrival of Mexicans leaving behind the revolution at home. Migration from Latin America increased in the 1960s. By 1990 Latinos made up more than half the Mission's population.

In the Castro District, street life makes people-watching the main attraction. Gays began flocking here in the 1970s. In that decade the city passed the Gay Bill of Rights against housing and employment discrimination, and gays decided to strut their stuff, rather than hide their sexual orientation.

A hilly district, graced with Victorian houses, and somewhat isolated because it lacked major transit, the Castro made a perfect "separate world" for gays. Men lovingly restored old Victorian houses, barhopped and boogied all night, and opened

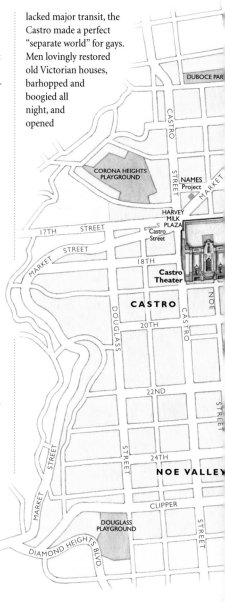

businesses. Harvey Milk rose from the Castro to become the nation's first openly gay elected official. In 1978 his assassination and the murder trial that followed it, galvanized gay political activity. Today San Francisco has more than 120,000 gay and lesbian residents, with the Castro as their capital. ∎

Area of map detail

Mission Dolores is a reminder of the city's humble beginnings.

Mission Dolores

SAN FRANCISCO'S OLDEST BUILDING, FINISHED IN 1791, Mission Dolores exudes an air of the past. Swing open the wooden door to the chapel. Adobe walls three feet thick damp the noise of the outside world. Incense smoke rises toward a beamed ceiling painted in zigzag stripes of gray, white, red, and ocher, a design taken from the baskets of the Ohlone Indians who lived here before the Spanish came.

Mission Dolores

- See map pp. 198–99
- 16th St. & Dolores St.
- 415/621-8203
- $
- Bus: 14, 22, 33, 49; Streetcar: J; BART: 16th St. or 24th St.

The sixth of the 21 California missions founded by Franciscan padres between San Diego and Sonoma, it is officially called Mission San Francisco de Asís. The mission was originally established in 1776 about two blocks east, near a small stream the Spanish named Nuestra Señora de los Dolores (Our Lady of Sorrows). Hence the mission's popular name, Mission Dolores. Padre Francisco Palou designed the adobe chapel. The roof is supported by the original redwood logs, lashed together with rawhide (and later reinforced with steel). At the front of the chapel, the baroque *reredos* (decorative altar) was brought from Mexico in 1796, the two gilded side altars in 1810.

Outside the north door a **diorama,** made for the 1939 Golden Gate International Exposition, depicts the mission quadrangle in 1799 in its original pastoral setting. (From this passageway you can detour into the adjacent 1918 parish church, designated a **basilica,** or honorary church of the Pope, by Pius XII in 1952. Of extravagant Churrigueresque style, it has a large stained-glass window of St. Francis of Assisi.)

In the mission **museum,** a patch of the wall's cement overlay has been removed to reveal the actual adobe, a mixture of clay and straw. Building the chapel took 36,000 sun-dried adobe bricks. Religious articles from the mission era are on view, with a book listing people buried in the cemetery outside. Some 5,500 Indians lie in unmarked graves. Buried in places of honor are the first Mexican governor of Alta California, Capt. Luis Antonio Arguello, and Padre Palou. A statue depicts Junipero Serra, founder of the mission system.

MISSION NEIGHBORHOOD

A mix of residents makes for a lively neighborhood and a great mix of food, with varied restaurants serving up the fare of Mexico, Peru, Cuba, Brazil, and other spicy countries. The Mission District throws itself into celebrations: Cinco de Mayo (first weekend in May), Festival de Carnaval (Memorial Day weekend), and Día de los Muertos (Day of the Dead, November 1).

Southward on Dolores from the Mission are palms planted in 1910 by John McLaren (see pp. 156–57). **Mission Dolores Park** (*18th-20th Sts.*) was until 1905 the site of two Jewish cemeteries, then became a park. (Around this time the

deceased throughout San Francisco were removed beyond the city limits to Colma.) The park has an unexpected view of the Financial District skyscrapers. On the corner of 18th Street stands the 1926 **Mission High School** designed by John Reid, whose mission revival architecture—white walls, red tile roof, arcades—reflects a style popular across California then and now.

Liberty Street (*part of the Liberty Hill Historic District between Dolores, Mission, 20th, & 23rd Sts.*) offers a walk through Victorian architectural styles. Note No. 159 (1878, Italianate), No. 123 (1890s, Queen Anne), and Nos. 111–121 (1880s, Stick).

A few blocks east on **Valencia Street** (*16th to 22nd Sts.*), a visitor has a view into a neighborhood that mixes cultures (Hispanic, bohemian, feminist/lesbian) and businesses (thrift stores, coffee shops, bookstores) along a main thoroughfare in the Mission District.

For Latin street life, head to **24th Street** (*Mission St. to Potrero Ave.*). Small restaurants cater to locals (from Mexico and Guatemala), the air is scented with freshly cooked *churros* (like fried donuts), Latino music blasts from record shops, and grocery stores overflow with such delicacies as cactus leaves (*nopales*) and chilis. Near Bryant stands **Galeria de la Raza,** an established gallery showing Chicano and other Latino art. ■

Father Junipero Serra, founder of the mission system

Galeria de la Raza
✉ 2857 24th St.
☎ 415/826-8009

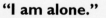

Commemorative stained glass at Mission Dolores

"I am alone."

From the mission look across Dolores Street at the former Notre Dame School, and try to imagine when it was part of the *rancheria,* or compound, where Indians were corraled to live during mission times. Separated from their own people, forced to stay in one spot rather than roam, exposed to European diseases, the Indians quickly succumbed. By 1850 (about 75 years after the mission was founded) only one local Indian remained to be counted. "I am all that is left of my people," he said. "I am alone." ■

Murals of the Mission District

A longstanding tradition in Latin America, outdoor murals add color to the streets of the Mission District. Some illustrate Latino daily life, family, work, and play. Others give groups without "media access" a way to express their political views, or to depict the struggles and achievements of their races. Some murals simply celebrate personal fantasies. Perhaps 200 murals adorn everything from banks and schools to garage doors.

Mural painting has been going on in San Francisco at least since the 1930s, when noted Mexican muralist Diego Rivera created work at the San Francisco Art Institute and the Pacific Exchange. An influence on both style and technical handling was David Alfaro Siqueiros (1896–1974), a Mexican mural painter who depicted political protest and revolution. In the 1960s he improved the technical methods of outdoor painting. Mural

Mission neighborhood mural

painting in the Mission District took off in the following decade.

Some Mission murals were funded by the city for their cultural and artistic merit; others are spontaneous, funky, and homemade.

Precita Eyes Mural Arts Center *(2981 24th at Harrison Sts., tel 415/285-2287, www.precitaeyes.org)* sells a "Mission Mural Walk Map" and leads walking tours. The Precita Avenue branch *(348 Precita Ave., tel 415/285–2311)* holds classes.

Murals & where to see them

Balmy Alley *(off 24th St. between Harrison St. and Treat Ave.):* On garage doors, fences, and walls, colorful murals with names such as "Indigenous Eyes" reflect Latin American political concerns. Other murals are fanciful. The first murals here were painted by schoolchildren, and in the 1980s a group called PLACA (slang for a graffiti artist's "tag") created nearly 30 new murals. Sadly, gang-style graffiti has been spray-painted on some of the artwork. This is a service alley without many people around; use reasonable caution when visiting.

Carnaval Mural *(24th St. at Van Ness Ave.):* The Carnaval festival (Memorial Day weekend) celebrates Latin American and Caribbean cultures in flamboyant style.

BART Station Mural *(24th St. at Mission St.):* In depicting a BART commuter train running across the bent backs of "the people," this 1975 mural protests about the extra sales tax that paid for San Francisco's rapid transit, which in turn threatened the Mission District with high-rise development.

"500 Years of Resistance" *(24th St. at Florida St.):* A study of racial and economic struggle, the mural shows such figures as Mexico's Padre Miguel Hidalgo and Martin Luther King.

"Inspire to Aspire: Tribute to Carlos Santana" *(22nd St. at Van Ness Ave.):* As colorful as a parrot, this city-funded mural honors the great Latino rock guitarist. It shows musicians and an Aztec pyramid set against the Transamerica Pyramid—a meeting of two worlds.

"New World Tree" *(Mission Playground pool, 19th St. near Valencia St.):* A tree with a man, woman, and children suggests an Eden of mixed cultures.

Other murals are at: Mission Cultural Center *(2868 Mission St.);* Taquería San Francisco *(24th St. at York St.);* Cesar Chavez Elementary School *(22nd St. at Shotwell St.);* Little Hollywood Launderette *(Market St. at Laguna St.).* ■

The Castro

THE CASTRO IS THE ELECTRIC-PINK HEART OF SAN Francisco's gay and lesbian community. Bounded by Market, Noe, 20th, Diamond, and 17th Streets, it looks much like any other affluent neighborhood—if not in its social life, then in its streets, shops, and houses. On special occasions there's plenty of local color: Just consider the studded bikers, cowboys, and high-heeled drag queens who take part in the Castro Street Fair on the first Sunday in October.

The Castro

See map pp.
198–99

Bus: 24, 33, 35, 37;
Streetcar: F

In the 1980s the catastrophe of AIDS put a damper on the gay party mood. Social services appeared in the neighborhood alongside the bars and campy shop-window displays. Lately lesbians have become more of a presence, but the neigh-borhood is definitely not as flamboyant as in former days.

Optimism and good humor reign, despite the specter of illness and loss. For a sample, stroll around the Castro on a Saturday, when residents are doing errands. Or see a

Castro, the color-
fully outrageous
Main Street of
gay life in San
Francisco

movie at the Castro Theater, where the audience often creates a participatory theater of its own.

In this part of town, you'll definitely see things you don't see every day. One comfortable introduction to the neighborhood is via the **Cruisin' the Castro tour.**

The neighborhood's main thoroughfare is **Castro Street** (*Market St. to 19th St.*). At the busy intersection with Market Street, **Harvey Milk Plaza** was named for the city's first out-of-the-closet gay supervisor, a former Wall Street financial analyst elected in 1977. Milk ran a camera store in the Castro whose sign read: "Yes, We Are Very Open." He was killed in 1978. During protests and celebrations, traffic at this intersection usually grinds to a halt, with Castroites takin' it to the street. The plaza also serves as the entrance to the underground Muni Metro station. The trees along the street are Canary Island palms, planted when the F streetcar line was installed in the mid-1990s.

Along **Market Street** (*Castro St. to Church St.*), shops proffer trendy clothing, furniture, home accessories, gay and lesbian books, designer flowers, and more. Look for shops with revealing, funny names such as All American Boy.

Cruisin' the Castro tour
☎ 415/550-8110
$ $$$$$ (includes lunch and access to Castro Theater)
🕐 No tours Sun.–Mon.

Castro Theater

Castro Theater
- ✉ 429 Castro St.
- ☎ 415/621-6120
- 🚌 Bus: 24, 33-
  Stanyan, 35, 37;
  Streetcar: F, K, L, M

Noe Valley
- 🚌 Bus: 24, 48;
  Streetcar: J

The neighborhood and tens of thousands of visitors all come together at June's **San Francisco Lesbian, Gay, Bisexual, Transgender Pride Parade & Celebration** *(Tel 415/864-3733, www.sfpride.org)*, a one-day extravaganza that starts with a parade featuring such entrants as the San Francisco Women's Motorcycle Contingent (a group of more than 500 women originally known as Dykes on Bikes), queer cheerleading squads, zanily costumed revelers, support groups, politicians, the media, and celebrities. The event continues with a celebration on cordoned-off blocks around the Civic Center that features more than a dozen stages, music, booths, and food and drink.

On Castro Street near 17th, the **Castro Theater** is a classic 1922 movie palace, with a pink neon sign that serves as a beacon for the Castro District. Designed by Timothy Pflueger in Spanish Renaissance Revival style, the building has a highly ornamented facade; the sign and marquee were added in 1937. Inside, the 1,450-seat theater is often compared with an Arabian Nights fantasy, the plaster ceiling like a fanciful Bedouin tent with drapery, ropes, and tassels. A Wurlitzer organ ascends from the orchestra pit for performances,

usually with plenty of audience participation. The theater shows independent films, silent movies, and campy cult classics, and holds screenings for the San Francisco Film Festival.

Just south on Castro Street, you'll reach the **village center** around 18th Street. Past 20th Street there's a string of Victorian houses. Also explore side streets, such as Liberty, to see Victorian cottages with gingerbread trim.

If you follow Castro to 24th Street, you reach the main shopping strip in **Noe Valley.** Just south of the Castro, quiet Noe Valley, bounded by 20th, Dolores, 30th, and Douglas Streets, attracts young professionals with families to its Victorian cottages. They replaced the hippies of the 1970s (when the area was nicknamed "Granola Valley") and brought wine shops and latte dispensaries with them.

Daily life focuses around 24th Street, a place of baby strollers and bookshops and cafés. Try to picture the corner of 24th and Noe in the 1840s, when the main feature was the adobe ranch house of José de Jesús Noe, the city's last Mexican mayor. This was the hub of Noe's 4,000-acre land grant, which also took in the Castro District. Development took place after a cable car line came over the Castro Street hill in 1887. ■

When you weary of San Francisco's city life, you can quickly escape to landscapes and towns that are utterly different.

Excursions

Wild mustard blooms in wine country vineyards

Excursions

VENTURE ALMOST ANY DIRECTION FROM SAN FRANCISCO, AND YOU'LL FIND enriching places filled with cultural wonders and natural beauty. And you don't just have to look: There are plenty of opportunities for active breaks.

SOUTH & EAST

On the San Francisco Peninsula are the park-like campus of Stanford University and a country estate called Filoli, created by the possessor of a gold rush fortune. In Silicon Valley, where rolling hillsides were once covered in fruit-producing orchards, industrial parks crowd around San Jose, turning out chips and software. For tourists, San Jose's attractions include the Tech Museum of Innovation and the spooky Winchester Mystery House.

Farther south, the Monterey Peninsula is considered by many to be one of the world's most beautiful shores, and it is also home to two intriguing towns. In Monterey's historic quarter you'll find Spanish adobe buildings and Cannery Row, once the haunt of novelist John Steinbeck and now a commercialized tourist magnet. The innovative Monterey Bay Aquarium boasts a million-gallon indoor ocean and around 360,000 sea creatures. Defining the word "quaint" (perhaps a bit too insistently), Carmel-by-the-Sea shelters fairy-tale cottages, fine restaurants, galleries, and California's loveliest mission. Nearby Point Lobos unveils a natural realm of rugged shores, basking sea lions, and windblown headlands with Monterey cypress trees.

To the east of San Francisco, in Oakland, you can follow the shore of Lake Merritt to the Oakland Museum of California, which tells the story of the golden state through history, natural science, and art. Facing the busy port, Jack London Square bustles with restaurants, shops, and sites related to its namesake author. Famously liberal Berkeley (birthplace of 1960s student protest) is home to the 30,000-student campus of the University of California, and it also offers an abundance of street life, cafés, restaurants, and campus cultural activities.

NORTH

Across the Golden Gate Bridge in Marin County lies Sausalito, a small harbor town with a sophisticated atmosphere and a Mediterranean look. Beyond trendy Mill Valley stand the thousand-year-old trees of Muir Woods, and beyond them is the tree-covered summit of Mount Tamalpais, reputed to be the birthplace of mountain biking. Along the Pacific shore you'll find beaches, wildlife lagoons, and the 67,000-acre Point Reyes National Seashore.

NORTH EAST

This is the California wine country: In excess of 250 wineries dot the Sonoma and Napa Valleys, to the east of Marin County, many welcoming visitors with tours and pouring samples to taste. Innovative restaurants and relaxing inns, serving food that complements the local wine, complete the picture. The town of Sonoma has an old Spanish mission and plaza, early hotels, and other buildings. Nearby, Jack London's ranch displays the personal belongings of the author of *The Call of the Wild*. Napa Valley towns include Calistoga, with its hot springs, and St. Helena, the tony hub of wine touring.

FARTHER AFIELD

Yosemite National Park in the Sierra Nevada is a sublime kingdom of granite peaks, ancient groves, waterfalls, and wildflower meadows. Also to be found here is the 1927 Ahwahnee Hotel, perhaps the grandest rustic lodge in any national park. Farther north, Lake Tahoe is an alpine lake, so deep that its waters could flood the whole of California to a depth of 14 inches. Tahoe lies cradled between two mountain ranges. Wooded shores, mountain trails, ski areas, historic residences, and gambling casinos on the Nevada shore—there's something for everyone here. Due to their distance from San Francisco, these two excursions are more suitable for a weekend stay than a day trip. ∎

The island of Fanette sits like a jewel in the deep blue waters of Lake Tahoe.

San Francisco Peninsula & Silicon Valley

Filoli
www.filoli.org

211 4B
86 Cañada Rd., Woodside
650/364-8300
Closed Sun.–Mon. & Nov.–mid-Feb. Guided tours by reservation
$ $$

SAN FRANCISCO OCCUPIES THE NORTHERN TIP OF THE peninsula that separates the ocean from the bay. People and their enterprises, from education to high tech, pack this strip of land, which is only a few miles wide.

Tending Filoli's formal gardens

Stanford University
www.stanford.edu
211 4B
Palm Dr., Palo Alto
650/723-2560 (tours)
Tours 11 a.m. & 3:15 p.m., except mid-Dec. through the first week of Jan.

Silicon Valley & San Jose
211 4C
San Jose Visitor Information Center
www.sanjose.org
150 W. San Carlos
408/977-0900
Closed Sun.

FILOLI

Gold-mining heir and utilities magnate William Bowers Bourn II built Filoli (short for his motto, "Fight for a just cause, Love your fellow men, Live a good life"), a 43-room Georgian Revival mansion by Willis Polk, around 1917. With its French windows and carved moldings, it ranks among the great American country houses. Filoli's enticing gardens (designed by Bruce Porter and Isabella Worn) suggest a series of rooms, variously decorated with foliage and flowers. Guided nature walks through the grounds can be arranged (call in advance). For those who remember (or care anymore), Filoli was the setting of the television mini-series *Dynasty*.

From San Francisco head south on I-280 and turn right at the Edgewood Road exit, then turn right again onto Cañada Road.

STANFORD UNIVERSITY

In the 1880s "Big Four" railroad baron Leland Stanford transformed his horse farm into a university dedicated to his son, who had died of typhoid fever. The landscaping was planned by Frederick Law Olmsted, designer of New York's Central Park. At the heart of the spacious campus is the Richardsonian Romanesque **quad,** an arched colonnade of sandstone classrooms with Spanish red-tile roofs. By the quad entrance, a visitor information booth supplies maps and is the starting point for free walking tours. Dominating the quad is **Memorial Church** (1903), with Byzantine biblical mosaics and stained-glass windows.

To get the big picture of the prestigious campus and its backdrop of oak-studded hills, ride the elevator ($) up 285-foot **Hoover Tower,** designed by Bakewell & Brown; in the lobby are memorabilia of Stanford alumnus Herbert Hoover. Around the campus look for artwork by Henry Moore and Alexander Calder. The **Rodin Sculpture Garden,** which contains more than 20 Rodin sculptures, including "The Gates of Hell," is adjacent to the **Leland Stanford Jr. Museum,** which displays art and family artifacts; note the Asian pieces, and the gold spike driven by Leland Stanford to complete the transcontinental railroad in 1869.

To reach Stanford from San Francisco, head south on U.S. 101 to the Embarcadero exit and turn west.

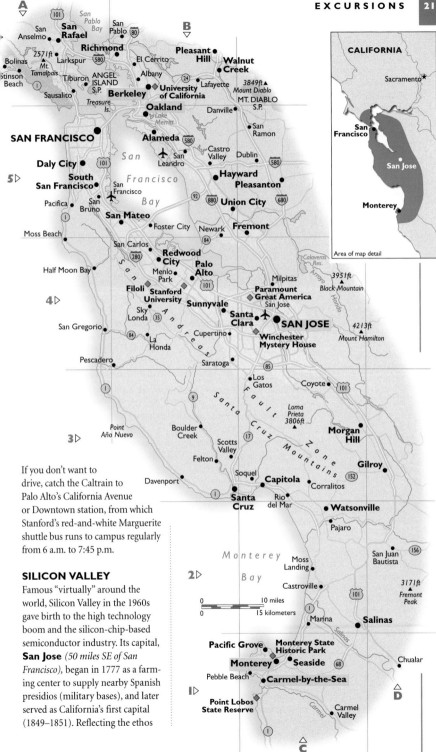

If you don't want to drive, catch the Caltrain to Palo Alto's California Avenue or Downtown station, from which Stanford's red-and-white Marguerite shuttle bus runs to campus regularly from 6 a.m. to 7:45 p.m.

SILICON VALLEY

Famous "virtually" around the world, Silicon Valley in the 1960s gave birth to the high technology boom and the silicon-chip-based semiconductor industry. Its capital, **San Jose** *(50 miles SE of San Francisco),* began in 1777 as a farming center to supply nearby Spanish presidios (military bases), and later served as California's first capital (1849–1851). Reflecting the ethos

The Tech Museum of Innovation brings complex science into the real world.

Tech Museum of Innovation
www.thetech.org
✉ Market St. & Park Ave., San Jose
☎ 408/294-8324
🕐 Closed non-holiday Mondays from Labor Day through March
💲 $$

Rosicrucian Egyptian Museum & Planetarium
www.egyptianmuseum.org
✉ 1342 Naglee Ave.
☎ 888/726-5673
🕐 Closed Mon.
💲 $$

Winchester Mystery House
www.winchestermystery house.com
🅰 211 4C
✉ 525 S. Winchester Blvd.
☎ 408/247-2101
💲 $$$$

Children's Discovery Museum of San Jose
www.cdm.org
✉ 180 Woz Way
☎ 408/298-5437
🕐 Closed Mon.
💲 $$

San Jose Museum of Art
www.sjmusart.org
✉ 110 S. Market St.
☎ 408/294-2787
🕐 Closed Mon.

San Jose Historical Museum
www.historysanjose.org
✉ Kelley Park, 1600 Senter Rd.
☎ 408/287-2290
🕐 Closed Mon.
💲 $$ weekends only. Tours on weekends.

of Silicon Valley, the **Tech Museum of Innovation** bills itself as a theme park for your brain, with four interactive galleries (partly developed with the help of explorers and scientists such as astronaut Buzz Aldrin and physicist Stephen Hawking). Among other activities, visitors can design virtual roller coasters, make 3D computer portraits of themselves, and use a jet-pack simulator to move in a "weightless" environment. There's also an IMAX dome theater.

The **Rosicrucian Egyptian Museum & Planetarium** has an air of mystery, like a Boris Karloff mummy movie. This fine institution boasts architecture out of the temple at Karnak and is a repository for mummified priests (and cats!), amulets and Egyptian jewelry, and a reproduction of a 4,000-year-old rock tomb.

A haunting (and perhaps haunted) 160-room Victorian mansion, the **Winchester Mystery House** has stairs that rise to the ceiling, doors that open to blank walls, and a Tiffany window with a spider web design. It's said that a spirit medium told

heiress Sarah Winchester that her husband had been killed by the spirits of men killed by Winchester rifles. She should build a room for each spirit, and she would live as long as construction continued—which it did, from 1884 until she died in 1922. A firearms museum displays Winchester weapons.

At the **Children's Discovery Museum of San Jose,** kids can tinker with 150 interactive exhibits focused on the arts, humanities, science, and culture. The **San Jose Museum of Art** displays 20th-century works from the Whitney Museum of American Art, ranging from Edward Hopper's starkly realistic works to the early modernist imagery of Georgia O'Keeffe, New Mexico's most famous painter. The **San Jose Historical Museum** fills 25 acres with well-reproduced houses and businesses of the late 19th century. The downtown arts and entertainment district is called **SoFA** (South First Area), a five-block section of South First Street, south of San Carlos Street and north of Gore Park. It has nightlife, restaurants, art galleries, coffee shops, and theater. ■

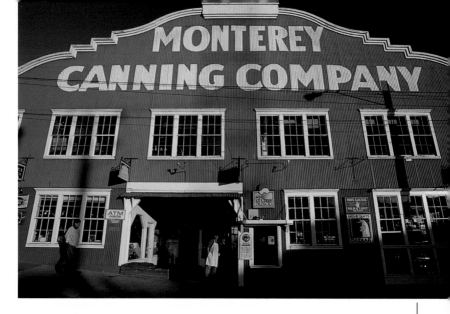

Monterey Peninsula

A 1920s cannery survives on Cannery Row.

FEW PLACES BLEND NATURE AND HISTORY AS BEAUTIFULLY as this peninsula 120 miles south of San Francisco, with its rocky coastal scenery and long parade of cultures. (Here nature comes first: Anyone caught harming a Monarch butterfly will be fined $1,000. Carmel-by-the-Sea prohibits neon signs and billboards that would blight the scenery.) Visitors will find a world-class aquarium, upscale restaurants and cozy inns, and 18 golf courses, including world-famous Pebble Beach.

MONTEREY

The capital of California under Spanish, Mexican, and U.S. flags, Monterey treasures its historic adobes downtown.

Monterey State Historic Park encompasses several of the buildings described below. The **Custom House** (1827), California's oldest public building, displays early cargo. At the Stanton Center, the **Maritime Museum of Monterey** traces local seagoing history, with model ships and an 1887 Fresnel lighthouse lens made of 1,000 prisms, whose light shone for 24 miles. Monterey's oldest building is the 1795 **Royal Presidio Chapel** (*Church St. at Figueroa St.*), built of stone and adobe. A touch of New England, **Colton Hall** (*559 Pacific St.*) is where delegates in 1849 framed California's first constitution. Noteworthy houses include the 1835 **Larkin House** (*510 Calle Principal*), an example of the Monterey colonial style that fused Spanish adobe construction and New England design; it operates as a house museum. Also look in at the **Robert Louis Stevenson House** (*530 Houston St.*), an 1830s adobe where the Scottish author rented a room in 1879 while courting Fanny Osbourne. A collection of Stevenson memorabilia is on display.

Monterey County Convention & Visitors Bureau
www.montereyinfo.org
☎ 888/221-1010

Monterey State Historic Park
www.mbay.net/~mshp
✉ 20 Custom House Plaza
☎ 831/649-7118

Maritime Museum of Monterey
☎ 831/373-2469
💲 $

Monterey Bay Aquarium

www.mbayaq.org

✉ 886 Cannery Row

☎ 831/648-4888 or 800/756-3737 (advance tickets)

💲 $$$$

Cannery Row

www.canneryrow.com

☎ 831/649-6690

The extraordinary **Monterey Bay Aquarium** reveals the world beneath the sea. Highlights: jellies presented as living artworks; a forest of kelp, which can grow six inches a day; a million-gallon tank whose denizens include sunfish that can weigh 1.5 tons. A new shark exhibit presents rarities (puffadder shysharks, pajama catsharks) and looks at worldwide cultural traditions (e.g., headdresses worn by African boys costumed as hammerhead sharks for an initiation ceremony).

A tidal wave of tourism has swamped **Cannery Row,** the site of former sardine canneries along Monterey Bay, leaving a wrack of T-shirt shops, saltwater taffy vendors, and factory outlets. From the 1920s to the 1950s (when the sardines gave out), this industrial zone was a place John Steinbeck characterized as "a poem, a stink, a grating noise, a quality of light…a dream" (*Cannery Row,* 1945). Steinbeck fans should make a pilgrimage to the **Pacific Biological Laboratory** (*800 Cannery Row),* which was run by Steinbeck's friend and protagonist, Ed "Doc" Ricketts.

For a funkier, less plastic tourist experience than Cannery Row offers, try nearby **Fisherman's Wharf,** a pier with shops and seafood eateries. ■

Monterey provides both informative entertainment in the guise of the aquarium (left) and scenic beauty (below).

Carmel Mission
has been exten-
sively restored.

**Carmel-by-the-Sea
visitor information**
🅰 211 IC
✉ San Carlos St. bet.
Fifth & Sixth Sts.
☎ 831/624-2522

**Mission San Carlos
Borroméo de
Carmelo**
✉ 3080 Rio Rd.
☎ 831/624-3600
💲 $

17 Mile Drive
✉ Carmel gate: Hwy.
1; Pacific Grove
gate: Hwy. 68 West
💲 $$

**Tor House & Hawk
Tower**
✉ 26304 Ocean View
Ave.
☎ 831/624-1813
🕐 Open Fri.–Sat. Tours
by reservation only
💲 $$

Carmel-by-the-Sea

AN ARTISTS' COLONY TURNED UPSCALE RESORT, CARMEL has a village atmosphere with cottages on tree-lined streets, fancy shopping and dining along Ocean Avenue, tuck box inns, and a curve of white sand on a turquoise ocean (which isn't safe for swimming).

The **Mission San Carlos Borroméo de Carmelo** has sandstone walls, a Moorish-domed bell tower, and walled gardens, and in a mysterious way these elements add up to something ineffable, beyond simply a historic mission. Completed in 1797, it captures the romance of mission days in old California. Padre Junipero Serra, founder of the California mission system, chose this as his headquarters and is buried in the sanctuary.

Poet Robinson Jeffers designed **Tor House** to look like a Tudor barn he had seen in England. Granite for its walls was hauled up by horses from the cove below; he also built the stone **Hawk Tower.** From Carmel, the **Seventeen**

Mile Drive takes you through 8,000-acre Del Monte Forest. The road passes multimillion-dollar houses and legendary golf courses (Pebble Beach, Spyglass Hill, Cypress Point), and traces a rugged shore. The oft-photographed Lone Cypress stands on a rocky point.

One of the most inspiring places on the California coastline, **Point Lobos State Reserve** (Tel 831/624-4909, $) protects rocky headlands, tide pools, meadows, and Monterey-cypress groves, as well as 750 acres offshore, one of the first underwater preserves in California. Look for seals, sea lions, and playful sea otters. For a close look at Point Lobos, walk the trails that wind through the reserve. ∎

Berkeley

OPENED AS AN "ATHENS OF THE WEST" IN 1873, THE University of California at Berkeley defines the city with its academic air and sprawling campus. With the bay in front and craggy hills behind, nature provides a backdrop to a vibrant metropolitan scene.

The city was named in 1866 for Irish prelate George Berkeley (author of the line, "Westward the course of empire takes its way"). The hills showcase fine regional architecture, particularly the rustic shingled houses of architects Bernard Maybeck and John Galen Howard in North Berkeley.

On the gastronomic front, the birthplace of California cuisine was Alice Waters' **Chez Panisse** (see p. 258) in an area nicknamed Gourmet Ghetto for its many restaurants. Telegraph Avenue is thronged by students, hippies (both aging and retro), the homeless, and the tattooed and pierced.

UC Berkeley's
Sather Gate and
Campanile

Berkeley
🅰 211 5B
Visitor information
www.berkeleycvb.com
✉ 2015 Center St.
☎ 510/549-7040 or
800/847-4823
🕐 Closed Sat.–Sun.
🚇 BART: Downtown
Berkeley

Hearst Memorial Mining Building at Berkeley

University of California
www.berkeley.edu
Visitor Center
✉ 101 University Hall,
   Oxford St. at
   University Ave.
☎ 510/642-5215

Museum of Paleontology
✉ Valley Life Sciences
   Bldg.
☎ 510/642-1821

Phoebe Hearst Museum of Anthropology
✉ Kroeber Hall
☎ 510/643-7648
🕐 Closed Mon.–Tues.
💲 $

Berkeley Art Museum
✉ 2626 Bancroft Way
☎ 510/642-0808
🕐 Closed Mon.–Tues.
💲 $$

Bancroft Library
✉ Doe Library annex
☎ 510/642-3781
🕐 Closed Sun.

Lawrence Hall of Science
✉ Centennial Dr.
☎ 510/642-5132
💲 $$

First Church of Christ Scientist
✉ 2619 Dwight Way
☎ 510/845-7199
🕐 Open 1st Sun. by
   tour only

Vendors sell crafts and tie-dyed clothes. (For true sixties authenticity, flash the peace sign.)

UNIVERSITY OF CALIFORNIA

With 465 buildings on 1,350 acres, this is a big campus; get your bearings with a walking-tour booklet at the visitor center. Called Cal, the 1873 university was the first in the University of California system and now has 30,000 students and top graduate programs. During the sixties the university made headlines as the birthplace of the Free Speech Movement and a crucible of Vietnam War protests.

Demonstrations took place on Sproul Plaza, still a soapbox for protesters, preachers, street performers, and assorted loonies (e.g., "Hate Man," who wears a skirt, bra, and high heels and says he basically hates everything). To join the three-ring circus, stand in the plaza's "extraterritorial zone," a six-inch circle fancifully proclaimed free from outside authority.

Granite-and-bronze **Sather Gate** serves as the university's ceremonial front door. For a bird's-eye view of Cal, take the elevator *($)* up the 307-foot **Campanile,** or Sather Tower, designed by John Galen Howard in 1914. The white granite bell tower was inspired by that in Venice's Piazza San Marco.

Museums reflect the university's scholarship. The **Museum of Paleontology** has a few public exhibits, notably a complete skeleton of a *T. rex.* The **Phoebe Hearst Museum of Anthropology** shows artifacts from California, Peru, Egypt, and Mediterranean Europe, and items associated with Ishi, the last Yahi Indian. The **Berkeley Art Museum** is devoted to Asian and modern artists, notably abstract expressionist Hans Hofmann. Across the street the **Pacific Film Archive** shows independent, classic, and world films. Among treasures of the American West at the **Bancroft Library** are the nugget reputed to have started the California gold rush, and many of Mark Twain's papers. The **Lawrence Hall of Science** is full of holograms, lasers, and hands-on fun, plus a planetarium.

OTHER BERKELEY SIGHTS

Just outside the campus, **People's Park** *(E of Telegraph Ave. between Dwight and Haste Sts.)* was a vacant lot planted in 1969 by students who clashed with the National Guard when the university announced plans to build on it. Today it is the grubby haunt of hippies and homeless people. Across the street stands the **First Church of Christ Scientist**, designed by Bernard Maybeck in 1910. Draped with wisteria, the church has been compared to "a Japanese pagoda in a Gothic forest." ∎

Oakland

NAMED FOR ITS OAK GROVES, THE CITY BECAME THE western terminus of the transcontinental railroad in 1869. It was linked to San Francisco by the Bay Bridge in the 1930s, then boomed with the Kaiser Shipyards during World War II. But within two decades Oakland was plagued with racial discord (it was the birthplace of the Black Panthers) and serious crime. In 1989, part of I-880 collapsed during the Loma Prieta earthquake.

These days things are looking up, with restored residential and commercial buildings, a tourism hub at Jack London Square, a fine regional museum, and the economic boon of Oakland's port, which has nearly 20 miles of berths and terminals. With a large black community, Oakland spawned a school of rap music through stars like MC Hammer and Tupac Shakur.

Lovers of Victorian architecture should stroll around **Old Oakland** *(between Washington St. and Broadway, from 8th to 10th Sts.),* the original 1870s downtown; its buildings are now occupied by shops and cafés. Victorian houses were moved from the path of I-990 to **Preservation Park** *(between Castro St. and Martin Luther King Jr. Dr., from 12th to 14th Sts.).* You

Oakland's colorful past comes alive at the First & Last Chance Saloon.

Oakland
🅰 211 5B
Oakland Convention & Visitors Bureau
www.oaklandcvb.com
✉ 463 11th St.
☎ 510/839-9000
🚉 BART: 12th St./City Center

Oakland Museum of California

www.museumca.org

✉ 1000 Oak St. at 10th St.

☎ 510/238-2200 or 888/625-6873

🕐 Closed Mon.–Tues.

$ $$

🚇 BART: Lake Merritt

Urban Lake Merritt (below) and the Paramount Theater (opposite) adorn Oakland.

can visit the **Pardee Home Museum** *(11th St. at Castro St., tel 510/444-2187, closed Sun.–Tues. & Thurs., by reservation only, $)*, an 1868 Italianate house built by an early Oakland mayor.

A classic art deco movie palace (Timothy Pflueger, 1931), the **Paramount Theater** *(2025 Broadway, tel 510/465-6400, tours 1st & 3rd Sat., $)* is faced with a tile mural of marionettes. Inside are bas-relief warriors and maidens, a glass sculpture, and a women's smoking lounge in black lacquer.

On the shore of **Lake Merritt** (formerly a tidal slough) are gardens, paths, and 122-acre **Lakeside Park.**

JACK LONDON SQUARE

Also known as **Jack London Waterfront** *(foot of Broadway)*, this tourist haunt overlooking the port commercializes the author of *The Call of the Wild* and other works, an Oakland resident for much of his life. As a boy London hawked newspapers at **Heinold's First & Last Chance Saloon** *(56 Jack London Square, tel 510/ 839-6761)*, which was built with wood from a whaling ship in 1883; its floors were tilted by the 1906 earthquake. As a Yukon prospector in 1897, the writer lived in the **Jack London Cabin,** now relocated to the square and occupied by a bookstore.

President Franklin D. Roosevelt's "floating White House," the 165-foot **Potomac** *(Tel 510/627-1215, tours Wed., Fri., & Sun., $)* is docked close by. Other attractions at the square: restaurants, hotels, movies, and the ever popular Sunday farmers' market.

OAKLAND MUSEUM OF CALIFORNIA

One of the world's great regional museums fills an innovative, three-tiered structure designed in 1969 by Kevin Roche and constructed so that the roof of each level becomes a garden and terrace for the one above. The museum addresses the natural environment, history, and art of California.

Dioramas in the **Hall of California Ecology** (first level) allow you to take a simulated walk across California, from the Pacific seashore through the interior valley, over the high sierra, and into the desert. Topographical models show the physical characteristics of each zone, while informative displays make clear the interrelated lives of plants and animals. The **Aquatic California Gallery** covers the state's watery environments—not

The Port of Oakland is a major container-ship facility.

The gardens at the Oakland Museum of California

just the ocean, streams, lakes, and estuaries, but even hot springs and snow banks.

Through the use of crafts, tools, costumes, furniture, machines, decorations, games, and vehicles, the **Cowell Hall of California History** (second level) examines the Native American, Spanish-Mexican, and American periods. You'll see a gold rush assay office, a pumper from the 1906 San Francisco fire, a Beat generation coffeehouse scene, the cultures of Hollywood and the car, and the inevitable computer.

The **Gallery of California Art** (third level) exhibits paintings, sculpture, prints, illustrations, photographs, and decorative arts

by California artists and others who deal with California themes. The collection spans the state's history, from sketches by early artist-explorers to massive panoramic landscapes, such as Albert Bierstadt's views of Yosemite Valley.

Other 19th-century landscape artists featured here include Thomas Hill and William Keith. Among the styles on view are impressionism (work by the Society of Six, who exhibited in the 1920s), abstract expressionism, Bay Area figurative painting (David Park, Richard Diebenkorn, Elmer Bischoff), pop, and funk.

CHABOT SPACE & SCIENCE CENTER

In 2000 the **Chabot Space & Science Center** (*10000 Skyline Blvd., tel 510/336-7300, www.chabot space.org, closed Mon., $$*) features the nation's largest public refractor telescope; a 36-inch reflector telescope that has more dramatic views of the cosmos; one of the world's most advanced planetariums; and a large-screen theater.

There is also a six-acre environmental education center and nature trail, together with other scientific exhibits. ■

Marin County

ON CALIFORNIA'S SOCIOLOGICAL MAP, MARIN IS A LOTUS land colored mellow yellow and sunny green. Residents became famous for grooving on hot tubs, massage, and, of course, themselves. Locals still seek out organic food and any spiritual movement of the moment. But mellow Marin has also become a place of purring BMWs, cell phones, and remarkable wealth. Real estate prices are among the highest in the nation.

Marin County
🅰 224 E2
Marin County Convention & Visitors Bureau
www.visitmarin.org
✉ 1013 Larkspur Landing Circle, Larkspur
☎ 415/499-5000

Bay Area Discovery Museum
www.baykidsmuseum.org
🅰 224 F2
✉ East Fort Baker
☎ 415/487-4398
🕐 Closed Mon.
💲 $$

Marin Headlands Visitor Center
✉ Fort Barry Chapel, Field & Bunker Rds.
☎ 415/331-1540

Marin's sunshine and tranquil beauty attract creative corporations and software companies, as well as upscale shops and restaurants for wealthy residents. Yet nearly 40 percent of Marin County has been protected as parks and open space, including Muir Woods and Point Reyes National Seashore. Cities include Sausalito, trendy Mill Valley, exclusive Ross, and pragmatic San Rafael (home of the **Marin County Civic Center,** designed by Frank Lloyd Wright).

MARIN HEADLANDS
Beyond Golden Gate Bridge lies a world far removed from urban life. The Marin Headlands offer nearly 12,000 acres of rolling coastal hills with miles of hiking and mountain biking trails, views, and old military installations to explore.

In a cove beneath the Golden Gate Bridge, **East Fort Baker** was built to guard the nearby strait. Its Battery Yates (1905–1946) had six rapid-fire guns to trade shots with enemy ships (which never appeared). Enjoy a picnic on the bluffs or go fishing from the pier. Or just watch ships come and go through the Golden Gate; Lime Point (west of the fort area) gives you an eye-to-porthole view of passing ships. Younger children enjoy the **Bay Area Discovery Museum,** whose hands-on lessons in local history and ecology include a crawl-through sea tunnel.

For spectacular vistas of the bridge and city, follow Conzelman Road along the bluffs westward from the Golden Gate. About 1.8 miles along, a fire road leads to **Hawk Hill,** where 20,000 birds of prey pass by during their autumn journey down the coastal flyway; look for red-tailed and Cooper's hawks, turkey vultures, and peregrine falcons.

Conzelman Road continues toward Point Bonita, where a half-mile walk takes you to Land's End. Here the 1855 **Point Bonita Lighthouse** (Closed Tues.–Fri.) warns fogbound ships away from the rocky shore. (A cannon once boomed every half hour around the clock; now an automated light does the work.)

An artist captures the Marin Headlands with paint and canvas.

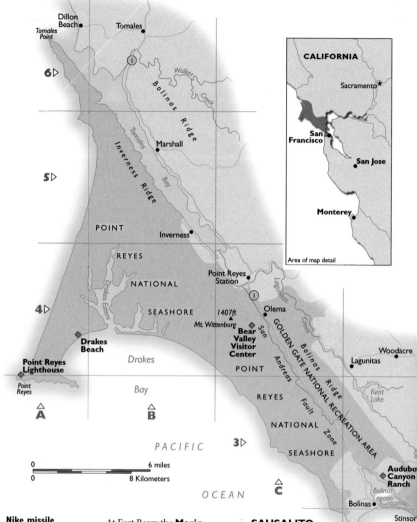

CALIFORNIA

Sacramento ★

San Francisco

San Jose

Monterey

Area of map detail

Dillon Beach
Tomales
Tomales Point

6▷

Bolinas Ridge

Walker Creek

Marshall

Tomales Bay

Inverness Ridge

5▷

POINT

Inverness

REYES

NATIONAL

Point Reyes Station

4▷

SEASHORE

1407ft
Mt. Wittenburg

Drakes Estero

Drakes Beach

Drakes

Point Reyes Lighthouse

Point Reyes

A

Bay

B

PACIFIC

0 ——— 6 miles
0 ——— 8 Kilometers

OCEAN

Olema

Bear Valley Visitor Center

San Andreas Fault Zone

POINT

REYES

NATIONAL

3▷

SEASHORE

C

GOLDEN GATE NATIONAL RECREATION AREA

Bolinas Ridge

Lagunitas Creek

Woodacre

Lagunitas

Kent Lake

Audubon Canyon Ranch

Bolinas Lagoon

Bolinas

Stinson Beach

Duxbury Point
Bolinas Bay

D

Gulf of the

Nike missile launch site

☎ 415/331-1453
🕐 Closed Sat.–Tues. except 1st Sun.

Sausalito

🅰 224 F2

Visitor information

✉ 780 Bridgeway Blvd.
☎ 415/332-0505
💲 $$ for the ferry
⛴ Ferry: 30 minutes from Ferry Building at foot of Market St. or Fisherman's Wharf (tel 415/923-2000)

At Fort Barry the **Marin Headlands Visitor Center** explains the area's natural and human history. Nearby is the nation's only restored **Nike missile launch site,** part of a Cold War defense system from 1954 to 1974. Visitors can see a missile raised into firing position. (The engines and warheads have been removed.) The five-ton Nike Hercules could fly at more than 3,200 miles an hour and had a range of about 90 miles. Nikes were made obsolete by intercontinental ballistic missiles.

SAUSALITO

A resort with a Mediterranean feel, this town clings to steep hills above a picturesque yacht harbor. Tourists congregate along Bridgeway, with its shops, galleries, restaurants, and fabulous views of San Francisco. Bars attract a colorful crowd, from yuppies and yachties to bikers and bohemians.

Hundreds of houseboats are moored at Gate 5 and other nearby locations. After World War II the Bay Area had a surplus of vessels, and adventurous locals turned them into houseboats, creating an artists' colony that included Zen philosopher Alan Watts. These days young professionals also live aboard houseboats, as an alternative to sky-high housing prices on shore.

At the **Bay Model Visitor Center** (*2100 Bridgeway Blvd., tel 415/332-3870*), a warehouse holds a vast model of the San Francisco Bay that compresses 400 square miles into a 1.5-acre simulation. Researchers use the model to study the effects of floods, drought, and development on the bay.

Sausalito developed as a ferry-boat connection to San Francisco, and riding the ferry (see p. 224) remains an enjoyable and scenic way to come and go.

Houseboats in Sausalito

ANGEL ISLAND STATE PARK

Located north of Alcatraz, this island (*Tel 415/435-1915, ferry from San Francisco or Tiburon*) rich in beauty and history makes for great hiking, biking, picnicking, and even sunbathing on its beaches. The top of 781-foot **Mount Livermore** (a former Nike missile site) opens up panoramic views of the whole Bay Area.

Named Isla de Los Angeles by mariner Juan Manuel de Ayala in 1775, Angel Island has served as a Spanish cattle ranch, a U.S. military installation, a quarantine station, and the "Ellis Island of the West," an immigration station and detention center for 175,000 Chinese between 1910 and 1940. On a **tram tour** (*$$$*) or a walk around the 5-mile perimeter road, you'll see historical sites and military garrisons (some dating back to the Civil War), views, and beaches. At **China Cove** an immigration barracks contains a small museum.

MUIR WOODS NATIONAL MONUMENT

On the lower slopes of Mount Tamalpais, accessible via the Panoramic Highway, stands the Bay

Muir Woods National Monument

www.nps.gov/muwo
☎ 415/388-2596
💲 $

Mount Tamalpais State Park

🅼 224 D2–D3
Visitor information
☎ 415/388-2070
💲 $$ (parking)

Stinson Beach

🅼 224 D2
☎ 415/868-1034

Audubon Canyon Ranch

www.egret.org
🅼 224 D3
✉ 4900 Calif. Hwy. 1
☎ 415/868-9244
🕐 Open mid-March–mid-July Sat.–Sun.
💲 Donation requested

In the shade of giants, Muir Woods

Area's last virgin redwood forest. Some trees here are at least a thousand years old. The redwoods shelter ferns, a creek with crayfish and salmon, and varied trails. (The farther you walk from the parking lot, the fewer people you'll see—a good rule in any popular outdoor area.) **Cathedral Grove** and **Bohemian Grove** have the largest trees: The tallest rises 254 feet into the sky; the thickest measures nearly 14 feet across. The world's tallest living things, redwoods have thrived in northern California for 140 million years and grew when dinosaurs roamed the Earth.

MOUNT TAMALPAIS STATE PARK

The most visible point in Marin County is a lofty kingdom of chaparral and oak trees that is laced with more than 200 miles of trails. A quarter-mile path leads from the East Peak parking lot to a fire lookout on the 2,571-foot east summit, where you can scan both the Bay Area and the Pacific Ocean (and on a very clear day, the Sierra Nevada range 200 miles to the east).

PACIFIC COAST

Along Calif. 1, **Stinson Beach** boasts a 3-mile stretch of white beach that's safe for swimming; the village makes a good stop for sandwiches. Just north at **Bolinas Lagoon** you may see egrets and waterfowl, or spy harbor seals hauled out on Pickleweed Island. Bird-watchers might observe any of 115 species at **Audubon Canyon Ranch**, a 1,000-acre preserve on the lagoon where great blue herons and egrets nest in spring at the tops of redwood trees. At the north end of Bolinas Lagoon try to find the road to **Bolinas;** for decades, residents have sought anonymity by taking down the signs marking the turnoff to their town. It's a tranquil hideout with an organic-hippie-artistic-countercultural spirit, although it is now becoming upscale.

POINT REYES

Where the land juts to meet the ocean at Point Reyes, it seems you've stepped to the edge of the world. And maybe you have; the peninsula is separated from the mainland by the notorious San Andreas earthquake fault. Situated on the northward-moving Pacific tectonic plate, Point Reyes is heading for Alaska at the rate of two inches per year.

About 65,000 acres of wild beauty embrace steep cliffs, a rocky coastline with thunderous surf and hidden beaches, open meadows of wildflowers, and windswept hillsides. This area is protected as the **Point Reyes National Seashore.** Just off Calif. 1 near Olema, the **Bear Valley Visitor Center** gives an overview. Here you can trace the actual big bad San Andreas Fault on an interpretive trail. Miwok Indian life is re-created through redwood bark houses and an underground sweat lodge.

Fifteen miles west, just off Sir Francis Drake Boulevard, **Drakes Beach** offers wind-sheltered sand and a visitor center with exhibits on the ocean environment and 16th-century maritime exploration. You can ponder whether explorer Sir Francis Drake really beached his ship, the *Golden Hind*, in surrounding Drakes Bay in 1579, a debate that still occupies historians.

The boulevard goes a few miles farther west to the tip of Point Reyes and the 1870 **Point Reyes**

House in Bolinas

Lighthouse, 296 feet above the ocean. The lighthouse is a perfect perch for watching gray whales migrate (from late December to late April), but can be foggy in summer. Exhibits focus on whales and lighthouse gear, including a massive Fresnel lens. Bring a jacket for wind, and be aware that you must walk down (and climb back up) 309 steps to reach the lighthouse. ■

Point Reyes National Seashore
🅰 224 B4–B5
Visitor information
✉ Bear Valley Rd., Point Reyes Station
☎ 415/464-5100

Point Reyes Lighthouse
🅰 224 A4
☎ 415/669-1534
🕐 Closed Tues.–Wed.

Gray whales in motion

Each year 18,000 gray whales migrate from Alaska along the California coast to their breeding and birthing waters in Baja California. Their 12,000-mile round-trip trek is the longest annual migration in the animal kingdom. The whales swim 5 miles an hour and cover 80 miles a day. To spot a whale, look for a spout of vaporized water as it surfaces to breathe. Gray whales can grow 50 feet long and weigh up to 45 tons. ■

Napa Valley

THIS VALLEY 50 MILES NORTH OF SAN FRANCISCO PRO-
duces some of the world's greatest wines, but that's not the only
reason readers of *Wine Spectator* rank it above Burgundy, Bordeaux,
and Tuscany as their "favorite wine region for vacationing in
the world." It helps that the valley is a lovely sight, bordered by
the mountains of the Coast Range, carpeted with yellow mustard
flowers in late winter, and dotted with picturesque wineries that open
their tasting rooms to visitors. Charles Krug established the first
winery here in 1861; today more than 300 wineries dot Napa Valley.
The grape harvest and crush take place in autumn.

Napa Valley
🅰 233 D1
**Napa Valley
Conference &
Visitors Bureau**
www.napavalley.com
✉ 1310 Napa Town
Center, Napa
☎ 707/226-7459

Charles Krug
🅰 233 B3
✉ 2800 Main St.,
St. Helena
☎ 707/967-2200

Beringer Vineyards
🅰 233 B3
✉ 2000 Main St.,
St. Helena
☎ 707/963-4812

**Hess Collection
Winery**
🅰 233 C2
✉ 4411 Redwood Rd.,
Napa
☎ 707/255-1144

Enhancing its appeal, the valley
also boasts epicurean restaurants
and such hybrids as the winery/art
gallery. Napa Valley is also the
world's most heavily traveled hot-air
balloon corridor. Sunrise ascensions
are usually followed by champagne
brunch. There are ten championship
golf courses, notably the **Silverado
Country Club** (*1600 Atlas Peak
Rd., Napa, tel 707/257-0200*).
Calistoga's hot springs have attracted visitors since the early 1900s.

Geographically, Napa Valley is a
cornucopia of wine grapes that
spills southward from 4,343-foot

Mount St. Helena. The rich, porous
soil and dry Mediterranean climate
provide ideal grape-growing conditions. Many celebrated wineries
(Beringer, Beaulieu, Charles Krug,
Robert Mondavi) lie along the
valley's main road, Calif. 29, which
links the main towns: Napa,
Yountville, Oakville, Rutherford,
St. Helena, and Calistoga (see map
p. 233). This "rural" highway is
often jammed with cars, though,
especially in spring, fall, and on
weekends. A quieter, less trafficked
route is the parallel **Silverado
Trail,** to the east. The **Napa**

Valley Wine Train *(Tel 707/253-2111 or 800/427-4124, $$$$$)* makes a three-hour round-trip from Napa to St. Helena in 1915–1950 dining and lounge cars, with gourmet meals and local wines. The train runs on a route established in 1864.

NAPA VALLEY WINERIES

The valley's oldest wine producer is **Charles Krug,** founded in 1861 and now operated by the Peter Mondavi family. **Beringer Vineyards** ranks as the valley's oldest continuously operated winery (1876). Tastings are conducted in a German mansion with a slate roof and wonderful stained-glass windows; the wines age in caves tunneled 1,000 feet into the hillside.

Fine contemporary art complements the wine at the **Hess Collection Winery. Domaine Chandon** produces sparkling wine by the classic *methode champenoise*, which involves a second fermentation in the bottle; the method was invented in the 1600s by the blind Benedictine monk Dom Perignon.

Tours at the **Robert Mondavi Winery** range from an hour-long overview to a four-hour "advanced winegrowing tour"; the winery presents concerts in summer and winter. New and old meet at **St. Supéry Wine Discovery Center & Winery.** In the modern winery, the Wine Discovery Center teaches visitors about winemaking and such matters as varietal aromas; there's also a Queen Anne-style Victorian mansion furnished as a living museum of the 1880s. The **Niebaum-Coppola Estate** focuses around the 1882 stone winery known as Inglenook; the operation now belongs to moviemaker Francis Ford Coppola, who displays wine and film artifacts.

The valley's first hillside winery, the 1862 **Schramsberg Vineyards,** makes sparkling wines. After Robert Louis Stevenson visited in 1880, he wrote about the winery and founder Jacob Schram in *The Silverado Squatters.* To visit **Sterling Vineyards,** you ride an aerial tram from the parking lot to the top of a 300-foot knoll.

Late winter in Napa Valley

Domaine Chandon
- 233 C2
- 1 California Dr., Yountville
- 707/944-2280

Robert Mondavi Winery
- 233 C3
- 7801 St. Helena Hwy., Oakville
- 707/226-1335

St. Supéry Wine Discovery Center & Winery
- 233 C3
- 8440 St. Helena Hwy., Rutherford
- 707/963-4507

Niebaum-Coppola Estate
- 233 C3
- 1991 St. Helena Hwy., Rutherford
- 707/968-1100

NAPA & YOUNTVILLE

The front door to the valley, **Napa** grew up on the Napa River as a shipping hub for valley wines. The old part of town is worth a look for its Victorian neighborhoods—one of the state's largest collections of pre-1906 architecture.

Named for George Yount, who planted the valley's first vineyard in 1833 (and is buried in the pioneer cemetery), the small town of **Yountville** now caters to an upscale crowd with inns, shops, and restaurants. Exhibits at the **Napa Valley Museum** take visitors through a year in the winemaking process and reveal the geographical and cultural influences on the valley; artifacts on display range from Pomo Indian basketry to railroad memorabilia and viticultural implements.

ST. HELENA

Hub of the wine-growing region, St. Helena dates from 1853. Some shops and restaurants on historical Main Street occupy buildings of native stone erected before the end of the 19th century. Streetlights were installed right after being demonstrated at the 1915 Panama-Pacific International Exposition.

Fans of the writer Robert Louis Stevenson shouldn't miss the **Silverado Museum,** which displays his childhood toy soldiers, together with his handwritten manuscript pages, letters, photographs, and first editions. Works by Stevenson (1850–1894) include *Treasure Island, Dr. Jekyll and Mr. Hyde,* and *A Child's Garden of Verses.* In 1880 the writer honeymooned with his bride, Fanny Osbourne, in a cabin on nearby

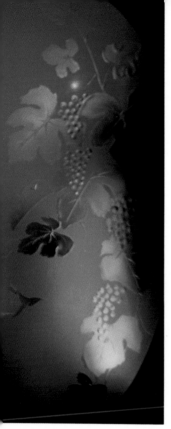

Mount St. Helena (see Robert Louis Stevenson State Park, this page), which he later described in *The Silverado Squatters*.

You can eat the homework at the **Culinary Institute of America,** which trains chefs at the former Greystone Cellars, built in 1889 and once operated by the Christian Brothers. (The institute displays nearly 2,000 corkscrews collected by one of the brethren.) Dine at a gourmet restaurant that has institute-trained chefs, or stroll through the herb garden.

A 36-foot waterwheel turns at **Bale Grist Mill State Historic Park.** Built by Dr. Edward Turner Bale in 1847, it was used to grind the grain of local farmers. Visitors can see the original grindstones in use, and purchase the flour that they produce.

CALISTOGA & BEYOND

At the north end of the valley, Calistoga is famous for its mineral-rich hot springs and purifying mud baths. Spa treatments are a cottage industry, an enterprise that began in 1859 when California's first millionaire, Sam Brannan, built a resort for well-to-do San Franciscans. Legend says the spa got its name when the colorful Brannan rose to his feet at a banquet after imbibing freely and announced that his resort would be the "Saratoga of California"—at least, that's what he meant to say. His tongue twisted, and he called it the "Calistoga of Sarafornia."

The resort era comes to life at the **Sharpsteen Museum** through dioramas created by an early Disney artist and a furnished cottage from the old resort.

One of three geysers in the world guaranteed to go off like clockwork (in this case every 14 minutes), the private **Old Faithful Geyser of California** shoots water and steam 60 feet high. About 4,000 gallons of sulfurous water spew forth at 350°F.

Another natural wonder, the **Petrified Forest** resulted from an eruption of Mount St. Helena around three million years ago. Uprooted trees were buried by ash and lava, then permeated by water and silica. Over many millennia, this turned the trunks to stone—one measuring 108 feet long.

For a vigorous hike, great views, or a brush with history, visit **Robert Louis Stevenson State Park** on Mount St. Helena. A rough trail leads to an abandoned silver mine, near which Stevenson honeymooned in a mining shack in 1880. The trail continues to the summit (4,343 feet), from which you can see Napa Valley, the Pacific Ocean, the Bay Area, and (if it's clear) the Sierra Nevada. ■

Silverado Museum
- 1490 Library Ln., St. Helena
- 707/963-3757
- Closed Mon.

Culinary Institute of America
www.ciachef.edu/greystone
- 2555 Main St., St. Helena
- 707/967-1010

Bale Grist Mill State Historic Park
- 3369 St. Helena Hwy. North, St. Helena
- 707/942-4575
- Phone for hours
- $

Sharpsteen Museum
www.sharpsteen-museum.org
- 1311 Washington St., Calistoga
- 707/942-5911

Old Faithful Geyser of California
www.oldfaithfulgeyser.com
- 233 A4
- 1299 Tubbs Ln.
- 707/942-6463
- $$

Petrified Forest
www.petrifiedforest.org
- 233 A4
- 4100 Petrified Forest Rd.
- 707/942-6667
- $

Robert Louis Stevenson State Park
- 233 A5
- 707/942-4575

Napa & Sonoma Valley wines: a taster's guide

Wines of the Napa and Sonoma Valleys have achieved a worldwide reputation. Each part of the valley has its own distinctive wines, produced using a number of different varieties of grape.

Top of the line in red grapes is Cabernet Sauvignon. The wine has a full-bodied fruit flavor, but also the balance that comes from tannins.

Increasingly popular Merlot is a smooth, drinkable red wine with a rich fruit taste. Its ideal "finish"—a term for the palate sensation or aftertaste remaining after you swallow—is like velvet on your tongue.

The same grapes that the French grow in Burgundy go into California's Pinot Noir. Here it has a lighter color and body, as well as a fruitier flavor and aroma.

California's premier white wine, Chardonnay has a velvety texture and a flavor that suggests apples or pears. If the wine has been aged in

Guided tours and wine tastings are available at most vineyards and wineries.

oak barrels, it may gain a buttery flavor with traces of vanilla or cloves. Chardonnay has enough intensity to suit a fine meal, yet it can also go with a light lunch or picnic.

WINE TASTING MADE EASY

There is no reason to be intimidated by a bottle of wine—especially when you can unlock its secrets very easily. Use your senses.

Sight

You can learn a lot about a wine from visual clues. A wine buff holds the glass by the stem, with the base flat on the table, and swirls the wine. Why? When the wine runs down the sides of the glass, it shows its "legs," a term referring to stripes or columns of liquid. A wine with "good legs" is thicker and has more substance than wine that slides down the glass in sheets (an indication that it is thin and lacks interest for the oenophile).

Each wine variety has an ideal color. Chardonnay should be a rich gold; if pale, it probably tastes weak or watery. The staff at a winery tasting room can tell you the ideal color for each variety.

Smell

Another reason for swirling the wine is to mix it with air, which volatilizes the alcohol and releases chemical compounds you can smell. The human nose can detect thousands of different odors in wine. As for wine terms: "Aroma" is the smell of the grape itself; "Bouquet" refers to the fragrances created during winemaking (the yeast used in fermentation, the type of oak used for barrel aging, and so forth). The sum of all the aromas in a wine is called its "nose."

Before you drink a bottle of wine, don't forget to sniff the cork: if the wine has turned sour, this is an early warning system.

Taste

Human taste buds detect just four flavors: sweet (front of tongue), sour (edges), salty (middle), and bitter (back). To taste sweetness, draw a sip of wine up the middle of your tongue. Wine tastes sweet at a level of 0.7 percent residual sugar; below that, "dry" (which means free of sugar, not to be confused with astringent or tart). Roll another sip around the edges of your tongue and notice the acid, which gives a wine tartness and life; a wine without acid components is called "flabby." If the wine has an agreeable proportion of acidity, sugar, and other elements, it is said to have "balance."

To serve a bottle of wine properly, uncork it a while before serving it. This airing gets rid of chemical vapors and also adds oxygen to mellow the flavors and allow them to meld.

Feel

Warm a sip of wine in your mouth for a moment, then judge its weight, or "body"—how thick or thin it feels. Some wines have a lush feel that tasters try to capture with words like "velvet." In red wines, especially, you'll detect the dry, puckery feeling of tannins, which are natural preservatives produced by the skins of grapes. The term "big" is used for a wine that fulfills the senses.

No two people have the same proportion of taste buds, so no wine tastes the same to everyone. If you like it, nothing else matters. ■

Map of the Napa and Sonoma valleys wine region, showing wineries and landmarks including Calistoga, St. Helena, Yountville, Napa, and Sonoma.

Sonoma Valley

THE BIRTHPLACE OF THE CALIFORNIA WINE INDUSTRY and a producer of world-class vintages, Sonoma Valley (approximately 10 miles west of Napa Valley across the Mayacamas Mountains) remains a more easygoing, down-home place than trendy Napa Valley. Farmers grow everything from vine-ripe tomatoes to Christmas trees.

The town of **Sonoma** dates from 1823, when padres founded a mission here. After Mexico secularized the California missions in 1834, Gen. Mariano Vallejo surveyed the adjacent plaza as part of his charge to establish a pueblo and distribute lands. Sonoma wine growing dates from the 1825 planting of Franciscan mission grapes. Large-scale winemaking began in 1857 when Hungarian nobleman Agoston Haraszthy brought cuttings of Old World grapes to his Sonoma vineyard.

Sonoma Valley
◭ 233 B1-B2
Sonoma Valley Visitors Bureau
www.sonomavalley.com
✉ 453 First St. East
☎ 707/996-1090

Sonoma State Historic Park
◭ 233 B1
☎ 707/938-1519
$ $ includes all sites

SONOMA STATE HISTORIC PARK
Sonoma Plaza is the largest Hispanic square in California, and forms part of the Sonoma State Historic Park. In the plaza's northeast corner a bronze figure holds a flag to commemorate a ragtag group of Americans who staged the Bear Flag Revolt in June 1846. Thirty horsemen rode into Sonoma, took Mexico's General Vallejo prisoner, and without firing a shot declared California an independent republic. Their muslin flag

had a red star and stripe (made from a petticoat), a crudely drawn grizzly bear, and the hand-scrawled words "California Republic." The new republic lasted just 25 days, until U.S. forces stormed the Mexican capital at Monterey and claimed California. In Sonoma the Stars and Stripes took the place of the Bear Flag. The bear lives on, however, on the flag of California.

Mission San Francisco Solano (*corner of Spain & 1st Sts., at NE corner of the plaza*) was the last link in California's chain of 21 Franciscan religious outposts. It lay at the northern end of El Camino Real, the "king's highway" that connected the missions. Uniquely, the Sonoma mission was built under the rule not of Spain but of Mexico (to which Spain had ceded California in 1822), whose government wanted to fend off Russian incursions from Fort Ross, 40 miles away. Today the padres' quarters, adjoining the adobe chapel, is the oldest building in Sonoma (1825). In the 1880s the mission fell on hard times and was sold; over the years it became a hay barn, winery, and blacksmith shop. Restoration began in 1903.

Across First Street East is the 1841 **Sonoma Barracks,** which housed Mexican and then American soldiers. Inside it now you'll see a history museum, a re-created bunkroom, and a film about Mexican General Vallejo. Next door stands the wood-frame **Toscano Hotel,** a former-boarding house. Nearby, at 133 Spain Street East, the adobe **Blue Wing Inn** was built in 1840. Into its saloon swaggered such Western characters as Kit Carson and bandit Joaquin Murietta.

Half a mile from the Plaza, via Spain Street West, is General Vallejo's house, **Lachryma Montis** (*Spain St. W. at 3rd St. W.*), which reveals how the Mexican commandante adapted to American rule. Moving out of his adobe house on the plaza, in 1851 he built this New England-style house, with a pitched roof and carved ornamental eaves. The storehouse where Vallejo kept wine and olives is now a museum.

HISTORIC WINERIES

Sebastiani Vineyards incorporates some of the mission vineyard. Founded in 1904, this is one of California's oldest family wineries; it displays a huge collection of hand-carved wine casks, some dating from the mid-1800s.

In 1857 Count Agoston Haraszthy began premium wine production at what is now the **Buena Vista Winery.** Tastings are held in the stone Press House, built in 1862 and thought to be California's oldest winery building.

VALLEY OF THE MOON

Ten minutes north of Sonoma is **Glen Ellen,** where the **Jack London State Historic Park** celebrates the author of *The Call of the Wild* and many other books. Jack London moved to the 835-acre Beauty Ranch when he became "tired of cities and people." Having been an author, sailor, prospector, socialist agitator, railroad hobo, and adventurer, London took to farming here on the ranch. Today you can picnic or walk among oaks, madrones, and redwoods. Visit the **House of Happy Walls** (built by London's widow in 1919) to see his mementoes, South Pacific artifacts, typewriter, and (every writer's nemesis) publishers' rejection slips. The Londons had earlier built **Wolf House,** which burned in a mysterious fire before they moved in. Its evocative stone walls still stand. London wrote about Glen Ellen in his 1913 novel, *The Valley of the Moon.* ■

Sebastiani Vineyards

🅰 233 B1

✉ 389 4th St. East, Sonoma

☎ 707/938-5532

Buena Vista Winery

✉ 18000 Old Winery Rd., Sonoma

☎ 707/252-7117

Jack London State Historic Park

✉ 2400 London Ranch Rd., Glen Ellen

☎ 707/938-5216

Ⓢ $

Yosemite National Park

Yosemite National Park

www.nps.gov/yose

Visitor information

✉ Headquarters, Yosemite National Park

☎ 209/372-0200 (24-hour updates on weather & trail conditions); 800/436-7275 (campground reservations)

$ $

ONE OF EARTH'S NATURAL CATHEDRALS, YOSEMITE enshrines a trinity of wonders: Yosemite Valley, groves of sequoias, and the High Sierra. In this park of nearly 1,200 square miles, you can see waterfalls, climb granite peaks, camp under the stars, picnic in wildflower meadows, or just stand awestruck before the scenery.

YOSEMITE VALLEY

A mighty granite fortress, Yosemite Valley is edged with cliffs, pinnacles, and rounded domes. Seven miles long, it was glacially sculpted; you can tell by its "U" shape. (River canyons are "V" shaped.)

Unyielding against the forces that eroded the surrounding terrain, granite **El Capitan** stands as one of the world's largest exposed monoliths.

Rising 3,245 feet from its base, it is the tallest unbroken cliff on the planet. Look for climbers high on the face.

Curry Village provides food, accommodations, and camping. Trails from here lead to 317-foot **Vernal Fall** and 594-foot **Nevada Fall;** both cascades appear to have jumped right off postcards. **Mirror Lake** shows a silvery reflection of surrounding cliffs, a sight popular with photographers.

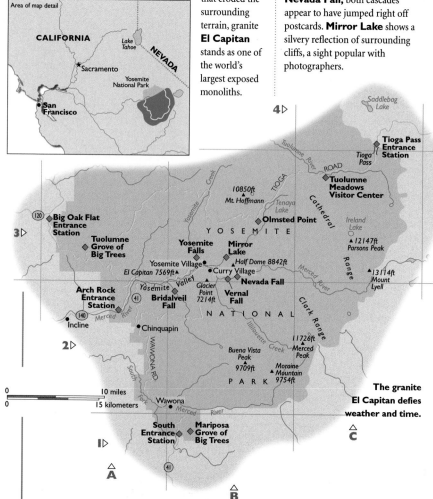

The granite El Capitan defies weather and time.

**Mariposa Grove
of Big Trees**

🅼 236 B1

🕐 Closed mid-
Sept–mid-May

Tram from visitor
center

💲 $ (for tram)

(Shoot pictures on a windless morning or moonlit evening. The lake has water in spring and early summer.)

Above the lake rises legendary **Half Dome.** Originally a complete dome, its sheer cliff face was cracked away by Ice-Age glaciers. The summit seems to touch the sky, 4,748 feet above the valley floor.

Yosemite Village encompasses park headquarters, restaurants, shops, and the **Valley Visitor Center,** with exhibits on natural and human history. Pick up a map while you are here.

A lodge whose architecture is a match for the majestic landscape is the 1927 **Ahwahnee Hotel** (see p. 259). For its grand but rustic design, architect Gilbert Stanley Underwood called for ten million pounds of native granite, plus "redwood" timbers (actually stained concrete). The interior is decorated with designs from Indian baskets, stylized with a touch of art deco. The dining room, with log pillars 40 feet high, has floor-to-ceiling windows overlooking Yosemite Valley.

Take the free tram from the visitor center to one of the world's highest waterfalls. **Yosemite Falls** drops 2,425 feet in three stages. (The Lower Fall alone, at 320 feet, is twice as high as Niagara.) In spring and early summer the falls roar with snowmelt; by August they're often dry, as if someone turned off the tap.

Want to stroll through a tree trunk? Visit the **Tuolumne Grove of Big Trees** (at the western end of Tioga Road), a walking route among giant sequoias, ponderosa pines, and incense cedars.

WAWONA ROAD

Take Wawona Road south out of the valley. You'll see **Bridalveil Fall,** which drops 620 feet from a "hanging valley," a canyon that was

stranded high above the Yosemite Valley floor when glaciers ground away the lower section. Turn up Glacier Point Road to sublime **Glacier Point,** which presents a view unparalleled in the world. Peaks seem to levitate beyond an empty chasm. You can see Half Dome and three waterfalls (Vernal, Nevada, Yosemite). Yosemite Valley lies far below you, at the bottom of a 3,200-foot cliff. Imagine the days when the "Firefall" was staged nightly for visitors below in Curry Village. A bonfire was pushed over the edge, creating a cascade of sparks and streaming fire.

Historic cabins, an 1875 covered bridge, an old jail—all are part of the **Pioneer Yosemite History Center** (in Wawona, to the south of the park on Wawona Road), which portrays valley life in the 19th century. In the **Mariposa Grove of Big Trees**, some of the trees have been alive for nearly 3,000 years. These aptly named giant sequoias—some weighing more than two million pounds— are the world's largest living things. Yosemite's biggest tree, with a 96-foot circumference, is the **Grizzly Giant,** ragged with age after 2,700 years. The 209-foot tree stands so high above the forest that it was hit by lightning six times during a single storm. You can visit by tram from the visitor center, or on foot.

TIOGA ROAD

Tioga Road leads eastward across the high country. Stop at **Olmsted Point,** where a trail leads to a lookout over Half Dome and Tenaya Lake. In **Tuolumne Meadows** (8,575 feet) the Tuolumne River winds through summer wildflowers. There is a **visitor center** and trailheads leading to the Pacific Crest and John Muir trails. The road crosses 9,945-foot Tioga Pass before leaving the park. ■

Lake Tahoe

SUSPENDED BETWEEN THE PEAKS OF THE SIERRA NEVADA and the Carson Range at 6,225 feet above sea level, Lake Tahoe straddles two states, California and Nevada. As the lake deepens from the shore to a maximum of 1,645 feet, its hue changes from aquamarine to rich lapis lazuli.

South Lake Tahoe Visitors Authority
www.bluelaketahoe.com
1156 Ski Run Blvd.
530/544-5050 or 800/288-2463

North Lake Tahoe Resort Association
www.mytahoevacation.com
380 N. Lake Blvd., Tahoe City
530/583-3494 or 888/434-1262

U.S. Forest Service Visitor Center
239 B2
Calif. 89, near Fallen Leaf Rd.
530/543-2674
Closed Nov.–May

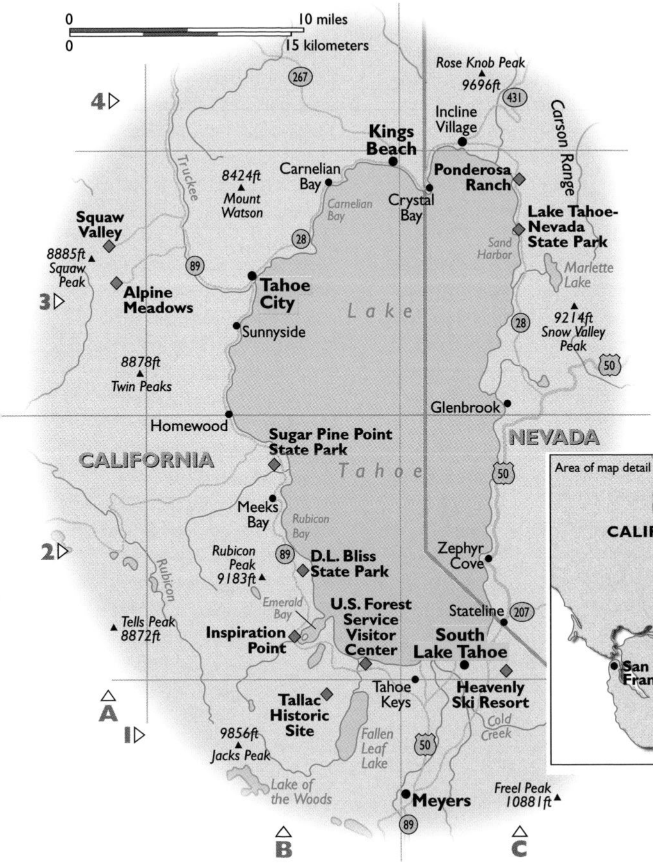

0 10 miles
0 15 kilometers
Rose Knob Peak 9696ft
Incline Village
Kings Beach
Carson Range
Carnelian Bay
Ponderosa Ranch
Crystal Bay
8424ft Mount Watson
Truckee
Carnelian Bay
Squaw Valley
Lake Tahoe-Nevada State Park
Sand Harbor
8885ft Squaw Peak
Marlette Lake
Alpine Meadows
Tahoe City
Lake Tahoe
9214ft Snow Valley Peak
Sunnyside
8878ft Twin Peaks
Glenbrook
Homewood
NEVADA
Sugar Pine Point State Park
CALIFORNIA
Meeks Bay
Rubicon Bay
Rubicon Peak 9183ft
D.L. Bliss State Park
Zephyr Cove
Rubicon
Emerald Bay
U.S. Forest Service Visitor Center
Stateline
Tells Peak 8872ft
Inspiration Point
South Lake Tahoe
Tahoe Keys
Heavenly Ski Resort
Tallac Historic Site
Cold Creek
9856ft Jacks Peak
Fallen Leaf Lake
Lake of the Woods
Meyers
Freel Peak 10881ft
A B C
1 2 3 4

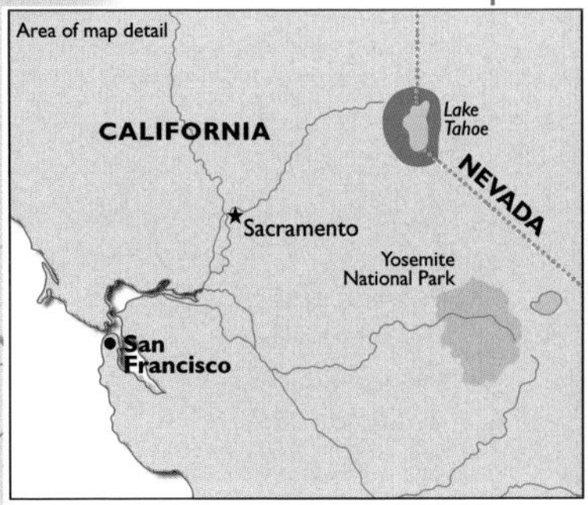

Area of map detail
CALIFORNIA
Lake Tahoe
NEVADA
Sacramento
Yosemite National Park
San Francisco

Lake Tahoe has recreation and mountain scenery written large on every page of its calendar. In the summer hiking and mountain biking are popular in the hills around the lake, as is boating on the water. Winter means skiing. After an energetic day, relax in casinos on the Nevada side, which offer gambling and big-name entertainers.

THINGS TO SEE & DO

South Lake Tahoe is the lake's largest community. The gondola at **Heavenly Mountain Resort** offers a view of the lake—called the "fairest picture the whole earth affords" by Mark Twain—as you ride 2,000 feet up Monument Peak.

Going clockwise around Lake Tahoe from there:

Heavenly Mountain Resort Gondola
239 C2
US 50 just W of Stateline
775/586-7000
$$$$

Tallac Historic Site
☎ 530/541-5227
🕐 Closed Sept.–mid-June
💲 $ to $$ (for tours)

Vikingsholm Mansion
☎ 530/525-7277
🕐 Closed Labor Day–Memorial Day
💲 $

D.L. Bliss State Park
🅰 239 B2
☎ 530/525-7277
💲 $$

Sugar Pine Point State Park
🅰 239 B2
☎ 530/525-7982
🕐 Closed mid-Sept.
💲 $$

Ehrman Mansion
☎ 530/525-7982
🕐 Closed Labor Day–Mem. Day
💲 $

Gatekeeper's Museum & Marion Steinbach Indian Basket Museum
✉ 130 W. Lake Blvd., Tahoe City
☎ 530/583-1762
🕐 Closed Oct.–May. Tours by appt. April–Sept.
💲 $

Watson Cabin Museum
✉ 560 N. Lake Blvd., Tahoe City
☎ 530/583-8717
🕐 Closed Labor Day–mid-June

At the **U.S. Forest Service Visitor Center** you can see below the surface of Taylor Creek without getting wet: The windows of a "stream profile chamber" reveal salmon, trout, and other creek denizens acting naturally.

The **Tallac Historic Site** preserves rustic mansions built by wealthy San Franciscans. The oldest is the shingled **Pope Estate** (1894), which still has its coffered ceilings and paneling.

The log **Baldwin Estate** (1921) evokes the rustic elegance of an early summer retreat; there are exhibits on Washoe Indian culture and local history.

Emerald Bay is the most photographed spot at Lake Tahoe; try shooting from **Inspiration Point** along Calif. 89. Lora Josephine Knight's **Vikingsholm mansion** stands here, at the head of a bay that appropriately resembles a fjord. The 1929 Scandinavian-style castle has 38 rooms and a sod roof where wildflowers bloom. (Note: Visiting requires a 1-mile walk each way.) In the green water you'll see the lake's only island, Fanette, with an unusual stone teahouse also built by the heiress.

D.L. Bliss State Park has a good beach at Rubicon Bay, an early

1900s lighthouse (the nation's highest, at 6,235 feet), and the 130-ton Balancing Rock. Lumber magnate Bliss once cornered three-quarters of Tahoe's lakefront property.

Sugar Pine Point State Park shelters around 2,000 acres of its namesake trees, as well as incense cedars and other species. Indian fighter Gen. William Phipps built the 1872 Phipps Cabin, and a San Francisco financier erected the stone-and-wood **Ehrman Mansion** in 1902. You can join a tour of the interior (oak paneling, stone fireplace, 1930s furnishings); the lakeside lawn makes a nice picnic spot.

In **Tahoe City** the lake has its sole outlet, the Truckee River. See it from **Fanny Bridge,** so called for the rear view of gawkers leaning over the rail. Tahoe City is a gateway to ski areas at **Alpine Meadows** and **Squaw Valley** (site of the 1960 winter Olympics). Pioneer relics and guess what else are displayed at the **Gatekeeper's Museum & Marion Steinbach Indian Basket Museum**. Washoe Indians often came to use the grinding stone in front of today's **Watson Cabin Museum,** the oldest building in town (1909). ■

Amazing Lake Tahoe

- The nation's largest alpine lake, Tahoe measures 22 miles long by 12 miles wide and holds 39 trillion gallons of water. If you tipped out the contents, the water would flood an area the size of California to a depth of 14 inches.
- More than 60 streams flow into Lake Tahoe, but only one flows out, the Truckee River. Tahoe loses much of its water to evaporation: If the water that evaporates every day could be recovered, it could supply the daily requirements of a city the size of Los Angeles.
- Reputedly, the lake's water is 99.7 percent pure, about the same as distilled water. It is so clear that a dinner plate would be visible 75 feet below the surface. The lake's legendary clarity is threatened, however, by sediments washed in as land is cleared for development. ■

Travelwise

Lombard Street at dusk

TRAVELWISE INFORMATION

PLANNING YOUR TRIP

The city's major source for information, maps, and brochures is the San Francisco Convention & Visitors Bureau (Lower Level, Hallidie Plaza, 900 Market St., tel 415/391-2000; recorded daily events and activities, tel 415/391-2001). The bureau's web site (see below) offers information for visitors, plus a hotel booking service. Ask for "The San Francisco Book," which is mailed free upon request through the web site (below) or by phone; it takes four to six weeks to arrive, but you can request delivery within ten days for $6.10. *San Francisco Magazine* regularly publishes dining-guide and "Best Of San Francisco" issues; order by phone with a credit card (Tel 415/398-2800).

USEFUL WEB SITES

San Francisco Convention & Visitors Bureau:
www.sfvisitor.org
CitySearch:
www.citysearch7.com
San Francisco Magazine:
www.sanfran.com
San Francisco Chronicle:
www.sfgate.com

WHEN TO GO/CLIMATE

The weather in San Francisco is temperate year-round, generally ranging from 70°F (21°C) down to 40°F (5°C). But the weather isn't exactly predictable. The weather can sometimes change its mind several times during the course of a day, as fog rolls over the city or burns off under the sunshine. Some summer days top 80°F, yet summer is the foggiest season. Most rain falls from November through March. To prepare for quirky weather: Layer your outfits with a sweater and jacket, leave shorts and summer garb at home. (You should also bring good walking shoes for the hills.)

Most tourists descend on San Francisco in July and August. If they include you, reserve hotel rooms well ahead, and be prepared to stand in line at tourist spots and cable car stops. In other seasons be a contrarian: Explore the city on weekends (when business travelers leave...and hotel rates often drop); visit vacation areas such as Carmel and Napa Valley during the week (when they're less crowded with urban escapees).

MAIN EVENTS

FEBRUARY
Chinese New Year (Tel 415/982-3000) The date of Chinese New Year varies, and may fall in late January. Venture into Chinatown to see events such as a parade with firecrackers, a block-long dancing dragon, and the Miss Chinatown USA Pageant.

MARCH
St. Patrick's Day Parade Parade down Market Street, celebrating the patron saint of Ireland.

APRIL
San Francisco International Film Festival (Tel 415/561-5000; www.sffs.org) Various venues. Films and videos from many countries.
Cherry Blossom Festival (Japan Center, Civic Center, tel 415/563-2313) Parade, performances, food, crafts, martial arts.

MAY
Carnaval San Francisco (Tel 415/920-0125; www.carnavalsf .com) A two-day Latin American-style festival of dance and music, with a grand parade held in the Mission District.
Cinco de Mayo (Mission District, tel 415/826-1401) A 48-hour celebration of the Mexican victory at Puebla, complete with a parade, displays of traditional Mexican arts and crafts, food, and music.

Bay to Breakers Race (Tel 415/359-2800; www.bayto breakers.com) About 80,000 entrants race and/or show off wacky costumes during this 12K race, which starts in the Financial District and passes through Golden Gate Park on its way to Ocean Beach.

JUNE
Union Street Arts Festival (Union Street from Gough to Steiner, tel 800/310-6563) Arts and crafts, food, live music.
Dipsea Race (Tel 415/331-3550; www.dipsea.org) A 7.1-mile run from Mill Valley to Stinson Beach, via Muir Woods and around Mount Tamalpais.
North Beach Festival (Tel 415/989-2220) Music, food, and sidewalk chalk art in the North Beach area.
Lesbian, Gay, Bisexual, Transgender Pride Celebration (Tel 415/864-3733; www.sfpride.org) March through the Castro District down Market Street to the Civic Center Plaza, with numerous events (including a popular film festival at the Castro Theater).
Juneteenth Festival (Fillmore Street and Kimball Park, tel 415/931-2729) African-American cultural observance that includes a parade and a film festival.

JULY
Cable Car Bell-Ringing Championship They really do compete! Held in Union Square.
San Francisco Marathon (Tel 415/284-9653) Entrants run, jog, or stagger along the 26.1-mile route through the city. Sometimes early August.

SEPTEMBER
Shakespeare in the Park (Tel 415/422-2222; www.sfshakes.org) May start in late August. All performances are held in Golden Gate Park.
San Francisco Blues Festival (Tel 415/979-5588; www.sfblues .com) An open-air celebration of blues music held at Fort Mason and Justin Herman Plaza.
San Francisco Opera

opening night (War Memorial Opera House, tel 415/864-3330; www.sfopera.com) Gala with formal ball.

OCTOBER
Castro Street Fair (Tel 415/841-1824) Based around Castro Street and Market Street.
San Francisco Jazz Festival (Tel 415/398-5655; www.sfjazz.org) Various venues. Continues into November; also spring concerts March–June.
Italian Heritage Parade and Festival (Tel 415/703-9888) Held on Columbus Day. Parade, Blessing of the Fleet, and street stalls based around Fisherman's Wharf and North Beach.
Halloween (www.halloweensf .com) A major gay event, with far-out costumes, based around the Castro District.

NOVEMBER
Day of the Dead (Tel 415/826-8009) A Mexican festival, with a parade and other events based in the Mission District.

HOW TO GET TO SAN FRANCISCO

FROM THE AIRPORT
Served by 50 major airlines, San Francisco International Airport (Tel 650/821-8211; www.flysfo .com) lies 14 miles south of the city off US 101 (Bayshore Fwy.). For information on ground transportation (shared shuttles, buses, taxis, limousines), phone 415/817-1717. BART (Bay Area Rapid Transit, tel 415/989-2278; www.bart.gov) operates rail service to San Francisco until midnight; the station is on Level 3 of the International Terminal and is accessible from any terminal by riding the free AirTrain shuttle to the Garage G/BART Station stop. SFO Airporter buses (Tel 650/624-0500) run between the airport and downtown (5 a.m. to 11 p.m.). Taxis to San Francisco cost about $45 and can be shared.

In the East Bay, 17 miles from the city, smaller Oakland

International Airport (Tel 510/563-3300) has connections to San Francisco by BART, shuttle, and taxi (about $50–$60).

BY RAIL
Amtrak (Tel 800/872-7245; www .amtrak.com) has trains arriving and departing at the Oakland station, located at 245 Second St. in Jack London Square.

GETTING AROUND

BY PUBLIC TRANSPORTATION

For transportation information, dial toll-free from the Bay Area: 511; toll-free from elsewhere: 888/500-INFO; local toll: 415/ 817-1717. Web site: www.transitinfo.org

Muni The San Francisco Municipal Railway, aka Muni (Tel 415/673-6864; www.sfmuni.com) operates buses, streetcars, and cable cars. Route information is published in the *Yellow Pages*; route maps are available for $2 at newsstands and other outlets. Buses have the widest network and greatest convenience. Their numbers and destinations appear on the front; bus stops are indicated by signs and street markings. Muni Metro streetcars run underground through downtown and on surface streets beyond; there are six lines, of which the F-Market operates colorful historic streetcars on Market Street, from Castro Street to the Embarcadero and Fisherman's Wharf.

Cable cars (indicated by CC in text) follow three routes: The Powell-Hyde and Powell-Mason lines begin at Powell and Market Streets near Union Square; the former ends at Victorian Park near the Maritime Museum, the latter near Fisherman's Wharf at Bay and Taylor Streets. The California Street line follows California Street from Market Street through Chinatown to Van Ness Avenue. Tips: Board

along the route rather than waiting with a crowd at either terminus. For thrills, the Powell-Hyde line descends the steepest slope (on Hyde Street between Chestnut Street and Bay Street).

Muni fares are $1.25 for buses and streetcars (35¢ for seniors or children); free transfers are valid for two changes. Cable cars cost $2 for a one-way ticket. A Muni Passport costs $9 for one day, $15 for three days, $20 for seven days.

Around the city Bay Area Rapid Transit, or BART (Tel 415/989-2278; www.bart.gov), is a modern rail line with eight San Francisco stations linked to 29 East Bay stations. Maximum fares are $1.30 within the city and $5 to the East Bay.

Taxis Taxi fares run $2.85 for the first mile and $2 for each additional mile. The standard tip is 15 percent. Ask your hotel or restaurant to call you a cab. If calling yourself, you could try Yellow Cab (Tel 415/626-2345), Veteran's Cab (Tel 415/552-1300), or Luxor Cab (Tel 415/282-4141).

Ferries These operate to many points around the bay. The Blue & Gold Fleet (Pier 41 and Ferry Building, tel 415/705-5555; www.blueandgoldfleet.com) runs to Oakland's Jack London Square, Angel Island, Sausalito, Tiburon, and Vallejo (call for details). Golden Gate Ferry (Behind the Ferry Building, tel 415/923-2000; www.goldengate ferry.org) goes to Sausalito and Larkspur.

Out of town Golden Gate Transit (First and Mission Streets, tel 415/923-2000; www.golden gate.org) operates buses across the Golden Gate Bridge to Marin and Sonoma Counties. Caltrain (Fourth Street at King Street, tel 800/660-4287 or tel 415/817-1717; www.caltrain .com) runs trains between San Francisco and San Jose.

WALKING TOURS

For free walking tours contact the San Francisco Public Library's City Guides (Schedule: tel 415/557-4266, or www.sfcityguides.org).

DRIVING

Two words: Forget it.
If you ignore this advice, though, remember these tips: Give the right of way to pedestrians and cable cars. On hills, curb your wheels: Facing uphill, turn your tires toward the street; facing downhill, turn tires toward the curb. This precaution prevents a runaway vehicle (and also avoids a parking ticket).

Curb colors indicate parking regulations: Red (no stopping or parking), Green (10-minute limit), Yellow (commercial loading zone; parking permitted after 6 p.m.), White (passenger loading zone only), Blue (handicapped with permit), Towaway Zone (parking here will cost a ticket plus towing and storage fees).

Parking garages are situated near major tourist sites: Fisherman's Wharf (665 Beach St. near Hyde Street), Union Square (333 Post St., Mason Street at Ellis Street, 123 O'Farrell St.), Embarcadero Center (250 Clay St.), SoMa (833 Mission St.), Chinatown (433 Kearny St., 733 Kearny St.), and North Beach (735 Vallejo St.). Warning: Plan ahead, as public garages are expensive and will usually fill up early in the day.

All the major car rental companies operate in San Francisco, with offices in the city and at airports. Obtain phone numbers by dialing 800/555-1212 (toll-free directory), or look in the *Yellow Pages.*

The 49-Mile Drive winds through the city, touching on a combination of scenic and historical highlights. A succession of blue-and-white seagull signs guide you along the route.

PRACTICAL ADVICE

SAFETY

Although San Francisco is a relatively safe city, you should be cautious in—and avoid at night—the Tenderloin (an area near Union Square bounded roughly by Larkin Street, Mason Street, O'Farrell Street, and Market Street), the Western Addition (west of the Civic Center and south of Japantown), and the Mission District (east of Valencia Street and north of 16th Street). It is wise to avoid walking through any area that is isolated or badly lit at night.
Apply the usual rules of urban common sense:
• Do not give your bags to anyone in an airport or train/bus station other than authorized personnel, or your taxi driver while loading the trunk.
• Be alert to your surroundings, especially in crowds.
• Don't carry or flash large amounts of money. Keep your wallet in your front pocket, hold your purse securely with the clasp facing in, or use a concealed money belt.
• Do not use ATMs when there is no one around.
• If you are robbed, hand over your wallet and whatever else is requested without resistance, and call 911.
• Don't leave valuables in your car. If you do leave possessions there, ensure that they are stored out of sight. In case of mishap, contact the Crime Victims Hot Line at 800/842-8467.

EARTHQUAKE
Not likely. But if you feel a tremor, step into a doorway or crouch under a table, and stay away from windows. If outdoors, move away from buildings, trees, and electrical power lines.

TRAVELERS WITH DISABILITIES

For general city information, the San Francisco Convention &

Visitors Bureau maintains a TDD/TTY (textphone) line at 415/392-0328. The Independent Living Resource Center can be contacted at either 415/543-6222 or TTY 415/543-6698.

Muni operates more than 30 bus and streetcar lines accessible to disabled travelers (Tel 415/673-6864). For details of accessible bus and ferry services to Marin County, ask for Golden Gate Transit's "Welcome Aboard" handbook (Tel 415/923-2000, TDD 415/257-4554). Parking zones for people with disabilities are marked with signs and blue curbs. By law, public buildings must be at least partially accessible and provide toilets for visitors with disabilities. There are lowered curbs at most street corners.

EMERGENCIES & HEALTH CARE

• For police, medical, or fire emergencies, dial 911 (free call).
• Around-the-clock emergency rooms are available at the St. Francis Memorial Hospital (900 Hyde St., tel 415/353-6300), the Medical Center at the University of California, San Francisco (505 Parnassus St., tel 415/476-1037), and San Francisco General Hospital (1001 Potrero Ave., tel 415/206-8111).
• Other medical care available to travelers includes walk-in clinics such as The Physician Access Center (26 California St., tel 415/397-2881). The multilingual Traveler Medical Group (490 Post St., tel 415/981-1102) makes house calls to hotels.
• The San Francisco Dental Society has a referral service (Tel 415/421-1435).
• Pharmacies: Walgreen operates 24-hour pharmacies at 3201 Divisadero St. (Tel 415/ 931-6417) and 498 Castro St. (Tel 415/861-3136). The Four-Fifty Sutter Pharmacy (Tel 415/ 392-4137) and St. Francis Medical Center Pharmacy (Tel 415/776-4650) will deliver prescriptions to your hotel.

HOTELS & RESTAURANTS

Choose a lavish Nob Hill institution or a fashionable new boutique hotel near Union Square, a reasonably priced motel along Lombard Street or a neighborhood Victorian bed-and-breakfast. Your hotel won't be far from the city's attractions. An easy way to book a room (especially at busy times) is through San Francisco Reservations: tel 510/628-4450 or 800/677-1570; www.hotelres.com. Rooms can also be reserved through the San Francisco Convention & Visitors Bureau; 888/782-9673; www.sfvisitor.org.

Dining is a major attraction. (San Francisco is regularly named Favorite American City for Dining Out by the readers of *Bon Appetit* magazine.) More than 3,300 restaurants offer California cuisine (created in the Bay Area), French gastronomy, grills, humble burgers and tacos, and wonderful dishes from Italy, the Pacific Rim, Latin America, and other regions whose people immigrated to the city. You could eat at a different place every day for nearly ten years.

PRICES

HOTELS
An indication of the cost of a double room without breakfast is given by $ signs.

$$$$$	Over $300
$$$$	$200–$300
$$$	$150–$200
$$	$100–$150
$	Under $100

RESTAURANTS
An indication of the cost of a three-course dinner without drinks is given by $ signs.

$$$$	Over $50
$$$	$35–$50
$$	$15–$35
$	Under $15

USING THIS LIST

Hotels and restaurants are organized by neighborhood, then alphabetical order according to their price category. Restaurant closing days are included, but try to verify by phone; reservations are recommended. Most hotels, and some restaurants, have parking; check details with individual establishments. Ask hotels and restaurants about the extent of facilities for disabled guests, as these vary. Most hotels have both smoking and non-smoking rooms.

At upscale restaurants, lunch will cost at least 25 percent less than dinner, and some offer a prix-fixe menu. All restaurants in San Francisco are non-smoking.

FINANCIAL DISTRICT

HOTELS

🏨 MANDARIN ORIENTAL
$$$$$
222 SANSOME ST., 94104
TEL 415/276-9888
FAX 415/433-0289
www.mandarinoriental.com
Set in a dramatic location with great views of the city, this luxurious hotel consists of two towers linked by a glass skybridge. It occupies 11 floors of the city's third tallest building. Facilities include in-room faxes and top-flight service.
🛏 158 🅿 Valet 🔁 🔇
🛡 🅰 All major cards

🏨 PALACE
🍴 $$$$$
2 NEW MONTGOMERY ST., 94105
TEL 415/512-1111
FAX 415/543-0671
www.sfpalace.com
This grand old hostelry, dating from 1909, houses the famous Garden Court restaurant (with an art-glass ceiling and marble columns), and has an elegant bar with a must-see Maxfield Parrish mural. There is a skylighted swimming pool; large rooms have antiques.
🛏 552 🅿 Valet 🔁 🔇
🔇 🛡 🅰 All major cards

🏨 HYATT REGENCY
$$$$
5 EMBARCADERO CENTER, 94111
TEL 415/788-1234
FAX 415/398-2567
www.hyatt.com
This hotel is famous for its 17-story atrium lobby and glass-pod elevators. Floors are arranged in open tiers; many rooms have waterfront views, although the décor is rather businesslike. It is situated at the end of the California Street cable car line.
🛏 805 🅿 Valet 🔁 🔇
🛡 🅰 All major cards

🏨 OMNI
$$$–$$$$
500 CALIFORNIA ST., 94104
TEL 415/677-9494
FAX 415/273-3038
www.omnihotels.com

Located on the California cable car line two blocks from Chinatown, this "mini-Ritz" of a hotel, which occupies a 1926 building, exudes quiet luxury (330-thread count Egyptian cotton sheets) and modern business amenities (high-speed Internet, personalized voicemail).
🛏 362 🅿 Valet 🔁 🔇
🛡 🅰 All major cards

RESTAURANTS

🍴 AQUA
$$$$
252 CALIFORNIA ST.
TEL 415/956-9662
Celebrated, creative seafood. The signature dish is grilled tuna topped with foie gras in pinot noir sauce. A tasting menu and dessert sampler are available.
🍴 180 🅿 Valet 🔇
🔵 Closed L Sat.–Sun.
🅰 All major cards

🍴 ONE MARKET RESTAURANT
$$$$
1 MARKET ST.
TEL 415/777-5577
Farm-fresh seasonal American food served in a huge dining room. Recommended: Caesar salad,

oyster soup, mahi mahi with almond crumb topping and lemon sauce.

🔲 220 🕐 Closed Sat. L, all Sun. 🅿 All major cards

🍴 RUBICON
$$$$
558 SACRAMENTO ST.
TEL 415/434-4100
www.sfrubicon.com
Backed by Francis Ford Coppola and Robin Williams, this brick-and-wood restaurant offers à la carte and fixed-price menus (e.g., crispy skatewing with turnips, soybeans, cashews, and wine-ginger butter) and a stellar wine list.

🔲 100 🅿 Valet 🕐 L Wed. only; closed Sun. D 🅿 All major cards

🍴 TOMMY TOY'S CUISINE CHINOISE
$$$$
655 MONTGOMERY ST.
TEL 415/397-4888
A magnet for diners who enjoy elegant service, Chinese objets d'art, and a prix-fixe menu that blends French and Chinese approaches. Specialties include seafood bisque served in a coconut topped with puff pastry.

🔲 168 🅿 Valet 🕐 Closed Sat. & Sun. L 🅿 All major cards

🍴 THE WATERFRONT RESTAURANT
$$$$
PIER 7, THE EMBARCADERO
TEL 415/391-2696
www.waterfrontsf.com
Contemporary restaurant with views of the Bay Bridge (from windows and patio) and menu emphasizing classic seafood, as well as steaks, chops, wood-oven-roasted chicken, and pasta dishes.

🔲 160 🅿 Valet 🅿 All major cards

🍴 KOKKARI
$$$
200 JACKSON ST.
TEL 415/981-0983
www.kokkari.com

With the ambience of a country inn on the Aegean (fireplace, woodwork, flowers), Kokkari showcases seafood and meats. Notable: moussaka, grilled lamb chops with lemon-oregano vinaigrette.

🔲 185 🅿 Valet 🕐 Closed Sat. L, all Sun. 🅿 All major cards

🍴 PIPERADE
$$$
1015 BATTERY ST.
TEL 415/391-2555
www.piperade.com
Basque food by chef Gerald Hirigoyen is served in simple surroundings. A table set aside for communal dining adds interest. Typical dishes: seafood and shellfish stew in red pepper sauce; braised veal sweetbreads with Madeira.

🔲 60 🕐 Closed Sat. L, all Sun. 🅿 All major cards

🍴 PLOUF
$$$
40 BELDEN PL.
TEL 415/986-6491
Specializing in mussels with intriguing sauces, as well as clams and oysters, this casual spot (indoor/outdoor dining) also serves great starters, such as bacon-wrapped scallops.

🔲 65 🕐 Closed Sat. L, all Sun. 🅿 All major cards

🍴 TADICH GRILL
$$$
240 CALIFORNIA ST.
TEL 415/391-1849
This San Francisco institution is the city's longest continuously operating restaurant (since 1849). Good seafood includes sole, sand dabs, Hangtown fry, and their famous tartar sauce.

🔲 120 🕐 Closed Sun. 🅿 MC, V

🍴 YANK SING
$$$
101 SPEAR ST.
TEL 415/957-9300
49 STEVENSON ST.
TEL 415/541-4949
www.yanksing.com

Two words: dim sum. The helpful staff at both locations will explain the items on the trolleys; watch for Peking duck with scallions and plum sauce, lettuce cups with minced squab, and grilled avocado stuffed with curried chicken.

🔲 Spear St. 248, Stevenson St. 92 🕐 Closed D 🅿 MC, V

UNION SQUARE & NOB HILL

HOTELS

🏨 CAMPTON PLACE
$$$$$
340 STOCKTON ST., 94108
TEL 415/781-5555
FAX 415/955-5536
www.camptonplace.com
An intimate luxury hotel with intriguing architecture, personal service, stylishly furnished rooms, fine amenities (terry robes, French soaps), and a celebrated restaurant (see p. 250).

ℹ 110 🅿 Valet 🅿 All major cards

🏨 HUNTINGTON HOTEL
$$$$$
1075 CALIFORNIA ST., 94108
TEL 415/474-5400
FAX 415/474-6227
www.huntingtonhotel.com
Understated elegance and impeccable personal service combine with an easygoing and friendly atmosphere. Rooms have views of Nob Hill and antique furnishings. Room service from the celebrated Big Four restaurant (see p. 250). The hotel's Nob Hill spa has well-appointed treatment rooms and an indoor infinity pool.

ℹ 135 🅿 Valet 🔲 🔲 🔲 🔲 🅿 All major cards

🏨 PAN PACIFIC
$$$$$
500 POST ST., 94102
TEL 415/771-8600
FAX 415/398-0267
www.panpacific.com

A dramatic, sleek hotel whose lobby has a towering atrium and glass elevators. Elegant rooms contain marble baths. A personal valet and pillow-fluffing service are available.
(i) 329 **P** 🅑 ⬆ 🔟
🅑 All major cards

RITZ-CARLTON
$$$$$
600 STOCKTON ST., 94108
TEL 415/296-7465
FAX 415/291-0288
www.ritzcarlton.com/hotels/san_francisco
The dazzling lobby is a prelude to the grand, renovated 1909 neoclassical building. Elegant rooms and service (twice-daily maid, 24-hour multilingual concierge) are provided. Tea in the Lobby Lounge.
(i) 336 **P** Valet 🅑 🔟
🅑 All major cards

STANFORD COURT
$$$$$
905 CALIFORNIA ST., 94108
TEL 415/989-3500
FAX 415/391-0513
www.renaissancehotels.com/sfosc
Tucked away on a Nob Hill slope, the courtyard entrance and stained-glass dome in the lobby combine to create a discreet atmosphere. There are towel warmers and televisions in the bathrooms, morning newspaper and coffee at your door. The highly rated Fournou's Ovens restaurant is on the premises.
(i) 393 **P** Valet ⬆ 🅑
🔟 🅑 All major cards

THE FAIRMONT
$$$$–$$$$$
950 MASON ST., 94108
TEL 415/772-5000
FAX 415/772-5013
www.fairmont.com
A classic 1907 Nob Hill hotel that recalls old San Francisco. The lobby is opulent, with a gilt coffered ceiling, and marble columns. Tower rooms have the best views, but less charm.
(i) 600 **P** Valet ⬆ 🅑
🔟 🅑 All major cards

MARK HOPKINS INTER-CONTINENTAL
$$$$–$$$$$
1 NOB HILL, 94108
TEL 415/392-3434
FAX 415/421-3302
www.markhopkins.net
A Nob Hill landmark. Large rooms have dark furniture and marble baths. The famous art deco "Top of the Mark" cocktail bar has a panoramic view over the city.
(i) 380 **P** Valet 🅑 ⬆
🔟 🅑 All major cards

CLIFT
$$$$
495 GEARY, 94102
TEL 415/775-4700
FAX 415/441-4621
www.ianschragerhotels.com
This classic hotel has been given new owner Ian Schrager's standard trendy makeover, including deluxe room amenities (400-thread-count sheets, Philippe Starck bath fixtures). There are "digital paintings" in the 1933 Redwood Room cocktail lounge, whose interior was fashioned from a single tree.
(i) 374 **P** Valet ⬆ 🅑
🔟 🅑 All major cards

MONACO
$$$$
501 GEARY ST., 94102
TEL 415/292-0100
FAX 415/292-0111
www.monaco-sf.com
This 1910 landmark beaux arts building houses a hotel reflecting the 1930s. The registration desk resembles a classic steamer trunk, and the lobby has a two-story French inglenook fireplace. Guest rooms have beds with partial canopies, Chinese armoires, and bamboo writing desks.
(i) 201 **P** Valet 🅑 🔟
🅑 All major cards

PRESCOTT
$$$$
545 POST ST., 94102
TEL 415/563-0303
FAX 415/563-6831
www.prescotthotel.com

An intimate hotel with impeccable service. Ralph Lauren room décor and cherry furniture. Club Level guests enjoy complimentary cocktails and hors d'oeuvres from Wolfgang Puck's adjoining restaurant, Postrio (see p. 251), which also offers meals through room service.
(i) 164 **P** Valet 🅑 🅑
🔟 🅑 All major cards

WESTIN ST. FRANCIS
$$$$ (Tower $$$$$)
335 POWELL ST., 94102
TEL 415/397-7000
FAX 415/774-0124
www.westin.com
A 1904 grande dame on Union Square. The main building has charming guest rooms. Tower rooms have better views, but less charm. U.S. Presidents and royalty have sipped drinks at the Compass Rose bar.
(i) 1,192 **P** Valet 🅑 🅑
🔟 🅑 All major cards

CHANCELLOR HOTEL
$$$
433 POWELL ST., 94102
TEL 415/362-2004
FAX 415/362-1403
www.chancellorhotel.com
A good value hotel situated on the Powell cable car line. Modestly decorated, yet features some nice touches.
(i) 137 **P** Valet 🅑 🔟
🅑 All major cards

HOTEL DIVA
$$$
440 GEARY ST., 94102
TEL 415/885-0200
FAX 415/885-8842
www.hoteldiva.com
Futuristic Italian design. Beds have steel headboards, and high-tech gear in the rooms includes data ports and VCRs.
(i) 111 **P** Valet 🅑 🔟
🅑 All major cards

DONATELLO
$$$
501 POST ST., 94102
TEL 415/441-7100
FAX 415/885-8844

🅑 Air-conditioning 🅒 Closed 🅑Indoor/🅑Outdoor swimming pool 🔟 Health club 🅑 Credit cards **KEY**

HOTELS & RESTAURANTS

Large rooms with high ceilings. Some have terraces with flowers, others fine views. All have marble sinks and elegant amenities.
ⓘ 94 🔳 🚗 All major cards

🏨 GALLERIA PARK
$$$
191 SUTTER ST., 94104
TEL 415/781-3060
FAX 415/433-4409
www.galleriapark.com
European-style boutique hotel in a 1911 landmark building. The lobby has art nouveau touches. Rooms are decorated in deep hues with cream-striped walls. Rooftop park, complete with jogging track.
ⓘ 177 🅿 Valet 🔄 🚗 AE, MC, V

🏨 HANDLERY UNION SQUARE
$$$
351 GEARY ST., 94102
TEL 415/781-7800
FAX 415/781-0269
www.handlery.com
This is a boutique hotel decorated in neutrals. The newer Club section has fancier rooms, many overlooking the swimming pool and offering extra amenities.
ⓘ 377 🔄 🚗 All major cards

🏨 HOTEL TRITON
$$$
342 GRANT AVE., 94108
TEL 415/394-0500
FAX 415/394-0555
www.hoteltriton.com
This designers' playground includes features such as a lobby with whimsical pastel swirls on the walls, inverted sculpturesque columns, and contemporary furniture. Rooms are postmodern, with interestingly painted walls, CD players, Nintendo games. Special "EcoRooms" have environmentally friendly features. Frequented by an energetic, artsy crowd.
ⓘ 140 🅿 Valet 🔄 🚗
🔳 🚗 All major cards

🏨 NOB HILL LAMBOURNE
$$$
725 PINE ST., 94108
TEL 415/433-2287
FAX 415/433-0975
www.nobhillambourne.com
European style with American convenience and a "wellness" theme: Asian massage room, organic mini-bars, healthful continental breakfast, vitamins at turn-down.
ⓘ 20 🅿 Valet 🔄 🚗
🚗 All major cards

🏨 SAN FRANCISCO HILTON & TOWERS
$$$
333 O'FARRELL ST., 94102
TEL 415/771-1400
FAX 415/771-6807
www.hilton.com/hotels/SFOFHHH
Despite staffing a huge hotel filled with conventioneers and big-city bustle, employees remain remarkably personable. Tower rooms have large windows and (especially in Tower 1) stunning city views.
ⓘ 1,895 🅿 Valet 🔄 🚗
🔄 🔳 🚗 All major cards

🏨 SERRANO
$$$
405 TAYLOR ST., 94102
TEL 415/885-2500
FAX 415/474-4879
www.serranohotel.com
Although decorated with bright colors and a touch of exotica (striped draperies, Moroccan elements), this 1920s hotel retains its original Spanish Colonial style.
ⓘ 236 🅿 Valet 🔄 🚗
🚗 All major cards

🏨 VILLA FLORENCE
$$$
225 POWELL ST., 94102
TEL 415/397-7700
FAX 415/397-1006
www.villaflorence.com
Public areas are Italian-themed, while guest rooms are enlivened with warm colors and stripes. Situated on the Powell Street cable car line, it adjoins the popular Kuleto's Italian Restaurant,

which operates a lobby café.
ⓘ 183 🚗 All major cards

🏨 VINTAGE COURT
$$$
650 BUSH ST., 94108
TEL 415/392-4666
FAX 415/433-4065
www.vintagecourt.com
Themed around the Wine Country, this hotel serves complimentary evening wine beside the fireplace. Next door is the renowned Masa's restaurant (see p. 251), for which guests have the edge on reservations.
ⓘ 107 🅿 Valet 🔄 🚗
🚗 All major cards

🏨 WARWICK REGIS
$$$
490 GEARY ST., 94102
TEL 415/928-7900
FAX 415/441-8788
www.warwicksf.com
A pleasant boutique hotel with high beds with canopies, antiques, fireplaces, and touches of France.
ⓘ 80 🅿 Valet 🚗 🚗 All major cards

🏨 WHITE SWAN INN
$$$
845 BUSH ST., 94108
TEL 415/775-1755
FAX 415/775-5717
www.jdvhospitality.com
Emulating a London luxury hotel with dark wood paneling, floral carpets, a library, and afternoon tea. Bedrooms have comfy four-poster beds and fireplaces. Breakfasts are homemade.
ⓘ 26 🚗 All major cards

🏨 ANDREWS
$$
624 POST ST., 94109
TEL 415/563-6877
FAX 415/928-6919
www.andrewshotel.com
This 1905 building boasts a cage elevator. Small rooms feature peach pastel walls, floral curtains, and down comforters, creating a European-inn feeling. Good value; rate includes continental

breakfast at your door.
ⓘ 48 ⬍ 🅢 All major cards

🏨 CARLTON
$$
1075 SUTTER ST., 94109
TEL 415/673-0242
FAX 415/673-4904
www.carltonhotel.com
Decorated like an early San
Francisco estate: hand-painted
Moroccan tables, beaded
table lamps, ceiling fans,
wooden window blinds. Many
rooms have views; connecting
rooms available for families.
ⓘ 163 🅢 🅢 All major
cards

🏨 THE CARTWRIGHT
$$
524 SUTTER ST., 94102
TEL 415/421-2865
FAX 415/398-6345
www.cartwrighthotel.com
A boutique hotel with smallish
rooms containing antiques,
decorated with floral chintz.
ⓘ 114 🅢 🅢 All major
cards

🏨 COMMODORE
INTERNATIONAL
$$
825 SUTTER ST., 94109
TEL 415/923-6800
FAX 415/923-6804
www.thecommodorehotel.com
Artsy, funky, very hip hotel; the
lobby décor is a cartoonish
evocation of a cruise ship.
ⓘ 113 🅣 🅢 All major
cards

🏨 HOTEL COSMO
$$
761 POST ST., 94109
TEL 415/673-6040
FAX 415/563-6739
www.hotel-cosmo.com
This boutique property
describes itself as an "arts
hotel." The lobby has
whimsical geometric chairs
and a multihued glass-tile
reception desk; other public
areas feature art exhibits.
Rooms on higher floors have
city views.
ⓘ 144 🅿 Valet ⬍ 🅢 All
major cards

🏨 INN AT UNION
SQUARE
$$
440 POST ST., 94102
TEL 415/397-3510
FAX 415/989-0529
www.unionsquare.com
A stylish small inn. Thoughtful
touches include breakfast
rooms with fireplaces on
each floor, complimentary
umbrellas, around-the-clock
concierge service, and
down pillows. Room décor
varies from Georgian to
contemporary. No smoking.
ⓘ 30 🅿 🅣 🅢 All major
cards

🏨 JULIANA
$$
590 BUSH ST., 94108
TEL 415/392-2540
FAX 415/391-8447
www.julianahotel.com
A boutique hotel with friendly
staff, stylish lobby, and guest
rooms with striped walls and
appealing colors. Evenings,
wine is served by the fireplace.
ⓘ 107 🅢 🅣 🅢 All
major cards

🏨 KENSINGTON PARK
$$
450 POST ST., 94102
TEL 415/788-6400
FAX 415/399-9484
www.kensingtonparkhotel.com
This stylish boutique hotel
has spacious rooms and
marble-and-brass baths. The
lobby is shared with the
Theater on the Square, and
the hotel adjoins the hot,
upscale Farallon restaurant
(see p. 250).
ⓘ 88 🅿 Valet ⬍ 🅢 All
major cards

🏨 MAXWELL
$$
386 GEARY ST., 94102
TEL 415/986-2000
FAX 415/397-2447
www.maxwellhotel.com
A stylish Theater District
hotel with rooms decorated
in art deco Victoriana.
ⓘ 153 🅢 🅢 All major
cards

🏨 MONTICELLO INN
$$
127 ELLIS ST., 94102
TEL 415/392-8800
FAX 415/398-2650
www.monticelloinn.com
Federal-period lobby,
fireplaces, library, and rooms
decorated in florals.
ⓘ 91 🅿 Valet 🅢 🅢 All
major cards

🏨 NOB HILL INN
$$
1000 PINE ST., 94109
TEL 415/673-6080
FAX 415/673-6098
www.nobhillinn.com
An old-fashioned bed and
breakfast with Victorian
furnishings—and although the
inn is filled with antiques and
paintings, it offers bargain
rates on several smaller
rooms; other rooms cost
slightly more.
ⓘ 21 🅢 All major cards

🏨 PETITE AUBERGE
$$
863 BUSH ST., 94108
TEL 415/928-6000
FAX 415/673-7214
www.jdvhospitality.com
Intimate French country-style
inn, with a full breakfast
served in the garden room.
Many of the guest rooms
have fireplaces.
ⓘ 26 🅿 Valet ⬍ 🅣
🅢 All major cards

🏨 HOTEL REX
$$
562 SUTTER ST., 94102
TEL 415/433-4434
FAX 415/433-3695
www.thehotelrex.com
Fashioned after Manhattan's
Algonquin Hotel, this hotel
celebrates writers with old
books, leather chairs, and
writing desks. Rooms have
works by local artisans and
comfy pillow-top mattresses.
ⓘ 94 ⬍ 🅢 All major
cards

🏨 SAVOY
$$
580 GEARY BLVD., 94102

TEL 415/441-2700
FAX 415/441-0124
wwwthesavoyhotel.com
Designed like a small French country hotel, with featherbeds. Located in the Theater District.
[i] 83 [P] [elevator] [S] [S] All major cards

HOTEL UNION SQUARE
$$
114 POWELL ST., 94102
TEL 415/397-3000
FAX 415/399-1874
www.hotelunionsquare.com
The city's first boutique hotel, built for the 1915 Panama-Pacific Exposition, has been given a bold contemporary look. Rooftop penthouses have private view decks.
[i] 131 [P] [S] [S] All major cards

YORK HOTEL
$$
940 SUTTER ST., 94109
TEL 415/885-6800
FAX 415/885-2115
www.yorkhotel.com
Today it's a European-style boutique hotel. Earlier it was a speakeasy with subterranean passageways for San Francisco socialites. Alfred Hitchcock filmed scenes for *Vertigo* here.
[i] 96 [P] Valet [TV] [S] All major cards

ADELAIDE HOSTEL
$
5 ISADORA DUNCAN COURT (OFF TAYLOR ST.), 94102
TEL 415/359-1915
FAX 415/276-2366
www.adelaidehostel.com
In a quiet location on a cul-de-sac, this hotel is popular with Europeans, backpackers, and budget travelers; private rooms and dorm rooms, all with shared baths.
[i] 18 [S] AE, MC, V

CORNELL HOTEL DE FRANCE
$
715 BUSH ST., 94108
TEL 415/421-3154

FAX 415/399-1442
www.cornellhotel.com
A 1910 brick building decorated in French Provençal style. Breakfast included. The weekly package deal is a real bargain, including seven breakfasts and five dinners. No smoking.
[i] 60 [S] All major cards

GOLDEN GATE
$
775 BUSH ST., 94108
TEL 415/392-3702
FAX 415/392-6202
www.goldengatehotel.com
A friendly, cozy, turn-of-the-century hotel with wicker furniture; 14 rooms have private bathrooms. Continental breakfast.
[i] 25 [S] All major cards

HALCYON
$
649 JONES ST., 94120
TEL 415/929-8033
FAX 415/441-8033
www.halcyonsf.com
Highly rated by bargain travelers, this recently renovated hotel features private baths, microwaves, and refrigerators. Weekly package rates available.
[i] 25 [S] AE, MC, V

SAN FRANCISCO RESIDENCE CLUB
$
851 CALIFORNIA ST., 94108
TEL 415/421-2220
FAX 415/421-2335
www.sfresclub.com
A European-style, family-owned pension on Nob Hill with daily, weekly, or monthly rates. Shared or private baths available; some rooms have bay views. Homestyle meals are included. Sunny garden.
[i] 83 [S] No credit cards

RESTAURANTS

BIG FOUR
$$$$
1075 CALIFORNIA ST.
TEL 415/771-1140
www.huntingtonhotel.com

Situated in the Huntington Hotel, its dark wood, vintage railroad memorabilia and a clubby atmosphere set the scene for splendid American contemporary cuisine. Among the city's finest restaurants.
[seats] 60 [clock] Closed Sat. & Sun. L [S] All major cards

CAMPTON PLACE RESTAURANT
$$$$
340 STOCKTON
TEL 415/955-5555
www.camptonplace.com
In an elegant dining room decorated in warm earth tones, you'll find exciting French-influenced dishes such as Maine lobster with sweetbread cannelloni and asparagus à la Maltaise.
[seats] 70 [P] Valet [elevator] [clock] Closed Sun. L [S] All major cards

FARALLON
$$$$
450 POST ST.
TEL 415/956-6969
www.farallonrestaurant.com
Known for Pat Kuleto's undersea fantasy decor (jellyfish-shaped lamps, glowing columns of kelp), the restaurant serves coastal cuisine, roasted meats, and

[Hotel] Hotel   [Restaurant] Restaurant   [i] No. of guest rooms   [seats] No. of seats   [P] Parking   [elevator] Elevator

excellent desserts.
🔼 225 🅿 Valet ❄
🕐 Closed Sun. L ❄ All
major cards

🍴 FLEUR DE LYS
$$$$
777 SUTTER ST.
TEL 415/673-7779
www.fleurdelyssf.com
Highly regarded favorite for
French cuisine served in
equally rich surroundings.
Tasting and vegetarian meals
available.
🔼 80 🅿 Valet ❄
🕐 Closed L & all Sun.
❄ All major cards

🍴 MASA'S
$$$$
648 BUSH ST.
TEL 415/989-7154
Masa's presents a modern
spin on elevated French food,
using seasonal ingredients.
Stylishly minimalist décor.
🔼 120 🅿 Valet ❄
🕐 Closed L, all Sun. & Mon.,
also first 2 weeks of January
& week of 4th of July ❄ All
major cards

🍴 MILLENNIUM
$$$$
580 GEARY ST.
TEL 415/345-3900
www.millenniumrestaurant.com
Organic, gourmet vegan food.
Sample menu: Moroccan
spice-roasted portobello
mushrooms, chick pea-arugala
salad, apple-turmeric chutney.
🔼 150 🅿 Valet 🕐 Closed
L ❄ All major cards

🍴 POSTRIO
$$$$
545 POST ST.
TEL 415/776-7825
www.postrio.com
Dine on contemporary
American cuisine. Everything
is made on the premises,
from pasta to smoked salmon.
🔼 180 🅿 Valet ❄ ❄ All
major cards

🍴 LE COLONIAL
$$$
20 COSMO PL.

TEL 415/931-3600
www.lecolonialsf.com
French-Vietnamese food is
served in a 1920s atmosphere
of overhead fans and palm
fronds. Dishes range from
scallop-ginger potstickers to
pomegranate-glazed Peking
duck. The upstairs lounge,
with its outdoor veranda, is a
hot spot for cocktails and
appetizers.
🔼 320 🅿 Valet 🕐 Closed
L ❄ All major cards

HOTELS

🏨 GRANT PLAZA
$
465 GRANT AVE., 94108
TEL 415/434-3883
FAX 415/434-3886
www.grantplaza.com
One of the city's best buys,
near the entrance to
Chinatown off Union Square.
Simply but pleasantly furnished
standard rooms.
🛏 72 ❄ All major cards

RESTAURANTS

🍴 GREAT EASTERN
$$
649 JACKSON ST.
TEL 415/986-2500
A busy place known for
bargain seafood fresh from
the tanks along the walls.
🔼 250 ❄ AE, MC, V

🍴 HOUSE OF NANKING
$$
919 KEARNY ST.
TEL 415/421-1429
Szechuan cuisine so good that
even the locals put up with
the uninspiring decor and
sometimes ungracious service.
🔼 45 ❄ MC, V

🍴 HENRY'S HUNAN
$
924 SANSOME ST.
TEL 415/956-7727
674 SACRAMENTO ST.
TEL 415/788-2234
Hunanese food is hot and
smoky. These are popular and
modestly priced restaurants.
🔼 30 🅿 ❄ AE, MC, V

🍴 LUCKY CREATION
$
854 WASHINGTON ST.
TEL 415/989-0818
This tiny Chinese vegan
restaurant serves some of the
city's best vegetarian food.
🔼 35 🕐 Closed Wed.
❄ MC, V

NORTH BEACH, TELEGRAPH HILL, & RUSSIAN HILL

HOTELS

🏨 HOTEL BOHÈME
$$$
444 COLUMBUS AVE., 94133
TEL 415/433-9111
FAX 415/362-6292
www.hotelboheme.com
Imbued with the spirit of
North Beach, Ginsberg poetry
and 1950s artwork is on
view. Quiet, modern comforts.
No smoking.
🛏 15 ❄ All major
cards

🏨 WASHINGTON SQUARE INN
$$$
1660 STOCKTON ST., 94133
TEL 415/981-4220
FAX 415/397-7242
www.washingtonsquareinnsf.com
A cozy inn with European
décor and most rooms
facing the park (some with
shared baths). Near
restaurants and shops.
Continental breakfast, full
afternoon tea.
🛏 15 🅿 ❄ All major
cards

RESTAURANTS

🍴 ENRICO'S SIDEWALK CAFÉ
$$$
504 BROADWAY
TEL 415/982-6223
www.enricossidewalkcafe.com
The patio is a perfect spot to
sample an eclectic mix of
Italian dishes, tapas, seafood,
and meats.
🔼 110 🅿 Valet ❄ AE, MC, V

HOTELS & RESTAURANTS

🍴 CAFÉ JACQUELINE
$$$
1454 GRANT AVE.
TEL 415/981-5565
A small place focused on fabulous soufflés (e.g., black truffle and lobster or salmon and asparagus).
🍽 24 🕐 Closed L & Mon.–Tues. 🅰 All major cards

🍴 MOOSE'S
$$$
1652 STOCKTON ST.
TEL 415/989-7800
www.mooses.com
A handsome hub overlooking Washington Square Park. Moose's serves Californian dishes using fresh ingredients.
🍽 100 🕐 Closed Sun.–Wed. L 🅰 All major cards

🍴 YABBIES COASTAL KITCHEN
$$$
2237 POLK ST.
TEL 415/474-4088
Yabbie is Australian for crayfish, a featured menu item. Raw bar and Pacific Rim seafood.
🍽 50 🅰 D, MC, V

🍴 CAFFE SPORT
$$
574 GREEN ST.
TEL 415/981-1251
Great rural Italian pasta and seafood served in a festive atmosphere.
🍽 45 🕐 Closed Sun.–Mon. 🅰 None

🍴 IL FORNAIO
$$
1265 BATTERY ST.
TEL 415/986-0100
A popular Italian *trattoria*. Weekend brunch.
🍽 280 🅿 Valet 🅰 All major cards

🍴 L'OSTERIA DEL FORNO
$$
519 COLUMBUS AVE.
TEL 415/982-1124
A tiny kitchen serves up delectably authentic northern Italian dishes. Note: cash only.
🍽 28 🅰 None

🍴 ROSE PISTOLA
$$
532 COLUMBUS AVE.
TEL 415/399-0499
Nationally lauded Genoese and Ligurian cooking. Great local fish, as well as popular cioppino, wood-fired pizzas, and spit-roasted pork.
🍽 135 🅿 Valet 🅰 All major cards

🍴 SUSHI GROOVE
$$
1916 HYDE ST.
TEL 415/440-1905
Lovely presentation of sushi, fish, and salads in an artistically designed, small dining room.
🍽 50 🕐 Closed L 🅰 AE, MC, V

🍴 TOMMASO'S
$$
1042 KEARNY ST.
TEL 415/398-9696
Tommaso's has been serving brick-oven thin-crust pizza since the 1930s.
🍽 60 🕐 Closed L & Mon. 🅰 All major cards

🍴 MARIO'S BOHEMIAN CIGAR STORE
$
566 COLUMBUS AVE.
TEL 415/362-0536
A comfy neighborhood spot famous for focaccia sandwiches and cappuccino.
🍽 65 🅰 MC, V

🍴 MO'S GOURMET BURGERS
$
1322 GRANT AVE.
TEL 415/788-3779
The burgers are among the city's best. Also steaks, chicken.
🍽 40 🅰 MC, V

FISHERMAN'S WHARF

HOTELS

🏨 ARGONAUT HOTEL
$$$$
495 JEFFERSON ST., 94109
TEL 415/563-0800

FAX 415/563-2800
www.argonauthotel.com
This striking new hotel retains the old brick walls and wood beams of the restored 1909 warehouse it occupies. A real retreat from the bustle of Fisherman's Wharf.
🛏 252 🅿 Valet 🔼 🛗

🏨 TUSCAN INN
🍴 $$$
425 NORTH POINT ST., 94133
TEL 415/561-1100
FAX 415/561-1199
www.tuscaninn.com
European ambience, with a fireplace lobby, where complimentary morning coffee and biscotti and evening wine are served. Rooms are small, but richly decorated. Food is available in the Italian trattoria.
🛏 221 🅿 Valet 🔼 🛗 🅰 All major cards

🏨 WHARF INN
$$
2601 MASON ST., 94133
TEL 415/673-7411
FAX 415/776-2181
www.wharfinn.com
This independently owned inn (motel-like but nicely updated) offers free parking, and it's quieter and more personal than the usual Fisherman's Wharf accommodations.
🛏 51 🅿 🅰 All major cards

🏨 SAN REMO
$
2237 MASON ST., 94133
TEL 415/776-8688
FAX 415/776-2811
www.sanremohotel.com
Built in 1906 for homeless earthquake victims, this hotel has pension-style rooms that retain old-fashioned touches. There are shared baths (except in the penthouse, which has great views and is booked well in advance), but think European and ultra-clean.
🛏 62 🅿 🅰 All major cards

RESTAURANTS

SOMETHING SPECIAL

🍴 RESTAURANT GARY DANKO

Chef/owner Gary Danko's contemporary California/ French food stars at what is often ranked the city's best restaurant. The fixed-price menu (you can choose within categories) offers such dishes as lemon-herb duck breast with duck hash and rubarb compote. The food, décor, and attentive service create a memorable dining experience.

$$$$
800 NORTH POINT ST.
TEL 415/749-2060
www.garydanko.com
🔲 65 🅿 Valet 🕸 All major cards

🍴 A. SABELLA'S

$$$
2766 TAYLOR ST., 3RD FL.
TEL 415/771-6775
www.asabellas.com
Well prepared local seafood, overlooking the wharf. Choose shellfish fresh from the tank.
🔲 150 🕸 All major cards

🍴 MCCORMICK & KULETO'S

$$$
900 NORTH POINT ST.,
GHIRARDELLI SQ.
TEL 415/929-1730
www.mccormickandkuletos.com
An ocean-themed interior, a bay view, and a menu with fish and shellfish. Budget tip: Try the Crab Cake Lounge, serving seafood at lower prices.
🔲 475 🕸 All major cards

MARINA DISTRICT

HOTELS

🏨 HOSTELLING INTERNATIONAL FISHERMAN'S WHARF

$
FORT MASON, BLDG. 240, 94123

TEL 415/771-7277
FAX 415/771-1468
www.norcalhostels.org
Occupying a renovated Civil War building, this hostel has separate dorm rooms for men and women, a kitchen, and a common area with fireplace, piano, and pool table.
🛏 dorm rooms with 162 beds; 4 private rooms
🕸 MC, V

🏨 MARINA INN

$
3110 OCTAVIA, 94123
TEL 415/928-1000
FAX 415/928-5909
www.marinainn.com
An affordable European-style hotel, with pine beds, floral wall coverings, and junior suites suitable for families. Includes continental breakfast and afternoon cookies.
🛏 40 🔁 🕸 All major cards

RESTAURANTS

🍴 GREENS

$$$
BLDG. A, FORT MASON CTR.
TEL 415/771-6222
Famed for its organic vegetarian gourmet food and fine wine list. The airy dining room has bay views. Sunday brunch.
🔲 130 🅿 🕐 Closed Sun. D & Mon. L 🕸 D, MC, V

🍴 CAFÉ MARIMBA

$$
2317 CHESTNUT ST.
TEL 415/776-1506
This café serves Mexican dishes, which include a particularly good mole (pronounced MO-lay) and seafood tacos.
🔲 85 🕸 AE, MC, V

PACIFIC HEIGHTS & JAPANTOWN

HOTELS

🏨 HOTEL DRISCO

$$$$
2901 PACIFIC AVE., 94115

TEL 415/346-2880
FAX 415/567-5537
www.hoteldrisco.com
Built in 1903 and offering broad bay views, this upscale hotel has had guests ranging from author Kathleen Norris to President Eisenhower. Caveat: No parking available.
🛏 48 🔁 🔳 🕸 All major cards

🏨 RADISSON MIYAKO

$$$$
1625 POST ST., 94115
TEL 415/922-3200
FAX 415/921-0417
www.miyakohotel.com
A serene and luxurious hotel, with a Japanese garden and koi pond off the lobby. Many rooms have deep Japanese soaking baths and futon beds. Western-style rooms are plentiful too.
🛏 218 🅿 Valet 🔁 🔲 🔳 🕸 All major cards

🏨 ARCHBISHOP'S MANSION

$$$
1000 FULTON ST., 94117
TEL 415/563-7872
FAX 415/885-3193
www.thearchbishopsmansion.com
This 1904 manse has a stained-glass skylight, crystal chandelier, huge canopy beds, French antiques, and big bathtubs. Situated across from the much photographed "Postcard Row" of Victorian houses at Alamo Square.
🛏 15 🔁 🕸 All major cards

🏨 LAUREL INN

$$$
444 PRESIDIO AVE., 94115
TEL 415/567-8467
FAX 415/928-1866
www.thelaurelinn.com
Spare and stylish. There's free covered parking, and some units have kitchenettes and views. Safe neighborhood at the edge of Pacific Heights. The hip/chic G Bar cocktail lounge is in the house.
🛏 49 🕸 All major cards

🏨 THE MAJESTIC
🍴 $$$
1500 SUTTER ST., 94109
TEL 415/441-1100
FAX 415/673-7331
www.thehotelmajestic.com
Guest rooms have antiques, four-poster beds, and marble bathrooms with clawfoot tubs. Many rooms have fireplaces. Situated away from the downtown bustle.
🛏 57 🅿 Valet ⬍ 🚭
🚭 All major cards

🏨 QUEEN ANNE HOTEL
$$$
1590 SUTTER, 94109
TEL 415/441-2828
FAX 415/775-5212
www.queenanne.com
This 1890 hostelry has an oak-and-cedar lobby, and some guest rooms have bay windows or fireplaces.
🛏 49 🅿 ⬔ 🍽 🚭 AE, MC, V

🏨 UNION STREET INN
$$$
2229 UNION ST., 94123
TEL 415/346-0424
FAX 415/992-8046
www.unionstreetinn.com
This airy bed-and-breakfast in a 1904 Edwardian building has antique furnishings and a scented garden; cozy carriage house. Full breakfast.
🛏 6 🚭 AE, MC, V

RESTAURANTS

🍴 CAFÉ KATI
$$$
1963 SUTTER ST.
TEL 415/775-7313
www.cafekati.com
East meets West with imaginatively presented fusion cuisine, in a frescoed setting. Art on the walls is for sale.
🔲 70 🅿 🕐 Closed L, all Mon. 🚭 AE, MC, V

🍴 ELITE CAFÉ
$$$
2049 FILLMORE ST.
TEL 415/346-8668
Louisiana Cajun and Creole cooking includes baby back ribs, rich gumbo, and "Oysters in Hell" in a blackened crumb coating.
🔲 85 🕐 Closed L 🚭 All major cards

🍴 MERENDA
$$$
1809 UNION ST.
TEL 415/346-7373
There's a romantic air to this trattoria, which serves fixed-price dinners that might include such dishes as potato gnocchi in squab ragout.
🔲 42 🕐 Closed Sun.–Thurs. L 🚭 AE, MC, V

🍴 PLUMPJACK
$$$
3127 FILLMORE ST.
TEL 415/563-4755
A hot spot in Cow Hollow, it serves American/California cuisine—crab cakes, halibut with mashed potatoes—and popular devil's food cake.
🔲 55 🅿 Valet 🕐 Closed Sat.–Sun. L 🚭 All major cards

🍴 CLEMENTINE
$$–$$$
126 CLEMENT ST.
TEL 415/387-0408
Exquisite seasonal French cuisine. Entrees include honey-roasted quail with four spices and porcini mushroom raviolis. Incredible desserts. Located just beyond Pacific Heights toward the Richmond District.
🔲 49 🕐 Closed L, all Mon. 🚭 AE, MC, V

🍴 CASSIS BISTRO
$$
2120 GREENWICH ST.
TEL 415/292-0770
A low-cost French bistro in a neighborhood setting.
🔲 45 🕐 Closed L, Sun.–Mon. 🚭 None

🍴 CHEZ NOUS
$$
1911 FILLMORE ST.
TEL 415/441-8044
Small plates (tapa style) of Italian, Greek, Spanish, and French food served in a packed dining room.
🔲 42 🚭 MC, V

🍴 FLORIO
$$
1915 FILLMORE ST.
TEL 415/775-4300
www.floriosf.com
A warm neighborhood bistro where you can linger over comfort food, seafood, and dishes such as wild mushroom ravioli.
🔲 64 🕐 Closed L 🚭 AE, MC, V

🍴 ISOBUNE SUSHI
$$
1737 POST ST.
TEL 415/563-1030
Not the best sushi in town, but fun, because it passes by on little boats floating around a canal at the circular counter.
🔲 34 🅿 ⬍ 🚭 MC, V

🍴 LA MEDITERRANEE
$$
2210 FILLMORE ST.
TEL 415/921-2956
www.lamediterranee.net
Mediterranean food at value prices. Popular items include a sampler assortment of ten tapalike dishes and, for dessert, *datil amandra* (dates and nuts in warm phyllo dough).
🔲 45 🚭 AE, MC, V

PRICES

HOTELS
An indication of the cost of a double room without breakfast is given by $ signs.
$$$$$ Over $300
$$$$ $200–$300
$$$ $150–$200
$$ $100–$150
$ Under $100

RESTAURANTS
An indication of the cost of a three-course dinner without drinks is given by $ signs.
$$$$ Over $50
$$$ $35–$50
$$ $15–$35
$ Under $15

🏨 Hotel 🍴 Restaurant 🛏 No. of guest rooms 🔲 No. of seats 🅿 Parking ⬍ Elevator

PERRY'S
$$
1944 UNION ST.
TEL 415/922-9022
This was formerly one of the city's first "fern bars." Today it serves tasty grilled meats, bar food, and sandwiches.
🛏 235   ⬥ All major cards

SANPPO
$$
1702 POST ST.
TEL 415/346-3486
This small restaurant serves a well-prepared variety of Japanese standards and imaginative variations.
🛏 45   P   🅂   🕐 Closed Mon.   ⬥ MC, V

DOIDGE'S CAFÉ
$
2217 UNION ST.
TEL 415/921-2149
Breakfast and brunch. Nice standards such as pancakes, french toast, and omelettes.
🛏 43   🕐 Open breakfast & brunch only   ⬥ MC, V

MIFUNE
$
1737 POST ST.
TEL 415/922-0337
Inexpensive, popular, with delicious hot or cold noodles.
🛏 82   ⬥ All major cards

HAIGHT-ASHBURY & GOLDEN GATE PARK

HOTELS

VICTORIAN INN ON THE PARK
$$$
301 LYON ST., 94117
TEL 415/931-1830
FAX 415/931-1830
A Victorian house by the Panhandle of Golden Gate Park, some of whose rooms feature fireplaces and terraces.
🕐 12   ⬥ All major cards

RED VICTORIAN BED, BREAKFAST & ART
$$
1665 HAIGHT ST., 94117

TEL 415/864-1978
FAX 415/863-3293
www.redvic.com
Tie-dyed bed canopies and old rock posters recall the Haight's style in the sixties. Shared baths (except in six rooms). Family-style breakfast. No TVs. No smoking.
🕐 18   ⬥ AE, MC, V

STANYAN PARK
$$
750 STANYAN ST., 94117
TEL 415/751-1000
FAX 415/668-5454
www.stanyanpark.com
A restored Victorian. Many rooms have fireplaces, and some suites have kitchens, living rooms, and dining rooms. The area can be crowded at weekends. No smoking.
🕐 36   P   🔄   ⬥ All major cards

RESTAURANTS

EOS
$$$
901 COLE ST.
TEL 415/566-3063
www.eossf.com
California meets Asia in dishes such as curried freshwater shrimp and potato cakes or black soy sauce chicken in a clay pot.
🛏 125   🕐 Closed L   ⬥ All major cards

CHA CHA CHA
$$
1801 HAIGHT ST.
TEL 415/386-5758
The menu at this popular tapas bar changes daily, drawing on Caribbean, Cajun, and Mexican cuisines to create intriguingly spiced dishes such as Cuban roast pork and fish baked in banana leaves.
🛏 100   ⬥ All major cards

THEP PHANOM
$$
400 WALLER ST.
TEL 415/431-2526
Probably the best Thai cuisine in San Francisco.

🛏 49   🕐 Closed L   ⬥ All major cards

CIVIC CENTER & SOMA

HOTELS

FOUR SEASONS
$$$$$
757 MARKET ST., 94103
TEL 415/633-3000
FAX 415/633-3001
www.fourseasons.com
Large rooms with marble bathrooms, artwork, and business amenities. Guests can use a 100,000-square-foot fitness facility and spa.
🕐 277   P Valet   🔄   🅂   🏊   💪   ⬥ All major cards

W SAN FRANCISCO
$$$$$
181 THIRD ST., 94103
TEL 415/777-5300
FAX 415/817-7823
www.whotels.com
Hip style is everything here, but there's substance too (goose-down duvets, oversize work desks, high-speed Internet). Play board games in the sleek black-and-tan lobby.
🕐 423   P Valet   🔄   🅂   🏊   💪   ⬥ All major cards

HARBOR COURT
$$$$
165 STEUART ST., 94105
TEL 415/882-1300
FAX 415/882-1313
www.harborcourthotel.com
A 1907 building with a charming residential atmosphere. Rooms have canopied beds and many bay views. There is a business center, and a limousine service to the Financial District.
🕐 131   P   🔄   🅂   🏊   💪   ⬥ All major cards

HOTEL GRIFFON
$$$$
155 STEUART ST., 94105
TEL 415/495-2100
FAX 415/495-3522
www.hotelgriffon.com
Stylish, comfortable small hotel. The small rooms have

exposed brick walls and window seats; while many have bay or downtown views.

(i) 62 **P** ⊖ 🛎 📷 📺
🃏 All major cards

🏨 ARGENT HOTEL
$$$
50 3RD ST., 94103
TEL 415/974-6400
FAX 415/495-6152
www.argenthotel.com
An art deco lobby and guest rooms with expansive windows (great views from upper stories).

(i) 667 **P** Valet ⊖ 🛎
📺 🃏 All major cards

🏨 HOTEL MILANO
$$$
55 5TH ST., 94103
TEL 415/543-8555
FAX 415/543-5885
www.hotelmilanosf.com
Contemporary but calm Italian design. The health club includes a spa. Nintendo games are supplied in rooms.

(i) 108 📺 🃏 All major cards

🏨 INN AT THE OPERA
$$$
333 FULTON ST., 94102
TEL 415/863-8400
FAX 415/861-0821
www.innattheopera.com
Conveniently close to venues for opera, symphony, and ballet, with the inside track on some tickets. An elegant place, with refined artwork, antiques, and canopy beds.

(i) 46 **P** Valet ⊖ 🛎
🃏 All major cards

🏨 SAN FRANCISCO MARRIOTT
$$$
55 4TH ST., 94103
TEL 415/896-1600
FAX 415/486-8101
www.sfmarriott.com
Locally nicknamed the Jukebox for its glitzy Las Vegas design, the Marriott is well located for exploring SoMa. Many facilities.

(i) 1,500 **P** Valet 🛎 🚞
📺 🃏 All major cards

🏨 THE MOSSER
$
54 4TH ST., 94103
TEL 415/986-4400
FAX 415/495-7653
www.themosser.com
This family-run hotel dates from the 1915 Panama-Pacific International Exposition. Rooms aren't fancy but have appeal; those with private baths are more expensive. Weekly rates available. There's also a recording studio.

(i) 166 🃏 All major cards

🏨 PHOENIX HOTEL
$
601 EDDY ST., 94109
TEL 415/776-1380
FAX 415/885-3109
www.thephoenixhotel.com
This spoofed-up motel with tropical kitsch décor attracts rock musicians, and hip celebrities. Located in the unsavory Tenderloin district.

(i) 44 **P** 🛎 📷 🃏 All major cards

RESTAURANTS

🍴 BOULEVARD
$$$$
1 MISSION ST.
TEL 415/543-6084
www.boulevardrestaurant.com
New variations of traditional dishes. The menu changes frequently, and the wine list varies with it. Possible choices: Sonoma duck breast with applewood-bacon, lobster tart.

🍽 180 **P** Valet 🕐 Closed L Sat. & L Sun. 🃏 All major cards

🍴 FIFTH FLOOR RESTAURANT
$$$$
12 FOURTH ST. (HOTEL PALOMAR)
TEL 415/348-1555
French-inspired takes on meat and seafood in an elegant setting. Starters include seared sea scallops with sweet corn purée and crisp potato nuggets, while your entrée might be Argentinian filet mignon with Roquefort gratin. Extensive

wine list.

🍽 62 **P** Valet 🛎
🕐 Closed L, all Sun. 🃏 All major cards

🍴 JARDINIÈRE
$$$$
300 GROVE ST.
TEL 415/861-5555
www.jardiniere.com
The seasonal menu includes rich seafood chowders and imaginative treatments of meat and fish, with cheeses cellared on the premises. Pre-theater or concert quick menu. Interior designed by Pat Kuleto. Live music nightly.

🍽 155 **P** Valet 🛎
🕐 Closed L 🃏 All major cards

🍴 ABSINTHE
$$$
398 HAYES ST.
TEL 415/551-1590
Creative French bistro food with a California twist. Wide selection of oysters.

🍽 135 **P** Valet 🕐 Closed Mon. 🃏 All major cards

🍴 CALIFORNIA CULINARY ACADEMY
$$$
625 POLK ST.
TEL 415/216-4329
This leading school teaches European and global cooking, served in the elegantly vaulted Carême Room.

🍽 300 🕐 Closed Sat.–Mon.
🃏 AE, MC, V

🍴 FRINGALE
$$$
570 4TH ST.
TEL 415/543-0573
An unpretentious restaurant, serving delicious French bistro food with Basque-influenced seafood and sausages.

🍽 55 🕐 Closed Sat., Mon. L, all Sun. 🃏 AE, MC, V

🍴 HAWTHORNE LANE
$$$
22 HAWTHORNE ST.
TEL 415/777-9779
Former Postrio chefs' hot restaurant with arty ware-

🏨 Hotel 🍴 Restaurant **(i)** No. of guest rooms 🍽 No. of seats **P** Parking ⊖ Elevator

HOTELS & RESTAURANTS

house décor. An Asian slant on American-Mediterranean food (e.g., ginger seafood stew, maple-glazed quail). Don't forgo dessert.
⊞ 210 🅿 Valet ⊞ Closed Sat. & Sun. L ◈ All major cards

HAYES STREET GRILL
$$$
324 HAYES ST.
TEL 415/863-5545
www.hayesstreetgrill.com
This top seafood house serves fish grilled over charcoal and served with delectable sauces. It gets crowded before concerts at nearby Civic Center venues.
⊞ 120 ⊞ Closed L Sat. & Sun. ◈ All major cards

INDIGO
$$$
687 MCALLISTER ST.
TEL 415/673-9353
The California cuisine emphasizes seafood and local produce.
⊞ 120 ⊞ Closed L, all Mon. ◈ AE, MC, V

MOMO'S
$$$
760 SECOND ST.
TEL 415/227-8660
www.eatatmomos.com
This popular spot next to SBC Park serves new American food: maple-glazed chops, scallops with asparagus risotto. Dine indoors or on the deck.
⊞ 200 🅿 Valet ⊞ ◈ AE, MC, V

RESTAURANT LULU
$$$
816 FOLSOM ST.
TEL 415/495-5775
Californian-Mediterranean food, such as meats wood-roasted in brick oven. Serves a popular warm chocolate cake.
⊞ 270 ◈ All major cards

THE SLANTED DOOR
$$$
PERRY BLDG., MARKET ST. AT EMBARCADERO
TEL 415/861-8032
www.slanteddoor.com
Much praised modern Vietnamese cuisine that uses organic produce and other healthful ingredients.
⊞ 150 🅿 Valet ⊞ ◈ AE, MC, V

ZUNI CAFÉ
$$$
1658 MARKET ST.
TEL 415/552-2522
Features Judy Rodgers's much praised Mediterranean cooking: great Caesar salads, crispy *pommes frites*, and oysters.
⊞ 186 🅿 Valet ⊞ Closed Mon. ◈ AE, MC, V

CARTA
$$
1760 MARKET ST.
TEL 415/863-3516
A different world cuisine each month (India, Greece, Tuscany, Eastern Europe, etc.). Well-researched Sunday brunch.
⊞ 125 ⊞ Closed Sat. L ◈ All major cards

MISSION & CASTRO DISTRICTS

RESTAURANTS

FOREIGN CINEMA
$$$
2534 MISSION ST.
TEL 415/648-7600
www.foreigncinema.com
Foreign movies are shown on a wall outdoors as you dine on California/Mediterranean dishes. Inside seating also; weekend brunch.
⊞ 250 🅿 Valet ⊞ Closed Mon.–Fri. L, Mon. D ◈ All major cards

MECCA
$$$
2029 MARKET ST.
TEL 415/621-7000
www.sfmecca.com
Enjoy new American food (e.g., roasted rack of Colorado lamb, handmade fettucini). DJ and live music.
⊞ 150 🅿 Valet ⊞ Closed L ◈ All major cards

CHOW
$$
215 CHURCH ST.
TEL 415/552-2469
A packed spot for pasta, pizza, and roast chicken, sandwiches.
⊞ 74 ◈ MC, V

LUNA PARK
$$
694 VALENCIA ST.
TEL 415/553-8584
www.lunaparksf.com
Italian and French fare dominate at this reasonably priced Mission standby.
⊞ 49 ◈ AE, MC, V

SOUTH PARK CAFÉ
$$
108 SOUTH PARK ST.
TEL 415/495-7275
French café cooking that includes sautéed duck breast with spiced honey sauce and poached Bosc pear, and their own smoked king salmon.
⊞ 40 ⊞ Closed L, all Sun. ◈ All major cards

THIRSTY BEAR BREWING CO.
$$
661 HOWARD ST.
TEL 415/974-0905
www.thirstybear.com
Beers brewed on the premises and funky Spanish tapas draw a postwork crowd to this popular SoMa spot.
⊞ 300 ⊞ Closed Sun. L ◈ All major cards

TI COUZ
$$
3108 16TH ST.
TEL 415/252-7373
One word: crepes. More than two dozen fillings for entrees and dessert.
⊞ 100 ◈ MC, V

2223 RESTAURANT
$$
2223 MARKET ST.
TEL 415/431-0692
www.2223restaurant.com

Deft handling of seasonal food in styles ranging from American to Mediterranean to Caribbean—roast chicken with onion rings, seafood paella, crispy friend sweetbreads.
🍽 100 🕐 Closed L 💳 All major cards

🍽 UNIVERSAL CAFÉ
$$
2814 19TH ST.
TEL 415/821-4608
An unlikely industrial zone location for an airy, sunny place serving house-roasted coffees. Dishes include pizzas, or heartier fare.
🍽 40 🕐 Closed Tues.–Fri. L, all Mon. 💳 AE, MC, V

🍽 LA SANTANECA
$
3781 MISSION ST.
TEL 415/648-1034
Delicious Salvadoran-Mexican dishes, such as cheese-stuffed pupusas and chorizo soup.
🍽 44 💳 MC, V 🕐 Closed Mon.

EXCURSIONS

SAN JOSE

🍽 EMILE'S
$$$
545 SOUTH 2ND ST.
TEL 408/289-1960
An Old World standby specializing in refined versions of the classics such as osso buco and agnello rosmarino.
🍽 180 Ⓟ Valet 🔲
🕐 Closed L & Sun.–Mon.
💳 AE, MC, V

MONTEREY

🏨 SEVEN GABLES INN
$$$–$$$$
555 OCEAN VIEW BLVD., 93950
TEL 831/372-4341
An 1886 Victorian mansion and cottages converted to a bed-and-breakfast, with European antiques, gardens, and ocean views.
ⓘ 14 Ⓟ 💳 MC, V

🍽 MONTRIO
$$–$$$
414 CALLE PRINCIPAL
TEL 831/648-8880
www.montrio.com
An early 1900s firehouse is the setting for California bistro cuisine, with touches of France and Italy: crab cakes with remoulade, portabello with vegetable ragoût.
🍽 200 💳 All major cards

🍽 TARPY'S ROADHOUSE
$$
2999 MONTEREY-SALINAS HWY.
TEL 831/647-1444
www.tarpys.com
An atmospheric ivy-clad house serving "American" cooking such as roast rabbit and pecan-barbecued duck.
🍽 300 💳 All major cards

CARMEL

🏨 LA PLAYA HOTEL
$$$$
8TH AVE. & CAMINO REAL
TEL 831/624-6476
FAX 831/624-7966
www.laplayahotel.com
Beautiful gardens, great views, and plenty of charm.
ⓘ 75 rooms, 5 cottages Ⓟ
🔲 🔲 🏊 💳 All major cards

🍽 ANTON & MICHEL
$$$
MISSION & 7TH STS.
TEL 831/624-2406
One of the coast's top dining spots. Local vineyards featured on the wine list.
🍽 90 Ⓟ 💳 All major cards

🍽 MEDITERRANEAN MARKET
$
OCEAN & MISSION STS.
TEL 831/624-2022
A deli with great picnic fare.
Ⓟ 💳 AE, MC, V

BERKELEY

🍽 CHEZ PANISSE
$$$$
1517 SHATTUCK AVE.
TEL 510/548-5525
www.chezpanisse.com

The legendary birthplace of California cuisine presided over by Alice Waters. The prix-fixe menu features local organic ingredients and French technique in a Craftsman-style interior. À la carte meals available at the upstairs café.
🍽 Restaurant 50, Café 50
🕐 Closed Sun. 💳 All major cards

🍽 OLIVETO
$$$
5655 COLLEGE AVE.
TEL 510/547-5356
Chef Paul Bertolli prepares great rustic Tuscan dishes. Casual café downstairs.
🍽 110 🕐 Restaurant closed Sat.–Sun. L 💳 All major cards

🍽 RIVOLI
$$$
1539 SOLANO AVE.
TEL 510/526-2542
Trendy Mom & Pop cooking, including grilled wild salmon with potato gnocchi. Great desserts.
🍽 70 🔲 🕐 Closed L
💳 All major cards

OAKLAND

🍽 BAY WOLF
$$$
3853 PIEDMONT AVE.
TEL 510/655-6004
www.baywolf.com
Outstanding Mediterranean-style food in a lovely setting.
🍽 80 Ⓟ 🕐 Closed Sat. L & Sun. L 💳 All major cards

🍽 NAN YANG
$$
6048 COLLEGE AVE.
TEL 510/655-3298
Burmese food made with high-quality ingredients.
🍽 20 Ⓟ 🕐 Closed Mon.
💳 MC, V

SAUSALITO

🏨 THE INN ABOVE TIDE
$$$$–$$$$$
30 EL PORTAL, 94965
TEL 415/332-9535

FAX 415/332-6714
www.innabovetide.com
The Bay Area's only hostelry
on the water has rooms with
wide bay views. Many have
decks and fireplaces. Luxurious
amenities (pillow menu, DVD
players) and business needs
(large desks, office supplies,
wireless Internet). Continental
breakfast served in room.
[1] 29 [P] Valet [S] [S] All
major cards

🍴 CHRISTOPHE RESTAURANT FRANCAIS
$$
1919 BRIDGEWAY BLVD.
TEL 415//332-9244
www.christopherestaurant.com
French food set in a lovely old
house filled with art nouveau
furniture. The early bird prix
fixe is good value. Indoor and
outdoor dining.
[+] 120 [P] Valet [C] Closed
Sat.–Mon. L, Mon. D [S] All
major cards

NAPA

🍴 MUSTARD'S GRILL
$$$
7399 ST. HELENA HWY
TEL 707/944-2424
www.mustardsgrill.com
Called the cradle of Napa
California cuisine, Mustard's
offers dishes such as baby
back ribs with corn pudding
and delicious hamburgers.
[+] 60 [P] [S] [S] D, MC, V

YOUNTVILLE

🏨 YOUNTVILLE INN
$$$–$$$$
6462 WASHINGTON ST., 94599
TEL 707/944-5600
FAX 707/944-5666
www.yountvilleinn.com
Fieldstone fireplaces, elegant
linens, and some rooms with
private patios. Rustic setting
close to fine dining (see The
French Laundry, this page).
[1] 51 [P] [S] [S] [S] All
major cards

🍴 THE FRENCH LAUNDRY
Called the "best restaurant in
America." Reservations
required two months ahead. The
prix-fixe French-California
menu may include sautéed
moulard duck foie gras with
oven-roasted cherries; sweet
garlic-crusted cod with thyme-
roasted potatoes and
caramelized spring garlic; and
black pepper brioche.
$$$$
6640 WASHINGTON ST.
TEL 707/944-2380
www.frenchlaundry.com
[+] 62 [P] Valet [S]
[C] Closed L Mon.–Thurs.
[S] AE, MC, V

CALISTOGA

🏨 DR. WILKINSON'S HOT SPRINGS RESORT
$$
1507 LINCOLN AVE., 94515
TEL 707/942-4102
www.drwilkinson.com
Fifties-style motel with hot
springs, volcanic ash mud
baths, spa treatments.
Midweek specials offer mud,
aromatic whirlpool, mineral
steam, massage.
[1] 42 [P] [S] [S] [V]
[S] AE, MC, V

🍴 BRANNANS GRILL
$$$
1374 LINCOLN AVE.
TEL 707/942-2233
www.brannansgrill.com
Unpretentious food such as
ginger-honey braised short
ribs with pumpkin risotto.
[+] 190 [P] [S] [S] All
major cards

SONOMA

🏨 EL DORADO
🍴 $$–$$$
405 FIRST ST. W., 95476
TEL 707/996-3030
FAX 707/996-3148
www.hoteleldorado.com
A small hotel overlooking the

Plaza Sonoma where the Bear
Flag revolt (see p. 234) was
staged. Stylish Californian
guest rooms and delicious
breakfast. The Piatti restaurant
(tel 707/996-2351) serves
decent Italian cooking.
[1] 26 [P] [S] [S] [V]
[S] AE, MC, V

🍴 LA CASA
$$
121 E. SPAIN ST.
TEL 707/996-3406
www.lacasarestaurant.com
An old-fashioned Mexican
food hangout close to
Sonoma Plaza.
[+] 180 [P] [S] [S] All
major cards

YOSEMITE VALLEY

🏨 AHWAHNEE HOTEL & 🍴 RESTAURANT
$$$$$
1 AHWAHNEE WAY, YOSEMITE
NATIONAL PARK, 95389
TEL 866/646-0388
www.nationalparkreservations
.com/ahwahnee.htm
Make reservations several
months ahead for this
1920s mountain lodge, which
boasts Native American
decor. Also, book ahead for
the restaurant (dinner for
guests only), which serves
great American food.
[1] 127 [P] [S] [S] [S] All
major cards

LAKE TAHOE

🏨 INN BY THE LAKE
$$–$$$
3300 LAKE TAHOE BLVD.,
SOUTH LAKE TAHOE, 96150
TEL 530/542-0330
FAX 530/541-6596
www.innbythelake.com
Upscale motel near the bathing
beach, with free rides to the
casinos across the water.
[1] 100 [P] [S] [S] [S]
[S] All major cards

SHOPPING IN SAN FRANCISCO

The character of a San Francisco store is bound up with its neighborhood, each district having its own spin that is reflected in clothes, home furnishings, books, and so on. Shopping is a great excuse to explore these different worlds.

NEIGHBORHOODS

Union Square has department stores and exclusive designer boutiques. Don't forget Maiden Lane (an alley off Kearny), with its elegant shops and galleries. In nearby Chinatown, shops sell mostly ticky-tack for tourists, with some arts, linens, electronics, and intriguing food shops. Jackson Square in the Financial District is home to splendid antique shops. North Beach has eclectic, highly individual shops. Hayes Valley (along Hayes Street from Franklin to Laguna, and from Oak to Grove) is a happening area with a local feeling and has fun and funky clothes, crafts, furniture, trendy boutiques, jewelry, and galleries.

Along Upper Fillmore Street (from Post to Pacific) lies a strip of upscale shops for home furnishings, gifts, and the like, as well as great thrift shops that sell high-quality cast-off clothes cheap. Union Street in Cow Hollow furnishes young, well-to-do San Franciscans with chic clothes, housewares, antiques, jewelry, designer eyeglasses, and such. Funky, psychedelic Haight Street overflows with vintage clothes, books, music, and retro hippie paraphernalia. The Mission District has secondhand clothes, furniture, and thrift-shop items, as well as stores that reflect the neighborhood's Hispanic culture, such as Day of the Dead decorations. In SoMa you'll find numerous factory outlet stores, along with cutting-edge art galleries, a mix that reflects the neighborhood's personality.

On the mall front: The San Francisco Shopping Center (Market at 5th St.) is anchored by a colossal Nordstrom department store; in addition there are many upscale shops including Bloomingdale's. In the Financial District, the European-style Crocker Galleria (between Post, Kearny, Sutter, and Montgomery) shelters dozens of shops under a vaulted glass roof. The multiple buildings of the Embarcadero Center (foot of Sacramento St.) contain some 175 shops. Ghirardelli Square (west end of Fisherman's Wharf) is a complex of shops selling arts and crafts, clothing, housewares, and more. The Cannery is a similar collection of shops at Fisherman's Wharf.

Most of the businesses below are unique to San Francisco.

ANTIQUES & COLLECTIBLES

Bonhams & Butterfields, 220 San Bruno Ave. (SoMa), tel 415/861-7500, www.butterfields.com. Call for information about auctions and other special events at this well-known auction house's annex.
Don's Antiques, 572 Valencia St. (Mission), tel 415/586-3022. Closed Mon.–Fri. Vast jumble of furniture, household items, costume jewelry, silver, prints, and more.
Farinelli Antiques & Fine Art, 311 Grant Ave. (Union Sq.), tel 415/433-4823. Fine porcelain, carpets, and furniture.
Grand Central Station Antiques, 333 Ninth St. (SoMa), tel 415/252-8155. Spacious store filled with European antiques, primarily.
Mureta's Antiques, 2418 Fillmore St. (Pacific Heights), tel 415/922-5652. Closed Mon. Glassware, silver, and dishes.
Russian Hill Antiques, 2200 Polk St. (Russian Hill), tel 415/441-5561. Home furnishings and jewelry.

APPAREL

Aardvarks Odd Ark, 1501 Haight St. (Haight-Ashbury), tel 415/621-3141. Thrift shopping for apparel from past decades; a San Francisco favorite.
Agnes B., 33 Grant Ave. (Union Sq.), tel 415/772-9995. Paris imports with fashions for him and her.
American Rag, 1305 Van Ness Ave. (Pacific Heights), tel 415/474-5214. Designer labels, vintage clothing, and shoes. Not for bargain hunters.
Ambience, 1458 Haight St. (Haight-Ashbury), tel 415/552-5095. Kicky young dresses, accessories, and cotton knits.
Annie's, 2512 Sacramento St. (Pacific Heights), tel 415/292-7164. Ultra-fashionable boutique for women with great figures.
Anthropologie, 880 Market St. (nr. Union Sq.), tel 415/434-2210. Apparel, home decor, accessories, and clothes for kids.
Betsey Johnson, 160 Geary Blvd. (Union Sq.), tel 415/398-2516; 2033 Fillmore St. (Upper Fillmore), tel 415/567-2726. Stylish, kooky, freewheeling dresses and skirts.
Britex Fabrics, 146 Geary Blvd. (Union Sq.), tel 415/392-2910. Closed Sun. A vast collection of fine fabrics and accessories (more than 1,000 silks, 5,000 woollens, and 30,000 buttons in stock) for those who sew and know.
Brooks Brothers, 150 Post St. (Union Sq.), tel 415/397-4500. Conservative suits, button-down shirts, and sportswear for men; women's department.
Buffalo Exchange, 1555 Haight St. (Haight-Ashbury), tel 415/431-7733; 1800 Polk St., tel 415/346-5726. Used clothes with style at low prices.
Burberrys Ltd., 225 Post St. (Union Sq.), tel 415/392-2200. Raincoats, scarves, and more for men and women.

Burlington Coat Factory Outlet, 899 Howard St. (SoMa), tel 415/495-7234. Offering deep discounts; men and women.

Chanel Boutique, 155 Maiden Lane (Union Sq.), tel 415/981-1550. Find out how the other one percent lives at this ultraluxe purveyor of classic clothes, jewelry, and perfume.

Diesel, 101 Post St. (Financial District.), tel 415/982-7077. Italian high fashion streetwear.

Dottie Doolittle, 3680 Sacramento St. (Presidio Heights), tel 415/563-3244. Upscale clothes for little girls and infants.

Georgio Armani, 278 Post St. (Union Sq.), tel 415/434-2500. Closed Sun. Sleek couture for men and women. (The less expensive, younger style Emporio Armani is at 1 Grant Ave, tel 415/677-9400.)

Gianni Versace, 60 Post St. (Union Sq.), tel 415/616-0604. High-style Italian clothes and accessories for men and women.

Gimme Shoes, 416 Hayes St. (Hayes Valley), tel 415/864-0691; 2358 Fillmore St. (Upper Fillmore), tel 415/441-3040; 50 Grant Ave. (Union Sq.), tel 415/434-9242. European shoes and sports footwear for men and women.

Girlfriends, 1824 Union St. (Cow Hollow), tel 415/673-9544. Comfortable dresses, sweaters, skirts, and blouses.

Jessica McClintock, 180 Geary St., 4th Fl. (Union Sq.), tel 415/398-9008. For lovely bridal fashions.

Kenneth Cole, San Francisco Shopping Center, 5th at Market Sts. tel 415/227-4536; 2078 Union St. (Cow Hollow), tel 415/346-2161. High-fashion, original shoes for men and women.

Loehmann's, 222 Sutter St. (Financial District), tel 415/982-3215. Bargain-basement prices on good clothing for women.

Metier, 355 Sutter St. (Union Sq.), tel 415/989-5395. Young designer clothing and jewelry, high end. Closed Sun.

Next To New Shop, 2226 Fillmore St. (Upper Fillmore), tel 415/567-1628. Closed Sun. Junior League thrift shop, high-quality clothing at low prices.

Nida, 544 Hayes St. (Hayes Valley), tel 415/552-4670. Shoes, shirts, and other high-end clothing for men and women.

Peek-A-Boutique, 1306 Castro St. (Noe Valley), tel 415/641-6192. Used (not abused) children's clothes at low prices.

TSE, 60 Maiden Ln. (Union Sq.), tel 415/391-1112. Closed Sun. Cashmeres: sweaters, skirts, coats, dresses, jackets; men, women, children.

Urban Outfitters, 80 Powell St. (nr Union Sq.), tel 415/989-1515. Chain stocking men's and women's clothing, plus furnishings, jewelry, and unique gifts.

Wasteland, 1660 Haight St. (Haight-Ashbury), tel 415/863-3150. A fashionable place to buy vintage and trendy secondhand clothes at high prices.

Wilkes Bashford, 375 Sutter St. (Union Sq.), tel 415/986-4380. Closed Sun. Traditional, trendy, and sophisticated American and European fashions of high quality; men and women.

ARTS, CRAFTS, & GIFTS

Fumiki Fine Asian Arts, 272 Sutter St. (Union Sq.), tel 415/362-6677. A wide range of imari porcelain, baskets, chests, and embroidery.

Gump's, 135 Post St. (Union Sq.), tel 415/982-1616. Classic SF emporium showcases dinnerware, Asian and European antiques, crafts, jewelry, jade.

Hang, 556 & 567 Sutter St. (Union Sq.), tel 415/434-4264. Paintings, sculpture, and works on paper by emerging San Francisco area artists. "Emerging" means "affordable."

Twig-Gallery of American Crafts, 2162 Union St. (Cow Hollow), tel 415/928-8944. Home accessories, jewelry, ceramics, art glass.

Worldware, 336 Hayes St. (Hayes Valley), tel 415/487-9030. Recycled and natural products, from hemp clothing to aluminum-can picture frames.

Xanadu Tribal Art Gallery/ Folk Art International/ Boretti Amber & Design, 140 Maiden Ln. (Union Sq.), tel 415/392-9999. Fine arts and crafts from Asia, Africa, and elsewhere.

BOOKS

A Clean Well-Lighted Place for Books, 601 Van Ness Ave. (Civic Center), tel 415/441-6670. Well-run independent shop with large selection.

A Different Light, 489 Castro St. (Castro District), tel 415/431-0891. Gay, lesbian, and transgender publications.

Bound Together Book Collective, 1369 Haight St. (Haight-Ashbury), tel 415/431-8355. Anarchist, leftist, and subversive literature.

City Lights, 261 Columbus Ave. (North Beach), tel 415/362-8193. Landmark literary bookstore founded by poet Lawrence Ferlinghetti.

Green Apple Books, 506 Clement St. (Richmond District), tel 415/387-2272. Highly regarded for new, used, and rare books.

Harold's International Newsstand, 454 Geary St. (Union Sq.), tel 415/441-2665. Best selection of magazines and newspapers from all over.

William Stout Architectural Books, 804 Montgomery St. (Jackson Sq.), tel 415/391-6757. For books on both architecture and design. Highly regarded.

DEPARTMENT STORES

Macy's, Stockton at O'Farrell Sts. (Union Sq.), tel 415/397-3333. Occupies a whole city block: comprehensive, thronged.

Neiman-Marcus, 150 Stockton St. (Union Sq.), tel 415/362-3900. Fine clothing, flash, big-name designers.

Nordstrom, San Francisco Shopping Center, 5th at Market Sts. (Union Sq.), tel 415/243-8500. Five floors with great clothing, concierge, and restaurants.
Saks Fifth Avenue, 384 Post St. (Union Sq.), tel 415/986-4300. Quality clothing, couture, for women. (Men's store: 220 Post St., tel 415/986-4300).

FOR THE HOME

Biordi Art Imports, 412 Columbus Ave. (North Beach), tel 415/392-8096. Closed Sun. Italian majolica ceramics for table and home.
Crate & Barrel, 55 Stockton St. (Union Sq.), tel 415/982-5200. Reasonably priced household items.
Scheuer Linens, 340 Sutter St. (Union Sq.), tel 415/392-2813. Closed Sun. Elegant sheets with high thread counts, table linens; European and U.S. makers.
Sur La Table, 77 Maiden Ln. (Union Sq.), tel 415/732-7900. An Aladdin's cave of more than 14,000 items for professional and home chefs. There's a branch at the Ferry Building.
Zinc Details, 905 Fillmore St. (Pacific Heights), tel 415/776-2100. Contemporary ceramics, glass, dinnerware, lighting, accessories, with Japanese and Scandinavian qualities.

JEWELRY

Bulgari, 237 Post St. (Union Sq.), tel 415/399-9141. Closed Sun. Exclusive designs from a renowned Rome jeweler.
Dianne's Old & New Estates, 2181A Union St. (Cow Hollow), tel 415/346-7525. Engagement and wedding rings, necklaces, bracelets, earrings, vintage watches, estate china.
Shreve & Company, 200 Post St. (Union Sq.), tel 415/421-2600. Creating traditional jewelry designs since 1852.
Union Street Goldsmith, 1909 Union St. (Cow Hollow), tel 415/776-8048. Locally made gold and platinum jewelry; colored stones.

LEATHER

Bottega Veneta, 108 Geary St. (Union Sq.), tel 415/981-1700. Closed Sun. Italian handbags, luggage, wallets.
North Beach Leather, 224 Grant Ave. (Union Sq.), tel 415/362-8300. Factory shop with good deals and alterations on site.

OUTDOOR MARKETS

Ferry Plaza Farmers' Market, Ferry Bldg., Market St. at Embarcadero (Embarcadero), tel 415/291-3276. Tues., Thurs., Sat., Sun. Fresh farm products and food items.
Heart of the City Farmers' Market, Market St. between Seventh and Eighth Streets (Civic Center), tel 415/558-9455. Wed. and Sun. Fresh local produce, food items.

RECORDS, CDS

101 Basement, 513 Green St. (North Beach), tel 415/392-6368. Used records of all kinds.
Amoeba Music, 1855 Haight St. (Haight-Ashbury), tel 415/831-1200. Vast selection of new and used records and CDs.
Street Light Records, 2350 Market St. (Castro), tel 415/282-8000. Sell, trade, or buy from a varied collection.

TOYS & GAMES

Jeffrey's Toys, 685 Market St. (Union Sq.), tel 415/243-8697. Educational and not-so-educational toys and books.

MISCELLANY

Canton Bazaar, 616 Grant Ave. (Chinatown), tel 415/362-5750. A large and typical Chinatown store chockablock with souvenirs, porcelain, embroidery, arts and crafts.
Clarion Music Center, 816 Sacramento St. (Chinatown), tel 415/391-1317. Closed Sun. A huge variety of world instruments, from sitars to didgeridoos, drums, Chinese strings, and gongs.
Dudley Perkins Harley-Davidson, 66 Page St. (Civic Center), tel 415/703-9494. Closed Sun.; 2595 Taylor St. (Fisherman's Wharf), tel 415/776-7779. City's oldest Harley dealership (1914) also sells clothing, collectibles, videos, etc. Operated by women.
Ferry Building Marketplace, Embarcadero at Market St. (Embarcadero), tel 415/693-0996. Forage for all kinds of foods, from bread to oysters, from cheese to wine.
Flax, 1699 Market St. (Civic Center), tel 415/552-2355. San Francisco's best bet for art supplies, guaranteed to have anything you could wish for in the way of stationery, pens, paper, paint, ink, and brushes.
Gity Joon's, 1828 Union St. (Cow Hollow), tel 415/292-7388. Arts and antiques from Asian lands and spiritual traditions, especially religious devotional objects and figures; fountains, jewelry, clothing, books as well.
Golden Gate Fortune Cookie Factory, 56 Ross Alley (Chinatown), tel 415/781-3956. Freshly baked fortune cookies by the bag. For custom orders, bring your own fortunes to be inserted in cookies (good for parties, etc.).
Handle With Care Packaging Store, 200 Pine St., Ste. 160 (Financial District), tel 415/986-5568. Will pack and ship your purchases, especially valuable, fragile, awkward items.
Misdirections Magic Shop, 1236 Ninth Ave. (Sunset), tel 415/566-2180. For beginning conjurors as well as professional magicians, well stocked with tricks, books, and professional videos. Closed Mon.
Pipe Dreams, 1376 Haight St. (Haight-Ashbury), tel 415/431-3553. If you just have to visit a head shop, with its psychedelic posters and sixties-style paraphernalia, this is the oldest in the Haight.
Wine Club, 953 Harrison St. (SoMa), tel 415/512-9086. Reduced prices on wines.

ENTERTAINMENT & ACTIVITIES

In the performing arts, San Francisco entertainment venues present everything from world-class opera to cutting-edge theater, from dance to comedy to rock.

Nightlife is as varied as the city and its residents. Whether it's an old-time jazz club, a funky blues bar, a dance club for gay leather boys, a hotel ballroom with a big band and a city view, or a concert by rock 'n' roll superstars, you'll find it in San Francisco.

INFORMATION & TICKETS

For information on San Francisco events, call the San Francisco Convention and Visitors Bureau hotline at tel 415/391-2001. The *Sunday San Francisco Chronicle* "Datebook" section offers entertainment listings, as does the newpaper's web site: www.sfgate.com; also check www.sfarts.org, and widely available free tabloids such as the *San Francisco Bay Guardian* and the *SF Weekly*. Or phone individual venues.

Ticket agencies Call BASS Tickets for calendar listings or to charge tickets (adding a service charge): tel 415/478-2277 or 800/225-2277 outside California. TIX (Tel 415/433-7827 for information only, www.theatre bayarea.org,) sells half-price, same-day tickets for many theater, dance, and music events; the TIX booth is located at Union Square on the Stockton Street side; cash only; closed Mon.

It is a good idea to check with venues for house seats, single seats, or cancellations. Box offices are generally open during the day until after the performance begins.

THEATER

Productions run the gamut from big-name musicals and dramas in the downtown Theater District and the Civic Center to experimental works in neighborhood theaters.

THEATER DISTRICT

American Conservatory Theater/ACT, Geary Theater, 415 Geary St., tel 415/749-2228, www.act-sf.org. Nationally recognized, Tony-

Award-winning repertory company; from Shakespeare to Tennessee Williams, plus premieres of new works. The 1909 theater is a national historic landmark.
Curran Theatre, 445 Geary St., tel 415/551-2000, www.bestofbroadway-sf.com. Big musicals from Andrew Lloyd Webber, other Broadway hits; handsome 1922 theater.
Lorraine Hansberry Theatre, 620 Sutter St., tel 415/474-8800, www.lorraine hansberrytheatre.com. African-American theater that ranges from classical to experimental.

OTHER LOCATIONS

Beach Blanket Babylon, Club Fugazi, 678 Green St. (North Beach), tel 415/421-4222. Zany, long-running musical spoof of San Francisco and pop culture; outlandish hats and costumes.
Magic Theatre, Fort Mason, Bldg. D, Marina Blvd. at Buchanan St. (Marina District), tel 415/441-8822, www.magictheatre.org. American playwrights stage new works; performers range from stars to unknowns.
The Marsh, 1062 Valencia St. (Mission District), tel 415/641-0235. Small, avant-garde, hip productions and solo works.
Theatre Rhinoceros, 2926 16th St. (Mission District), tel 415/861-5079. Nation's oldest gay and lesbian theater company.

MUSIC

Grace Cathedral Concerts, Grace Cathedral, 1100 California St. (Nob Hill), tel 415/749-6350; www.gracecathedral.org. Fine choral and instrumental music, lovely surroundings and acoustics.
San Francisco Opera, War Memorial Opera House, 301 Van

Ness Ave. (Civic Center), tel 415/864-3330; www.sfopera .com. Spectacular, star-studded productions in renovated opera house. Season runs Sept.–Dec.
San Francisco Symphony, Louise M. Davies Symphony Hall, 201 Van Ness Ave. (Civic Center), tel 415/864-6000; www.sfsymphony.org. Michael Tilson Thomas is the resident conductor. The high standards attract top guest soloists. Runs Sept.–July.

DANCE

San Francisco Ballet, War Memorial Opera House, 301 Van Ness Ave. (Civic Center), tel 415/865-2000; www.sfballet.org. The nation's oldest ballet company presents classical and contemporary works. Runs Feb.–May; also Christmas season "Nutcracker."

NIGHTLIFE

Biscuits and Blues, 401 Mason St. (Union Sq.), tel 415/292-2583. Well-known, casual blues club.
Bimbo's 365 Club, 1025 Columbus Ave. (North Beach), tel 415/474-0365. Lush, plush environment for rock and jazz, often big names.
Boom Boom Room, 1601 Fillmore St. (Japantown), tel 415/673-8000. The late bluesman John Lee Hooker's down-home club presents both local and national performers.
Cobb's Comedy Club, The Cannery, 2801 Leavenworth St. (Fisherman's Wharf), tel 415/928-4320. Small, intimate venue. New talent. Popular spot.
Enrico's Sidewalk Café, 504 Broadway (North Beach), tel 415/982-6223. Jazz in a European atmosphere.
Fillmore Auditorium, 1805 Geary Blvd., tel 415/346-6000. Rock concerts at the famous psychedelic Sixties dance hall.
Great American Music Hall, 859 O'Farrell St. (Tenderloin), tel 415/885-0750. Rock, pop, R&B, and folk in an ornate turn-of-the-20th-century music hall.

ENTERTAINMENT & ACTIVITIES

Harry Denton's Starlight Room, Sir Francis Drake Hotel, 450 Powell St. tel 415/395-8595. Dancing to big band sounds, with a city view.
Jazz at Pearl's, 256 Columbus Ave. (North Beach), tel 415/291-8255. Jazz in old-time club atmosphere.
Ruby Skye, 420 Mason St. (Union Sq.), tel 415/693-0777. A vast art nouveau theater turned into a multilevel dance club, with DJs and live music. State-of-the-art sound system.
The Saloon, 1232 Grant Ave. (North Beach), tel 415/989-7666. A fun blues dive, in the city's oldest bar.
Slim's, 333 11th St. (SoMa), tel 415/255-0333. Boz Scagg's popular club devoted to blues and roots music, rock; some top performers.
Ten 15, 1015 Folsom St. (SoMa), tel 415/431-1200. Top-rated dance club with five theme environments.
The Warfield, 928 Market St. (Civic Center), tel 415/775-7722. Major rock groups in a relatively intimate concert venue.

OUTDOOR ACTIVITIES

From boating to biking to fishing, San Francisco offers a diverse bunch of options for outdoor enthusiasts. Head to the city's waterfront, parks, and trails, or to wilder environs nearby, particularly in Marin County.

SPECTATOR SPORTS

Oakland A's, Network Associates Coliseum, 7000 Coliseum Way, Oakland, 94621, tel 510/762-2255 (tickets). Baseball.
San Francisco 49ers, 3Com Park at Candlestick, tel 415/656-4900. Football.
San Francisco Giants, SBC Park, tel 510/762-2255. Baseball.
San Jose Earthquakes, San Jose State's Spartan Stadium, 7th St. between E. Alma Ave. & E. Humboldt St., San Jose, 9511, tel 408/985-4625. Soccer.

San Jose Sharks, San Jose Arena, 525 W. Santa Clara St. at Autumn St., 95113, tel 408/287-7070. Hockey.

WALKING & BIKING

Two of the nation's prettiest routes for people on foot or wheels are the Golden Gate Promenade (a 4-mile jaunt along the water with views of yachts and windsurfers, between Aquatic Park and the Golden Gate Bridge) and the Coastal Trail (a more rough-and-tumble 9-mile route from the bridge to Fort Funston, touching on headlands, city neighborhoods, and the beach). Other good places include the Presidio (which has a 2-mile Ecology Trail) and Golden Gate Park (whose main road closes to auto traffic on Sundays).

For regional trail information check out the Golden Gate National Recreation Area website: www.nps.gov/goga.

Although a network of bike lanes runs throughout the city (see the *Yellow Pages* phone book for a map), bikers must negotiate steep hills and dodge cars. Mountain biking enthusiasts flock to Marin; the sport was invented on trail-laced Mount Tamalpais, which offers stupendous views.

Avenue Cyclery, 756 Stanyan St. (Haight-Ashbury), tel 415/387-3155. Rent bikes next to Golden Gate Park.
Surrey Bikes & Blades, 50 Stow Lake Dr. (Golden Gate Park). tel 415/668-6699. Rent bikes and in-line skates.

GOLF

Courses that are open to the public include:
Presidio Golf Course, 300 Finley Road, tel 415/561-4653, www.presidiogolf.com. Privately managed course located in the Presidio. See p. 142 for more information.
Lincoln Park Golf Course,

34th Avenue at Clement Street, tel 415/221-9911; www.playlincoln.com.

WINDSURFING

Top-rated among windsurfers, the San Francisco Bay is blown by westerly winds from spring through fall. The best sites include Crissy Field (Presidio), Fort Point at the southern anchorage of the Golden Gate Bridge, Larkspur Landing (Marin), and the waters by 3Com Park (once Candlestick, south of the city). Be extremely cautious of the cold water, strong currents, and boat traffic.
Cityfront Boardsports, 2936 Lyon St. (Marina), tel 415/929-7873. Board rental for experienced windsurfers.

OTHER SPORTS

A good spot for boating is Golden Gate Park.
Golden Gate Park Boathouse, Stow Lake, tel 415/752-0347. Rent a rowboat or pedalboat (dogs allowed on rowboats only) by the hour. At the center of the lake is Strawberry Hill, an island with a Chinese pavilion and small waterfall; a path ascends to the 425-foot-high peak.

Another popular Golden Gate Park sport is lawn bowling.
San Francisco Lawn Bowling Club, near Sharon Meadow and the Carousel, tel 415/487-8787. This sport is easy to learn, yet competitive, for people of all ages. Free lessons are offered on Wednesdays at noon and at other times by appointment.

Consider a sports-fishing expedition from Fisherman's Wharf or pier fishing at Aquatic Park, Fort Mason, Crissy Field, and other locations.

Locals and visitors enjoy sailing and sea kayaking as much for the bay and city views these activities afford as for the fresh air and exercise. Many commercial operators offer trips and rentals.

ILLUSTRATIONS CREDITS

Abbreviations for terms appearing below: (t) top; (b) bottom; (l) left; (r) right; (c) center.

One of the world's largest nonprofit scientific and educational organizations, the National Geographic Society was founded in 1888 "for the increase and diffusion of geographic knowledge." Fulfilling this mission, the Society educates and inspires millions every day through its magazines, books, television programs, videos, maps and atlases, research grants, the National Geographic Bee, teacher workshops, and innovative classroom materials. The Society is supported through membership dues, charitable gifts, and income from the sale of its educational products. This support is vital to National Geographic's mission to increase global understanding and promote conservation of our planet through exploration, research, and education.

For more information, please call 1-800-NGS LINE (647-5463) or write to the following address:

National Geographic Society
1145 17th Street N.W.
Washington, D.C. 20036-4688
U.S.A.

Visit the Society's Web site at www.nationalgeographic.com.

Travel the world with National Geographic Experts:
www.nationalgeographic.com/ngexpeditions

Published by the National Geographic Society
John M. Fahey, Jr., *President and Chief Executive Officer*
Gilbert M. Grosvenor, *Chairman of the Board*
Nina D. Hoffman, *Executive Vice President,*
President, Books and School Publishing
Kevin Mulroy, *Vice President and Director, Book Division*
Marianne Koszorus, *Design Director*
Charles Kogod, *Director of Photography*
Elizabeth L. Newhouse, *Director of Travel Publishing*
Barbara A. Noe, *Senior Editor and Series Editor*
Cinda Rose, *Art Director*
Carl Mehler, *Director of Maps*
Joseph F. Ochlak, *Map Editor*
Gary Colbert, *Production Director*
Richard S. Wain, *Production Project Manager*
Lawrence Porges, *Editorial Coordinator*
Kay Kobor Hankins, Judith Klein, *Contributors*

Edited and designed by AA Publishing (a trading name of Automobile Association Developments Limited, whose registered office is Norfolk House, Priestley Road, Basingstoke, Hampshire, England RG24 9NY. Registered number: 1878835).
Betty Sheldrick, *Project Manager*
David Austin, *Senior Art Editor*
Victoria Barber, *Editor*
Keith Russell, *Designer*
Simon Mumford, *Senior Cartographic Editor*
Amber Banks, *Cartographer*
Richard Firth, *Production Director*
Picture Research by Zooid Pictures Ltd.
Area maps drawn by Chris Orr Associates, Southampton, England
Cutaway illustrations drawn by Maltings Partnership, Derby, England

Second edition 2005.

The Library of Congress has cataloged the first edition as follows:

Library of Congress Cataloging-in- Publication Data
Dunn, Jerry Camarillo.
The National Geographic Traveler : San Francisco / Jerry
Camarillo Dunn, Jr.
p. cm.
Includes index.
ISBN: 0-7922-3883-4
1. San Francisco (Calif.)--Guidebooks. I. Title.

F869.S33 D86 2000
917.94'610453--dc21
00-021659
CIP

National Geographic Traveler: San Francisco. Second edition 2005.
ISBN: 0-7922-3883-4

Visit the society's Web site at http:/www.nationalgeographic.com

Printed and bound by Cayfosa Quebecor, Barcelona, Spain. Color separations by Leo Reprographic Ltd., Hong Kong. Cover separations by L.C. Repro, Aldermaston, U.K.

The information in this book has been carefully checked and to the best of our knowledge is accurate. However, details are subject to change, and the National Geographic Society cannot be responsible for such changes, or for errors or omissions. Assessments of sites, hotels, and restaurants are based on the author's subjective opinions, which do not necessarily reflect the publisher's opinion. The publisher cannot be responsible for any consequences arising from the use of this book.

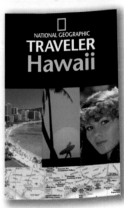

NATIONAL GEOGRAPHIC
TRAVELER

A Century of Travel Expertise in Every Guide

AVAILABLE WHEREVER BOOKS ARE SOLD